How to

Make and Sell Your Own Record

The Complete Guide to Independent Recording

DIANE SWARD RAPAPORT

JEROME HEADLANDS PRESS

TO *my friend and former publisher, the late Andrew Fluegelman of The Headlands Press, a man of great vitality and integrity. He inspired me to write this book and helped me persevere through many drafts to ensure a book that would endure.*

REVISED THIRD EDITION PRODUCED BY *Jerome Headlands Press, Jerome, Arizona. Original edition and revised second edition created and produced by The Headlands Press, Inc., Tiburon, California.*

COPYRIGHT © *by Diane Sward Rapaport, 1988; Copyright © by Diane Sward Rapaport and The Headlands Press, Inc., 1978, 1984. All rights reserved. No part of this book may be reproduced or transmitted in any form or by any means, electronic or mechanical, including photocopying, without permission in writing from the publisher: Jerome Headlands Press, PO Box N, Jerome, Arizona 86331.*

DISTRIBUTED TO THE BOOK TRADE BY *Perigee Books, The Putnam Publishing Group, 200 Madison Avenue, New York, NY 10016.*

DISTRIBUTED TO THE MUSIC TRADE BY *Music Sales Corporation, 24 East 22nd Street, New York, NY 10010.*

LIBRARY OF CONGRESS CATALOGING IN PUBLICATION DATA
Rapaport, Diane Sward
How to make and sell your own record
Jerome Headlands Press
Bibliography, p. 179
Includes index
1. Sound recording industry—United States
2. Music, Popular (Songs, etc.)—Writing and Publishing.
I. Title
ML3790.R36   338.4'7'7899120973   87-082953
ISBN 0-399-51430-9

EIGHTH PRINTING *(First Printing, Revised Third Edition) 1988*

ORIGINAL TEXT EDITED BY *Andrew Fluegelman*

REVISED THIRD EDITION APPENDIX AND CORRECTIONS EDITED BY *George Glassman*

DESIGNED BY *Howard Jacobsen/Triad*

PHOTOGRAPHS OR GRAPHIC ART BY *Andrew Fluegelman, pp. 2, 4, 15, 20, 27, 33, 38, 46, 54, 58, 61, 62, 68, 71, 77, 80, 81, 84, 86, 95, 102, 110, 120, 125; Vicki Vanderslice, 7: Karla Jo Keller, 8; Gary Lloyd, 9; Irene Young, 16; Marilyn Ward, 24; painting by Komar & Melamid; design by Drenttel Doyle, 29; Mark Hanauer, 32; Polyploid Sam and Don Gereux, 35; Curtis A. and Allen Beaulieu, 36; Pore Know Graphics, 40; Kerby Smith, 49; David Stahl, 55; John Coffman, 65; Sherry Rayn Barnett, 66; Sony Corporation, 75; Fostex, 79; Ellen Shumsky, 82; Jon Sievert, 83; Filmways/Heider Recording Hollywood, 96; Barry Brukoff and Anne Ackerman Robinson, 97; Kaz Tsurata, 98; Different Fur Recording Studios, 99; Lynda Gordon, 100; Alan McKittrick, 105; Trudy Fisher, 107; Eleanor Lawrence, 112; Rick Grosse, 117; Walter Van Voorhees, 120; Jackie Robbins and Kate Winter, 122; Ron Blanchette, 123; Lisa Wigoda, 131; Chas Krider, 163; Robert Swanson, 168.*

COVER PHOTOGRAPHS BY *Fred Lyon*

COVER PHOTO SPECIAL EFFECTS BY *LaserColor*

PHOTOGRAPHIC PRINTING BY *Chong Lee*

DIAGRAMS BY *David Bunnett and Susan Neri*

TYPESETTING BY *Type by Design, Fairfax, California and Archetype West, Point Reyes, California. Set in Bembo and Neufville Futura with Futura and Eras display.*

PRINTED AND BOUND BY *George Banta Company, Menasha, Wisconsin.*

Contents

ACKNOWLEDGEMENTS   vii

INTRODUCTION
A Guide to Independent Recording   1

1 Promotion   4

Identifying Your Audience   5
Researching the Media   6
  Print · Radio · Television
Mailing Lists   7
  Media List · Industry List · Fan List
Promotional Materials   9
  Your Record · Press Releases ·
  Photographs · Additional Materials
Performing   12
Reviews   14
Feature Stories   14
Airplay   15
Professional Services   16
Advertising   16
Sample Promotional Plan   17
Time and Money   17
  Tight Budgets

2 Sales   20

Format and Pricing   21
Selling at Performances   22
  Special Prices · Club Performances · Concerts ·
  Increasing Sales
Selling in Stores   24
  Obtaining Accounts · Discounts and
  Consignments · Servicing Accounts ·
  Having Friends Help
Record Distributors   27
  Finding a Distributor · Pricing and Payment ·
  Collection · Distributors and Promotion
Catalogs   32
  Schwann and Phonolog · Library of Congress
Mail Order Sales   34
  Audience · Mailing Lists · Mail Order Package ·
  Advertising · Federal Mail Order Regulations
Sample Sales Plan   36
Time and Money   36
  Tight Budgets

3 Printing   38

The Printing Process   39
  Color · Halftones · Color Separations ·
  Mechanicals · Negatives, Stripping and Proofs ·
  Checking Proofs · Printing · Fabrication ·
  Labels and Special Inserts
Choosing a Printer   41
Time and Money   42
  Tight Budgets

4 Graphics   46

The Graphic Designer   47
  Setting a Budget · Cover Concept ·
  Other Promotional Materials
The Production Process   49
  Illustrators and Photographers · Preliminary
  Design · Cover Copy · Copy Requirements ·
  Preparing Copy for Typesetting · Galleys ·
  Camera-ready Mechanicals
Choosing a Graphic Designer   54
Stock and Economy Covers   55
Time and Money   56
  Tight Budgets

5 Manufacturing   58

The Manufacturing Process   59
  Disc-mastering · Reference Lacquers · Plating ·
  Pressing · Test Pressings · Packaging · Shipping ·
  Storing Records
Choosing a Manufacturer   63
Time and Money   65
  Tight Budgets

6 Recording Procedures   68

Recording Equipment   69
  Specifications · Microphones · Pick-ups and
  Direct Boxes · Tape Recorders and Tape ·
  Tape Speed and Track Format · Multi-track ·
  Digital Recorders · Noise Reduction Systems ·
  Mixing Consoles · Signal Processing Equipment ·
  Speakers · Semi-professional Equipment
The Recording Process   79
  Preparing the Equipment · Set-up · Testing ·
  Record and Playback · Mixing ·
  Preparing for Disc-mastering

7 *Recording Options* 86

Arrangements 87

Recording Methods 88
*Direct to Two-track · Two-track with a Mixer ·
Multi-track/Ensemble · Multi-track/Overdubbing ·
Multi-track/Premixes and Ping-ponging ·
Direct-to-disc*

Recording Environments 94
*Recording Studios · Location Recording—
Concerts · Location Recording—Home ·
Home Studios*

Recording Personnel 97
*The Engineer · Arrangers · Studio Musicians ·
The Producer*

8 *Recording Time and Money* 102

Estimating Time 103

Recording Rates 103
*Recording Studios · Location Recording ·
Tape Costs · Payment · Home Studios*

Hiring Personnel 106
*The Engineer · Arrangers · Studio Musicians ·
The Producer · Band Members*

Making Sessions Work 107

9 *Song Rights* 110

Song Protection 111
*Copyrighting Your Songs · Copyright
Registration · Alternatives to Copyright
Registration · Copyrighting Your Record*

Song Exploitation 114
*Forming Your Own Publishing Company ·
Performance Rights · Mechanical Licenses ·
Selling Your Songs · Songsharks*

Using Other People's Songs 119

10 *Business* 120

Establishing Your Business 121
*Lawyer and Bookkeeper · Bank Account ·
Ledgers · Business Telephone · Postal Services ·
Stationery*

Government Regulations 123
*Fictitious Name Certificate · Sellers's Permit ·
Local Business License · Federal ID Number ·
Federal and State Tax Returns*

Joining the Industry 124
*Publications · NAIRD · NARM · NARAS ·
Labor Unions*

11 *Planning* 128

Time 129

Time Plan 130

Money 131

Worksheet 1, Promotion 133

Worksheet 2, Sales 135

Worksheet 3, Printing 137

Worksheet 4, Graphics 139

Worksheet 5, Manufacturing 141

Worksheet 6, Recording: Songs 143

Worksheet 7, Recording: Sessions 145

Worksheet 8, Recording: Costs 147

Worksheet 9, Song Rights 149

Worksheet 10, Business 151

Worksheet 11, Planning 153

APPENDIX I
Manufacturing Cassettes 155

APPENDIX II
Manufacturing Compact Discs 162

APPENDIX III
New Technologies 167

APPENDIX IV
Financing Recordings 169

APPENDIX V
Negotiating Record Contracts 172

APPENDIX VI
Selling Your Record in Foreign Markets 176

DIRECTORY AND BIBLIOGRAPHY 179

INDEX 180

FEEDBACK AND MAIL ORDER FORM 183

Acknowledge-ments

THIS BOOK WAS WRITTEN AND PUBLISHED WITH A GREAT deal of encouragement, advice, information and editing on the part of many people. It's wonderful to be able to thank them publicly.

I'd like to acknowledge, once again, the help extended to me by the late Andrew Fluegelman, founder of The Headlands Press. The idea for writing this book came out of a meeting we had to discuss how to improve distribution for *Music Works: A Manual for Musicians*. When Andrew saw the second edition of that magazine, dedicated to a dozen independent Bay Area record labels, he asked what it would take to write a book about the process of making and selling records. A few hours later, we shook hands on a deal. Every author and musician should have it so easy! Andrew took many of the excellent photographs that begin the chapters of the book. He was a multi-talented person of great integrity and it is to his standards of excellence that I am inspired to work.

I would also like to thank his wife Patricia Fluegelman who graciously made it possible for me to publish the third revised edition through my own publishing company in Jerome, Arizona; attorney Edward R. Hearn who helped with the maze of legalities; Editor Adrienne Ingrum and her assistant Anton Mueller, Perigree Books, Putnam Publishing Group, for their continuing enthusiasm and direction; and graphic designer Gary Romig of G/R Graphics, Jerome, Arizona, for the production of the final mechanicals for this edition.

As with the first and second editions, many people contributed knowledge and information. Thanks to Holger Petersen, Stony Plains Records, Canada; Craig Anderton, author of numerous technical books for recording musicians and composers; and attorneys Edward R. Hearn and J. Gunnar Erickson for the excellent articles they contributed to the Appendix of the revised edition.

Thanks also to Wan Seegmiller, Suzan Simone and Mindy Mull, LaserVideo; Patricia Harris, Grateful Dead Merchandising; Patricia A. Moore, Discovery Systems; Jim Cahalan and Mark Boddeker, Windham Hill Records; David Litwin, David Litwin Productions; Robert Swanson, San Francisco Bay Area photographer; John Braheny and Len Chandler, Songwriters Showcase; Marty Polon, Polon Research Associates; Augie Blume, Music Industry Resources; Randall S. Davis, The Creative Service Company; Global Pacific Records; Alan Penchansky, Geltzer & Company, Inc; Michael Schulhof and Jim Frische, Digital Audio Disc Corporation; Ken Pohlmann, Director, Music Engineering, University of Miami; Frank Jermance and Billy Porter, University of Colorado at Denver; Walter Rapaport, Rapasound; John Goddard, Village Music; Jesse's Books and Records; Jerry Richman, Richman Brothers; Jim Baskin, New Music Distribution Service; Fred Catero, Catero Records; Cynthia Saraniti, Electronic Industries Association; RIAA; NARM; Arnette Peel and Russell Smith, Mother Dubbers, Inc.; Brian Oxenreider, Spectrum Magnetics; Steve Katz, Audio Cassette Duplicating Company; Bob Fontana, TDK; Clete Baxter, Sound Recorders; Mary Anne Miller, Wakefield Manufacturing; Neil Cooper, ROIR Cassettes; Katie Lee, Katydid Records; Herb Wong, Palo Alto Records; Tam Martin, Olivia Records; Will Ackerman and Anne Robinson, Windham Hill Records; Hardy Fox, Ralph Records; Howie Klein, 415 Records; Peter Jesperson, Twin Tone Records; Fostex Corporation; TEAC Corporation; big band leader Rich Szabo; and Tim Owens, former award-winning producer for the now defunct Jazz Alive series on National Public Radio.

I'd like to specially thank Richard Flohil, editor of Canadian Composer, whose enthusiasm for the book led to a series of CAPAC sponsored seminars in major Canadian cities titled "How to Make and Sell Your Record." Top record and publishing company presidents, lawyers, producers, engineers, graphic designers and musicians participated, providing a stunning introduction to the very healthy Canadian music industry to thousands of musicians. I was honored to be a participant in all the seminars.

Special thanks to those contributing to the new look of the revised editions: David Schwartz of the *Mix* for suggesting Tres Virgo Studios; to Jerry Jacob, one of the owners of Tres Virgo, for his cooperation and enthusiasm; Fred Lyon, for his excellent photography; to the band Nancy and the Neighbors (Nancy Lualhati, Scoop McGuire and Tommy Kesecker) to designers Carol Hoover and Howard Jacobsen of Triad; copy editor and proofreader George Glassman; typesetter Michael Sykes, Archetype West; and to Gary Romig of G/R Graphics in Jerome.

It has been personally gratifying to meet and hear the music of so many musicians who started small record labels. The most satisfying feedback has been that they have read the book cover to cover.

I am very grateful to my family, friends and business associates for their continued enthusiasm and support.

Thank you!

Introduction
A Guide to Independent Recording

TEN YEARS AGO WHEN THIS BOOK WAS FIRST PUBLISHED, independent labels were just emerging. They provided music that had been unavailable from commercial outlets. Public familiarity with and access to music from these labels was limited. The prevailing attitude in the music industry, and among the public, was that if the music wasn't good enough for the major recording labels, it was amateurish. Making and selling your own record was compared to publishing books through vanity presses.

Today there are thousands of independent labels. They have become accepted breeding grounds for innovative music, contributing new vitality to music in every genre. They also serve as repositories of ethnic and traditional music.

Records from these firms can be found in chain and specialty record stores, bookstores, health food shops—and even in some toy, jewelry, and clothing stores. Recordings not available in stores can be ordered from a variety of mail order catalogs.

Some independent labels offer records from a variety of artists, but the most successful ones specialize in particular musical styles. For example, June Appal Records specializes in the sounds of old and new Appalachia. Olivia Records markets music for women. Arhoolie Records' catalog features Tex Mex border music, down home blues and Cajun rhythms. Still other labels profit from re-releasing old favorites from the 1920s to the 1980s on cassette or compact disc.

Many individual musicians and bands 'roll their own' and sell their music directly at performances or in record stores serving local audiences. Many show profits with sales of less than 500 cassettes, or 3,000 records, depending on their recording costs. Those artists who are able to keep expenses low and sell more than 10,000 records, cassettes or compact discs can make small fortunes. For them, small is indeed beautiful.

They also reap other benefits. Having a record of their music adds to their professional stature and can help them break out of the Thursday-through-Sunday bar gig routine into the concert arena. It also creates the opportunity for wider regional or national recognition. Most important, it gives them a unique opportunity to learn the techniques of recording and needed business skills common to small and large record companies that can lead to successful musical careers.

The majority of independents operate with budgets and sales expectations greatly scaled down from those of major record labels. Most involve no more than three people overseeing the entire operation, even when as many as twenty-five albums are released per year. Their sales may average from 5,000 records, cassettes or CDs a year to 50,000, with recording and promotion budgets appropriately scaled to result in profits. "Slow selling, long lasting," is Arhoolie Records' founder Chris Strachwitz's motto.

The success of the independents can be ascribed to their hard work in pursuing and building an audience that loves their music. This includes organizing a fan list and building up distribution and promotional networks through newsletters, mail order catalogs, specialty stores, distributors, concerts, festivals, and word of mouth.

Folk, jazz, women's music, reggae, blues, Tex Mex border rhythms, bluegrass instrumentals, minimalist compositions, meditation and religious music have been vitalized by the growth of alternative networks with strong commitments to the genre and to the audience served. With few exceptions, almost all these communication networks bypass popular promotional and distribution arteries (radio, television, major print media) reserved almost exclusively for major recording label artists.

A few independent labels show sales comparable to those of major recording labels. And a few independents have sold well over 100,000 records, cassettes or CDs, enough to generate handsome profits. The success of Mannheim Steamroller's Fresh Aire series, Kate Wolf's haunting folk ballads, Holly Near's political and social protests, or The Residents' outrageous new age/new wave sounds have helped widen distribution and promotion channels for artists wishing to market their music to similar audiences. It has also helped increase respect for artists recording outside the major label mainstream.

Although many musicians hope to leverage their local or regional success into major recording deals, stories of actual contracts are rare. Nevertheless, such exceptions as Laurie Anderson, UB-40, Romeo Void, the Police or Elvis Costello, whose successful independent singles and albums were very helpful in landing them contracts, continue to kindle hopes.

What has increased dramatically in the last decade is the signing of artists to such independent labels as Rounder or Kicking Mule who have built durable distribution networks. For this reason, the appendix in this edition carries information on recording contracts written by two prominent entertainment attorneys.

Many independent labels may eventually end up making distribution deals of their own with larger distribution arteries, such as a major recording label. The role model is Windham Hill Records whose success in promoting instrumental acoustic music led to a distribution deal with A&M records.

MARKETING MUSIC IN THE EIGHTIES

Sales of prerecorded cassettes and compact discs have been increasing dramatically since 1976.

According to statistics compiled by the Recording Industry Association of America (RIAA), shipments of prerecorded cassettes in 1976 totaled 21.8 million (net after returns) with a manufacturers' dollar value of $145.7 million dollars. In the same year, record shipments of LPs/EPs totaled 273 million (net after returns) with a manufacturers' dollar value of $1.663 billion dollars. In 1986, shipments of LPs/EPs had shrunk to 125.2 million units (net after returns) with a manufacturers' dollar value of $983 million dollars; while shipments of cassettes totalled 344.5 million with a manufacturers' dollar value of $2.4995 billion dollars. That figure is still rising.

The tremendous growth of prerecorded cassettes is matched with sales and accessibility of cassette-playback equipment in all price ranges and improvements in the fidelity of cassette tapes.

Both records and prerecorded cassettes, however, are analog formats that compete with digital formats, such as the CD, and in coming years with digital cassettes, or with formats that combine digital audio and video, such as the video disc.

The introduction of digital technology has been accompanied by massive marketing efforts aimed on the one hand towards musicians, recording producers and engineers and on the other towards consumers. The results are spectacular.

In 1983, the first year that the RIAA shows CD sales figures, shipments totaled 800,000 units with a manufacturers' dollar value of $17.2 million dollars; in 1986, shipments totaled 53 million units (net after returns) with a manufacturers' dollar value of $930.1 million dollars. Predictions from industry sources like the RIAA say those figures will continue to dramatically rise.

Both prerecorded cassettes and CDs deliver convenience, portability, durability, and compactness—factors that have also helped skyrocket sales and helped erode record sales.

Strong arguments have been advanced that CDs (and coming digital cassettes) sound better than analog records and cassettes. The reason most cited is that CDs and digital cassettes have a wider dynamic range than analog records or cassettes without sonic distortion, such as hiss, wow, flutter, modulation noise, frequency or mistrack distortion. When played on CD players or new digital cassette machines, background noises common to analog cassettes or records are also eliminated. To most consumers, the audible difference and clarity more than reinforces the marketing arguments.

Some people disagree, preferring a well mastered analog record to new digital formats. Their major argument is that the sound is 'tinny'; that acoustic instruments lose some of the important and pleasing harmonic subtleties; and that the ear tires of the mathematical sonic regularity of digital sound.

Diane Sward Rapaport was formerly an artists' manager with Bill Graham's Fillmore Management and, independently, for singer/songwriter Pamela Polland. She also founded, co-published, and edited three volumes of MusicWorks: A Manual for Musicians, which provided musicians business information on contracts, bookings, recording, and management. She is currently conducting music business seminars throughout the United States and free-lance writing. In 1980, Ms. Rapaport won the ASCAP–Deems Taylor Award for journalistic excellence in the field of music for an article published in 1979 in Contemporary Keyboard entitled "Making and Selling Your Own Record."

Given these factors, it's safe to predict that record companies are going to continue to give consumers their choice of analog and digital audio and video formats for many years to come. Those people who prefer the sound of their records will continue to buy them and will be increasingly courted by improvements in record quality—both in the recording end (digital) and on the manufacturing end (digital and half-speed mastering combined with premium vinyl).

The availability of records released in all available record and video formats has some negative marketing consequences for independent labels. The physical space large record stores can devote to independents has dwindled; and with it the number of stores that might have once been willing to stock music from new record labels. Record chain stores are also becoming larger and buying out their competition. In the last five years, a number of large independent distributors (like Pickwick) have shut their doors. This has been coupled with a consolidation of distribution systems back in to the hands of major labels. The consequence is that the number of distribution and store outlets once open to small independent labels has shrunk.

Promotional opportunities for small record labels have also dwindled. During the last ten years, commercial radio formats have narrowed to a basic four—country, album oriented rock, soul, and middle of the road. The same trends carry over into video programming. Almost all the music featured on major radio stations is from major labels. And almost all music from major labels corresponds to these formats. The reason is obvious: performance of music on radio and television leads to billions of dollars in sales of records and performance royalties. Moreover, radio programming, once the responsibility of local station owners, is increasingly centralized and computerized, the province of independent radio consultants.

Today, it is nearly impossible for independent labels to get their records, cassettes or compact discs aired over any commercial radio stations of any size or listening range.

Almost all video clips seen by consumers on major television networks are those provided free by the major labels. The money to make and distribute free promotional videos is not within the financial means of most independents.

The only antidotes to these disheartening trends are the following: Do it yourself. Do it well. Recognize the blockades and, when you can, help expose and tear them down. Establish personal business relationships with stores and distributors who love your music. Cooperate with other artists in building alternative distribution and promotional networks. Avoid getting caught up in record industry hype. Share information freely.

Most importantly, back releases of your records, cassettes or compact discs with a concrete plan for reaching your audience and generating sales. The choice of whether to manufacture records, cassettes, or compact discs, and in what quantity, must be carefully and realistically approached from the points of view of financing, marketing and promotion.

HOW TO USE THIS BOOK

The book is written "backwards"—the chapters on promotion and sales come first. Although you will be attending to these at the end of your project, this is where your thinking should start. In the excitement of creating music, it is hard to stay business oriented and easy to overlook practical considerations: how to assemble promotional materials and send them to the right people; how to get your records into stores; how to choose printers, manufacturers, graphic designers, engineers, and producers; how to establish yourself as a business and protect your original music.

In each chapter, basic procedures are explained first, followed by suggestions for hiring services or personnel and end with time and money considerations. In the chapter titled Planning, you will find a series of worksheets to help you project expenses mentioned in the book, as well as a guide for helping you plan your time.

One caution: prices given are an 'average' at the time this revision was updated. In these inflationary times, you should be sure to get up-to-date price information before you finalize your cost projections and make final plans.

The book won't make your music great or turn you into an overnight success. It will, however, spare you some of the frustrations which result from ignorance or trial and error, help you shape your fantasies, take charge of your career, and make it possible for you to share your music.

Chapter 1
Promotion

THE FIRST THING THAT MOST PEOPLE WHO MAKE THEIR own records do when they receive them neatly shrink-wrapped and boxed from the manufacturer is to call their families, their lovers, and their best friends with the news.

Letting other people know and getting them excited is called 'promotion'. Its purpose is to create a demand for your records (and your performances). You can start with as few as ten devoted fans and end up with your picture on the cover of *Rolling Stone*.

Promotion works by persuading people whose opinions are respected to share information and/or enthusiasm with others. A fan may spread the word to friends, a DJ may play cuts from your record on the radio, a critic may review it in the newspaper, or a reporter may interview you for a magazine. These people acquaint others with the music on your record and stimulate curiosity, interest, and excitement. They assure people that the money spent on your record will be worth it. They help dispel any lingering suspicions that a record from an independent label like yours might be amateurish—not quite up to the polish of records from major labels. These people also carry a great deal of credibility, especially since they are not presenting your music as advertising. At its most successful, promotion makes people want to buy your record.

Airplay and reviews seldom happen by chance. Many independent record makers still mistakenly believe that the very worthiness of their music will lead to its discovery and attention. In the music business, however, word is not magically passed along. Almost always, newspaper and magazine writers, DJs, and talent promoters are waiting in their offices for news to be brought to them in the form of press releases, free records, and invitations to performances and parties. You are expected to court them, feeding them the news you hope they will in turn feed to their audiences.

Promotion has sometimes been referred to as the art of gentle persuasion. In the music business, however, gentle persuasion has evolved into big business; the combination of money, personnel, power, and influence put out by major record labels for promotion resembles a military campaign in its complexity, intensity, and sophistication. You will be competing with their efforts for attention, as well as with hundreds of other records released each month. Staying home waiting to be discovered is not going to help.

Independent records are dark horses. You will have to work extra hard to attract the attention you need and (hopefully) deserve. You can succeed. Many independents already have, helping to open up access to the media and making your job easier.

A great deal of work needs to be done in advance of making your record. You need to identify your potential audience, to acquire a working knowledge of the media, to assemble mailing lists, and to design and print promotional materials, such as album covers, posters, or photographs. In addition, money should be set aside to meet expenses for promotional materials and such ongoing costs as telephone and postage. So many independents have spent their last dimes making their records sound beautiful and then have no money left to pay for an effective cover, much less for postage to send records to people on their mailing lists.

You will need to acquire a rudimentary knowledge of the promotional methods open to you and use them to gain performances, reviews, and airplay. By adding persistence, imagination, and old-fashioned *chutzpah*, you'll be surprised at the attention you can attract.

IDENTIFYING YOUR AUDIENCE

The first key to putting together a promotional plan is to determine which people are potential purchasers of your record. Although musicians dream that their music is so universal as to guarantee sales in the millions, most record sales start with a loyal following that can be identified.

Knowing your audience helps you assemble graphics and promotional materials that will appeal to them, research and approach the media they pay attention to, and book performances they will attend. By estimating how many of these people you can reach in the first six to eight months after you put out your record, you will be able to assess how many records to press initially. Ask yourself, "Who is going to like my music enough to spend the five to eight dollars on my record that might as easily be spent on another's?"

Begin by identifying the people who already listen to your music—your friends and your fans—and go from there. Try to describe them by age group, sex, social and political interests, occupation, financial status, lifestyle, hobbies, and their taste in music or art. See if you can isolate one or more characteristics that they share. Perhaps you'll find that all of them are guitar players or electronics wizards or that they all practice transcendental meditation and are working mothers. Isolating special interests may open up unusual avenues to follow in order to reach them.

Suppose you can't tell who your fans are. At your next performance, pick out some people at random and interview them. If you are shy about direct confrontation, devise a simple questionnaire that fits onto a postcard and hand it out at gigs, asking people to fill it out and turn it in before they leave. (If you do this, be sure to include a place for their names and addresses to add to your mailing list.)

If your music is similar to that of other recording artists in your community, ask these artists if they have ever analyzed their audience or if they have found any special ways to reach them.

RESEARCHING THE MEDIA

Once you have identified your potential audience, research the media that influences them. Spend some time reading various publications and listening to radio stations. At the same time, make a list of specific writers and DJs who might be sympathetic to your music so that you can personalize your approach and direct your energies towards them when your record is out.

Note the different styles and tastes of specific writers and DJs. Some music critics only review performances, others only pop records; some write regular columns devoted to news about recording studios or 'gossip', such as changes in personnel within a given band. On radio stations, although the program (or music) directors are chiefly responsible for selecting the playlist, each DJ may program distinctly different cuts. One DJ may always choose louder, more raucous songs, and another the more melodic, harmonious ones.

Print. First read the newspapers and magazines published in your community. Are critics only reviewing major label records and performances by major touring groups? How many reviews are given to local performers or records released by independent labels like your own? Are interviews or feature stories being written about anyone other than name performers? Does your community publish any specialty journals devoted to art or music? Don't neglect the Sunday supplements of daily newspapers which often have separate sections dealing with art and music news.

This kind of research will tell you whether you might be able to attract attention in your community, and if so, from whom. Certainly it is much easier to approach critics who have a history of reviewing independents than those who have never reviewed anyone without a big name.

If you find little or no space devoted to independents, you may be able to make your recording project a *'cause célèbre.'* You may be 'new' news, something the media dearly loves.

You may also notice that one person writes for several publications, which will identify him or her as a freelance writer. Freelance writers are good people to approach because they are often looking for fresh story angles for the various publications to which they contribute.

Next, read publications which serve specialized musical interests. These include magazines with circulations of under 100,000, such as *Synapse,* for electronic music lovers, *Mandolin World,* for mandolin artists, or *Paid My Dues,* for women composers and performers, as well as the major music magazines with circulations of well over 100,000, such as *Rolling Stone, Guitar Player, Downbeat, Modern Recording,* or *High Fidelity.* Include the trade magazines, such as *Billboard, Record World,* or *Cash Box,* which serve the recording industry.

As smaller publications may be hard to find in your community, we've listed some of them in the Bibliography. You can write to them directly for sample issues. These smaller publications are often willing to trade subscriptions for records, and offering to do so may open communications with them.

You'll find that the smaller publications regularly feature reviews and stories about alternative projects like your own and will be receptive to hearing from you. On the other hand, the big-time music magazines generally serve the interests of the major record companies. Notice particularly the correlation between the release of a new record from a major label and the barrage of interviews, feature stories, reviews of the album, and advertising that appear simultaneously in the principal music magazines. Some changes are beginning to occur, however, and reviews and stories about independents are occasionally included, particularly if they are felt to be of interest to the readers. Make a note of the writers who have helped break ground for independents on these publications so that you can later send your promotional materials to them.

By the time you finish your research, you should have a good working knowledge of print media people. You should also have a number of ideas about articles that might specifically interest different writers. Your ideas might range from a clever headline to a story about how you financed your project on a shoestring to a brainstorm for some madcap publicity stunt. Keep track of your ideas in your media notebook so that, when you release your record, you can follow through with them.

Radio. Spend a few days exploring the programming of local AM and FM stations to gain some knowledge of their style and tastes as well as to find out if any of them play music from independents. You'll probably find that the more popular AM and FM stations stick to the hits or new records from established artists.

Your best bet is to pay attention to the 'secondary' music stations, which have smaller audiences. They are not as deluged with records from major labels and are more receptive to independents. Other stations that might be researched in your area are listener-supported stations, which generally feature news and talk shows as well as a wide variety of music. College radio stations also tend to be more open to the music of independents, as they have fewer economic considerations. Programming on these stations is looser, politics a bit more casual, and competition for airplay not so fierce.

If you are determined to crack the major stations, listen to the late night DJs first. Their programming policies are less restrictive and occasionally they give airplay to new artists.

When you do discover DJs or radio stations that play music from independents, put their names on your priority media mailing list so you can remember to direct your promotional energies towards them first.

Television. The programming of video music is expanding rapidly, providing new exposure opportunities. Many programs feature a particular genre of music; MTV, for example, features rock and roll. Because music videos catalyze record sales so effectively, the competition for programming space has engendered an expensive barrage from the major labels. In many cases, major label video budgets exceed recording budgets. As a result, most video music programming features major label artists. If you are considering making video clips, investigate the video outlets thoroughly to make sure that some percentage of programming is given to non-major label artists.

Some good bets: public television and local cable or community television. Some night clubs are also beginning to produce and/or syndicate live shows for video programming. Appearing on one of these shows will increase your exposure within the community. It's great free publicity and a good place to direct your promotional efforts.

MAILING LISTS

To know where to send out your promotional materials, and which people to contact when, you

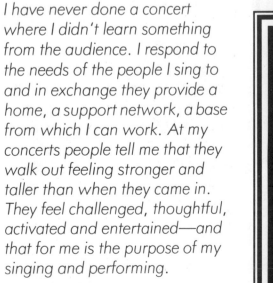

I have never done a concert where I didn't learn something from the audience. I respond to the needs of the people I sing to and in exchange they provide a home, a support network, a base from which I can work. At my concerts people tell me that they walk out feeling stronger and taller than when they came in. They feel challenged, thoughtful, activated and entertained—and that for me is the purpose of my singing and performing.

HOLLY NEAR
Redwood Records

should assemble three mailing lists. The first should consist of media contacts, the second of industry contacts, the third of the names and addresses of all your admirers—essentially a fan list.

Media List. While you are gathering information about specific writers and DJs, put together a list of the names, addresses, and phone numbers of the people at each publication and radio station you intend to approach. Each entry should also indicate the person's job title (e.g., record reviewer, program director, feature writer). You might list as many as ten names for one radio station or newspaper. People new at promotion often mistakenly assume that if one record or press release is sent to someone at a newspaper or radio station, it will automatically be shared with the rest of the staff. You should also make a note of freelance writers. A good media list takes time to assemble, but it is well worth the effort.

You will find it particularly helpful to divide your media list into two separate categories. The first is a priority category of the people who seem both accessible and sympathetic (a critic who has a reputation for writing feature stories or reviews of independents). This category might also include entertainment columns or announcements featured in newspapers, magazines, and radio stations, which advertise the date of your performances free of charge. All you have to do is to get the information in on time to the right person.

The other is a secondary category of the people who seem less accessible but who might be sympathetic and may in the future be able to give you the break you need (such as reviewers for *Rolling Stone* or *High Fidelity*). Some notable success stories have resulted from an important media person suddenly deciding to put a record on the turntable or to print a story.

Each of these two categories on your media list should be further broken down according to whether the contact is print, radio, or television, whether it is local, state, or national, and whether the publications are daily, weekly, or monthly. Note also how far in advance of publication each contact needs to receive information in order to meet their printing deadlines, usually referred to as 'lead time'. You can generally assume that a daily publication needs to have the information three to five days in advance; a weekly, from ten days to three weeks (depending on whether it is local or national); local monthly publications, three to four weeks; na-

tional monthlies, three to four months. If you're unsure, it's good to phone and ask about the lead time.

Sometimes other independents or friends in the business will share their media lists with you. Although this can save you time, you will still need to know whether the people on that list communicate with your potential audience. You should become familiar with what they write in their publications or program on their radio or television shows.

You might find it helpful to transfer your list onto file or Rolodex cards to facilitate finding or changing telephone numbers. Check your list for changes every three months.

Industry List. After you have assembled a media list, you should make another list of people who can help promote your record, hire you, use your songs, or book performances for you. This list should include names and addresses of club owners, promoters, booking agents, managers of groups who might invite you to be the warm-up act for their group, owners and managers of stores which might carry your record, record distributors, executives and producers at major record companies whose attention you might eventually attract, publishers and producers interested in

Most radio stations don't like to take chances. They'd rather play it safe and give the listener the already established hit artist or song. Entirely too many people in radio are more into playing the 'hits' than they are into music. They're more concerned with what's on the charts—with what's already been proven to have audience acceptability and familiarity. But the light continues to shine through at college and listener supported radio stations.

AUGIE BLUME
Music Industry Resources

Point of purchase (P.O.P.) promotion is important to help support stores that carry your record in depth. One of the members of the Subtle Hints band visited every store in areas where the band was performing and gave that store copies of the record for in-store play, buttons, and display material. Because of his local celebrity status, the visit made much more of an impact than one from the distributor or a label.

HOLGER PETERSEN
President, Stony Plain Records, Canada

buying new songs, and secretaries and assistants whose word in the right ear might help your record.

All these names are industry contacts and are people who can help further your career. Again, you should separate the particularly important contacts into a priority category, and always send them your promotional materials before the names in the less likely secondary category. For people not in your local community, research names in either of the two major music directories, *Official Talent and Booking Directory,* or *The Billboard International Buyers' Guide.* (See 'Publications' in the chapter on Business.)

Fan List. While assembling lists of important media and industry people, don't neglect your fans. Their loyalty, support, and enthusiasm are well worth courting. Find out who they are and send them promotional materials about both your record and your performances. A good fan list not only encourages stores to carry your record, but also provides solid evidence of a following to club owners and promoters and improves your chances of getting better gigs.

To start your list, write down the names and addresses of your family and friends. They are your most dedicated supporters and are the most likely to spread the word of your accomplishments. Next, gather the names of people who come to your performances, either by leaving a notebook they can sign close to the entrance or by passing out cards they can fill out and turn in when they leave. You can also add the names and addresses from the questionnaire postcards used in

researching your potential audience. If you add from five to ten names weekly to your fan list, after six months you will have an impressive collection.

Once you have assembled this list of fans, type the names and addresses onto masters that can be duplicated on self-adhesive mailing labels. This will save you time when you do mailings and will make it easy to change names and addresses when you update your list.

PROMOTIONAL MATERIALS

Effective promotional materials will greatly help you compete with the efforts of the major labels to capture the attention of the media and the public. These materials introduce your record, provide key information about you and your music, and arouse curiosity which will induce people to put your record on their turntables.

Your basic promotional materials should include 1) your record, 2) press releases, 3) photographs, and 4) posters, flyers, and similar printed materials to announce performances and advertise your record. At different times during your career, you will be using these materials either singly or in various combinations. Usually, the materials are placed inside a loose folder and referred to as a 'press kit'.

Your Record. The best promotional material you can have is a well-produced recording of your music. After all of your other efforts have convinced DJs, music critics, or major label executives to put your record on their turntables, there has to be something worth listening to.

Nevertheless, don't hide your music inside a poor cover. The first impression your album makes on anyone is visual; they see it long before they hear it. The album cover design is the single most important graphic on which to spend time and money. (The chapter on Graphics discusses cover design in detail.)

Giving your record away liberally is part of any promotional plan. The problem with give-aways is drawing the line. A common rule of thumb is to use them where they will accomplish tangible results: performances, airplay, reviews, in-store play, the promise of a store or distributor to carry the record. Your media list will help you make initial priority decisions. One of the reasons for assembling your media list in advance of the pressing of your record is to help you decide how many records you need for promotional purposes.

In a run of 5,000 records, it is not uncommon to give away as many as 750. That may seem like a lot, but bear in mind that each give-away can result in sales of many more records, can net you a high-paying gig or important review, or can attract a major label.

Press Releases. Most media people prefer information they receive to be capsulized in the form of a press release—a factual mini-story which tells who, what, where, when, and how, directly and simply. A good press release anticipates basic questions and takes responsibility for answering them.

Your first press release about your record should contain very little other than basic information:

► title

► principal musicians, singers, composers

► brief description of the music

► most important song or feature

► price

► how to get it; where it's being sold

► mail order address

All the rules of good journalism apply: a catchy headline and opening sentence; the most important facts first and the least important last; omission of hype and blatant opinions. There is one exception: if you have had some particularly favorable reviews from previous performances, you can include one or two key quotes somewhere towards the end of your press release. Leave out a history of where the musicians were born, what high school they attended, favorite hobbies, and similar information.

Many musicians shy away from trying to describe their music. The reason they often give is that they don't want their music to be labeled or typed. However, reviewers and DJs will describe your music anyway. If you want an accurate and complimentary description, take the time to literally put some words in their mouths. In fact, the more innovative your music is, the more you should try to give the media a handle on it.

Answering the following questions may help you discuss your music without categorizing it too narrowly:

► Who wrote the music?

```
                                    For immediate release
                                    May 7, 1979

THIS GOOD TONIGHT
NEW STEVE SESKIN ALBUM RELEASED

     Popular Bay Area singer/songwriter Steve Seskin has just
released his second album, entitled This Good Tonight, on his
own Bald Ego Records. Including the new, title song, the album
contains seven Seskin originals, as well as four songs penned
by other writers.

     Since the release of his first album, Steve Seskin & Friends
Greatest Hits, Steve has been spending time writing and
performing in Seattle and Los Angeles, as well as the Bay Area.
He will be appearing at San Francisco's Great American Music Hall
with Steve Goodman on May 15 and has a song ("Quiet Time")
slated for Helen Schneider's next album on Windsong Records.

     This Good Tonight was recorded in March at Corasound
Recording in San Rafael. Seskin, who does the vocals, piano, and
acoustic guitar, is joined on the album by Steve Gurr (electric
guitar and harmonica), Kent Middleton (percussion), and Jeff
Breeh (bass). The production is by Steve Seskin with engineering
done by Stephen Hart and Michael Raskovsky.

     This Good Tonight is available in record stores throughout
the Bay Area and the Pacific Northwest, as well as at gigs and
by mail order from Bald Ego Records, 531-4th Avenue, San Francisco,
California 94118.

                         * * *

                                    Please contact:
                                    Ken Baker, 415 864-2333
```

► What is the instrumentation and who are the chief musicians?

► Is the music primarily vocal or instrumental; do melodies, rhythms, or words dominate?

► Is the music highly orchestrated or arranged; does it feature vocal choruses, or large string or brass sections?

This press release for Steve Seskin's second album on Bald Ego Records presents information about Steve's songs, his performances, the recording of the album, personnel, and retail outlets—all in one page.

► Are there any musical styles with which the music has affinity?

► Does the music communicate ideas, causes, or specific moods or emotions?

► What is special about your music or musicians that would help people remember it or arouse interest (biographical information or unusual circumstances surrounding the recording of the album)?

► Have any unusual technical innovations been used (new recording techniques or special vocal or instrumental effects)?

In addition to helping you write your press releases, the answers to all of these questions will provide information that you may also want to use for the back cover copy of your album cover. (See the chapter on Graphics for details.)

Your press releases should be neatly typed, double-spaced, on your letterhead stationery. (The double-spacing makes it easy for reporters or critics to edit your copy.) Try to limit your press releases to one page; if you do need more space, use another page and not the reverse of the first page.

At the top left corner of your press release, write the date and the words, "For Immediate Release". At the top right or bottom left, include the name of a contact person and phone number with the words, "For further information:" written directly above.

It's important to follow these simple suggestions because the media likes to receive its information in this manner. It will show them that you know enough about their business to approach them professionally.

Type one copy of your press release on an electric typewriter to give it a clean, sharp look and to make it easy to duplicate. If you don't know anyone with this kind of typewriter, look in the Yellow Pages under 'Secretarial Services' for the names of people who will do part-time typing on their machines. You can then take your press release to an instant print facility and make as many copies as you think you'll need for a relatively low price. (See the 'Time and Money' section of this chapter for details.) To locate these facilities, look in the Yellow Pages under 'Printers'.

Photographs. The press needs good graphics to enliven its pages. Free publicity can be generated by having a newspaper in your area publish a good black and white photograph of you performing, or a copy of your album cover, if it is exceptionally well designed.

Technically, newspapers and magazines need black and white, non-grainy, glossy photographs with good contrast, preferably 8″ x 10″. Photographs should retain their impact when reduced (or cropped) to fit narrow columns or small boxes; hence, photographs featuring one musician at a time are much more effective than those attempting to include five band members. Action shots are preferable to standard portrait shots if the image is sharp and clear. Cluttered backgrounds are less desirable than plain ones.

For these reasons, it is wise to hire a professional photographer with experience in shooting musicians rather than a friend who has taken some good candid shots. The publicity generated when the photos are used by media will more than make up for the expense of acquiring them. Whenever submitting photographs to newspapers or magazines, credit the photographer.

Once you have chosen prints you like, you can have them reproduced inexpensively at a multiple photo facility. Firms that specialize in quantity photo duplication are listed in the Yellow Pages under the heading: 'Photographers: Commercial.' Obtain estimates since prices vary. (See the section on 'Time and Money' later in this chapter.) Provide lettering with the name of the artist, the title of the album, and a contact person and phone number. This can be stripped in at the bottom of the photos before they are reproduced. Multiple photo facilities can also make a black and white copy negative from your album cover and reproduce it on glossy paper.

Additional Materials. You might want to make a press kit cover as well as flyers, banners, postcards, or calendars to help you book and promote gigs and to draw attention to your album.

The time to assemble these materials is while working with a graphic designer on your album cover. Many of the basic designs he or she will supply you with can be used for multiple purposes. For example, when you are having your album cover printed, you can request an additional number to be printed on heavier paper. The extra charge for doing this will be minimal because the presses and inks are already set up, and you will pay only for the extra paper and press time. You can use these extra covers as mini-posters to enclose with sales letters and order forms to fans. The same graphic can be reduced and used for postcards, flyers, calendars, or as a cover for your press kit.

Using your album cover graphics as the basis for some of these extras will not only save you money but will help identify your group with that graphic image. Songwriter Margie Adam compiled an impressive press kit using the same black and white photograph on her album cover, on her press kit cover, and as part of a poster announcing her concert appearances.

Your initial investment for these extra materials may seem high, but you'll save a considerable amount of money by assembling them all at once. (See 'Other Promotional Materials' in the chapter on Graphics.)

PERFORMING

News of your record will get stale fast, and you will need a reason to keep hounding the media for attention. Regular performances serve this purpose. Exposure to large numbers of people over an extended period of time wins new fans and creates excitement among media people. Don't forget that performing is far more accessible to independents than airplay. Use your record and promotional materials to book club and concert performances—the bigger the better.

Mail or personally deliver free copies of your record and promotional materials to people on your industry mailing list who might hire you for performances. These will include club owners, concert promoters, booking agents, and managers of compatible performing groups with draws larger than yours who might be interested in using you as a warm-up act. Your materials will provide them with evidence of professionalism and success, as well as with the means to publicize any performances.

The most important publicity materials to send are 1) a press release with date, time, and place omitted, 2) a black and white photograph, 3) a flyer and/or performance poster with a space left blank for filling in the date, time, and place. Any extra promotional items, such as display posters or banners for use inside concert halls or clubs, should be mentioned in a personal letter emphasizing your need for bookings and your willingness to help publicize your performances. You can also offer to share your mailing list of fans. Follow up your efforts with phone calls.

Bookings will result. You may, however, be surprised at (and perhaps offended by) the low wages you are offered for playing key concerts or for touring with other groups. Remember that a good platform from which to create excitement can be worth a great deal more than a decent wage for your performance. It's a common trade-off in the music business. You might not realize that many first-album groups for major labels lose a great deal of money touring in their first year; in the balance, they gain attention from the media, increase their draw, add new fans, and sell records. Keeping your long-term goals in mind will help you make clear decisions about which performances are worth your while.

Once you have a performing contract, it is your responsibility to provide club owners or concert promoters with adequate publicity materials, weeks in advance of the show. Sometimes you will have to send out additional materials on your own. This is especially true if you are not the main act on a billing.

For each performance, write your own press release and send it to everyone on all three of your mailing lists. If the booking is very special (a particularly well-established concert hall, for instance), invite the press, DJs, record store owners, distributors, and other club owners to see you. Follow up your invitations with phone calls. Usually club owners and promoters will grant you a number of free passes for the media because it draws extra publicity for themselves as well. Even if you have to shell out some of your performing wages so that you can send tickets to nearby college promoters, recognize that one well-paid performance will more than compensate for the tickets you bought.

When you do invite guests to your performance, make absolutely sure that their names are on a guest list so that the person at the box office or at the door won't hassle them. In some cases, this mistake has led to adverse publicity. It's also good if you have press kits and extra records to hand out. Your album may have been shelved, filed obscurely, or given to a secretary the first time around. An extra copy to an important media person who shows up at your performance means that she or he will have it on hand when needed.

If guests do show up, call them the next day for feedback. Striking while the iron's hot may make the difference between getting a gig or review and not getting it. It's also good form.

When you do get reviews, make copies of them to mail to all the people on your media and industry

Margie Adam's press kit for Pleiades records makes use of a simple motif: a series of close-up, black and white photographs. Using these as full-page 'bleeds', her kit includes printed sheets containing information about Margie's album, her biography and personal philosophy, reviews, personal appearances, and glossy photos for reproduction. Copies of recent reviews are added to the kit regularly. The well-designed cover rounds out this press kit as a very effective personal presentation.

mailing lists. DJs and reviewers are impressed when you receive attention from others and it often prompts them into action. DJs and program directors often need a little extra input to decide to listen to your record and to give it airplay. Don't forget to add copies of these reviews to the promotional materials you use to book gigs.

Unlike the major labels, who concentrate their efforts on promoting new records for only a month or two after their release, you can take up to a year or more to get your record off the ground. Each booking gives you a new excuse to barrage the people on your mailing lists with press releases, photographs, flyers, and pleas for attention. This keeps your contact live over a long period of time. Eventually your persistence will bring reluctant reviewers or DJs to hear you or will persuade them to take your record down from their shelves and to put it on their turntables. If they like your music, they will review it or play your record on the air. This will lead to better gigs, more important reviews, more airplay, more excitement, more fans, and, ultimately, more sales.

REVIEWS

Media people are swamped with more news than they can handle. They need your press releases to write their articles, reviews, or interviews. The easier you make their job, the more likely they will be to give you their attention. You'll be surprised at how many articles or reviews are written directly from your press release, using your exact words.

Send your initial press kit to everyone on your media list. Include free copies of your record to people in the priority category of your media list. Ask for reviews or stories from them first, before you contact the people in the secondary category. Include a letter describing your project.

Don't stop with your first press release, even if there is no response. The more press releases you send out, the better are your chances of familiarizing the media with your name and eventually capturing their interest. Repetition works. Subsequent press releases can feature a brief biography of the musicians in the band, an account of how you made your record, a short interview with one of the principal musicians, a notice about changes in band personnel, or news of success in signing with a major booking agent. Each

new booking is a valid excuse for sending out a fresh press release.

Keep your press releases factual and straightforward; opinions and praise can be added by the press. With particularly newsworthy press releases, include a black and white photograph. The use of your photograph is great free advertising.

Follow up press releases with phone calls asking for attention. Be polite and brief, and *never* get angry with a media person for not using your press release or not showing up at a performance as promised, even if it is the tenth time it has happened. You will often be preempted by famous groups and more skilled promotional efforts. The press may feel guilty about not giving more coverage to alternative and independent efforts like your own, and eventually someone may give you the break you need.

FEATURE STORIES

Every newspaper and magazine uses regular staff or freelance writers whose job it is to find and write feature stories. Their names are easy to spot because, unlike regular news items, their stories are signed. It's your job to interest them with possible stories.

Feature stories include more information about a performer or group than do reviews or press releases. They can be done as interviews or biographies, can focus on a particular aspect of a performer or group, or can capture an event through a series of photographs. Although feature stories are usually reserved for name performers, exciting, controversial subject matter from less well-known groups can draw the attention of certain feature writers.

Dream up unusual angles on your endeavors and frame your ideas in the form of a brief cover letter. One or two enticing sentences should be enough to arouse their curiosity. With the cover letter, include your record and other promotional materials, especially a good photograph illustrating your suggestions. The more specific you can be about your idea for a story, the better. Here are some examples of short descriptions sent to feature writers:

► "Bronco busters and steer ropers aren't the only performers at a rodeo: California Zephyr, an independent recording group, makes its living on the rodeo circuit."

► "How did a Greek, a Scandinavian, and an outcast

Regular performances are essential to your promotion plan. Bread and Roses Festival, Berkeley, California.

from San Jose become the foremost balalaika trio in San Francisco?"

▶ "Janis Sherman built her recording studio from scratch before making her own record."

Follow up your letter with a phone call to check on their response and to provide additional information. Don't get discouraged if your ideas are rejected initially. Think up a new approach and try again.

Photo stories, which are a special form of feature story, can sometimes be placed in magazines or newspapers more easily than interviews or articles, simply because they are visually appealing and very few people take advantage of this accessible form of promotion. For example, a photo story showing how you recorded your album might make an excellent feature for a Sunday supplement or local music magazine, especially if you are not located in a music business center.

Finally, when a writer does respond to your ideas and prints a feature story about you or your group, write him or her a note of thanks. It is always appreciated, and helps cement your contact.

AIRPLAY

For independents like yourself, the most difficult, albeit effective, way to promote your record is to gain access to airplay. By exposing their audiences to a sample of the music on your record, DJs quickly create excitement and demand for it among large numbers of people. Approximately 70% to 80% of the public learns of a new record or artist through hearing it on the radio. In fact, in the record business, the word 'promotion' often narrowly refers to persuading DJs to play records on the air.

As you will have found in your research, priority on most major AM and FM radio stations is given to top hits by known artists in almost every musical category. However, you should have located some stations that will be receptive to your music, such as smaller FM stations and college radio stations. The names of their program directors and DJs should be on your priority media list, and you should first direct your energy towards them.

Before approaching a radio station, remember that airplay goes hand in hand with sales. If you do interest radio stations in playing your record, assure them that your record is available in the stores. Many radio stations will take a record off the air if listeners call in to say they can't find it anywhere.

Send your records to the program or music directors of the stations. They listen (as time and inclination allow) to many of the new releases they receive each week and from them choose what will be aired. Personal musical tastes of the stations' music directors greatly influence what gets played and how frequently.

Send at least three (or more) records to each program or music director. One will be his or her private copy; another will be placed in the music library so that there will be a 'clean' record in case airplay is desired; the third will be put out for the DJs to listen to. If you know any DJs who might be especially receptive to your music, send or leave extra copies with personal notes for them. Include a press release and promotional poster with each record. Follow through with calls and visits to remind them that you need their help.

One good reason for having a priority media list is to decide how many promotional records you will initially give away. Remember that your records are the cheapest form of promotion and advertising you have. Be liberal about giving them away to program directors and DJs.

Introduce yourself to the major FM stations on your secondary media list by sending them all your press releases and, if you can afford it, copies of your record. Let them know if you have received any significant airplay on any of the secondary stations as a way of encouraging them to listen to your record. At the same time, be aware that on these stations you are competing with major record companies for attention and that music programming is tightly controlled.

Repeated public performances, favorable reviews, fans who call up and request your record, and your own persistent mailings of press releases and promotional materials can pay off, even nine months down the road. You will also find that as soon as one major radio station 'goes' on your record, you can more easily persuade others to follow.

PROFESSIONAL SERVICES

Independent public relations firms work to stir up excitement in the media and to bring about articles and reviews, while independent record promoters try to gain airplay. Both can be very effective in your promotional plans and can take a big work load off your shoulders. The problem is that the good ones are expensive. (See the section on 'Time and Money' later in this chapter.)

The time to hire P.R. and promotion people is when your record has not only recouped initial expenses, but has made enough cash available to you to justify it. At that point, they will be able to take advantage of the groundwork you have already laid. Remember that results from promotional efforts often occur only over a long period of time. Six months of deluging the media with information before getting attention is not uncommon, even for a celebrity.

The best way to find a good P.R. firm or independent promotion company is to ask people who have used their services, particularly at the level you need. In all cases, be particularly wary of firms who promise to do large mailings of your album, but not the painstaking personal follow-through that brings results.

ADVERTISING

Advertising is the most costly means of letting people know your record is for sale. In the experience of many independents, it is not as effective as the other promotional methods outlined, especially when your album first comes out, because it puts you into direct competition with the major labels, who have more

Darol Anger / Barbara Higbie

Windham Hill Records

C-1021   Tideline

power, money, and advertising know-how than you as an independent can possibly hope to have. Until you know that every ninety dollars you might spend for a minute of advertising on a major FM station will reap you at least that much in sales in the stores, spend your money elsewhere. One-time print media advertising, except where it also publicizes an upcoming performance, has little initial effect.

Black and white photo posters featuring the same graphics used on album or cassette covers are inexpensive to print. Use the white space for gig announcements or for drawing attention to store and concert record sales. Quotes from good reviews add credibility.

There is one exception: many independents have found it useful to advertise their records in the classified sections of specialty publications. Notices there are inexpensive and good response has been reported. One country-label owner regularly advertises in a magazine aimed at private pilots—he claims they love bluegrass. Again, knowing your audience pays off.

SAMPLE PROMOTIONAL PLAN

The following sample plan outlines a schedule for staggered promotional mailings. It assumes that an important concert is scheduled for a month to six weeks after receiving your records from the manufacturer. This will allow time to get records into a few key stores. Note that each mailing contains a new press release and different promotional materials.

You can adapt this plan to your needs, but whatever plan you decide on, write it out. This will not only remind you when to send out mailings, but will also help you project expenses.

FOUR WEEKS BEFORE THE PERFORMANCE

► Send the record with a press release describing the record, together with a personal letter telling how this record was made and asking for attention. Limit this initial mailing to the people on the priority media list most likely to review the record or to give it airplay.

► Send a record and press kit geared to booking performances, together with a personal letter, to club owners or promoters most likely to offer additional bookings. If possible, deliver some of these personally.

► Follow up mailing of records with a phone call about three days after they should have been received.

► Send a press release describing the record and an order form to the rest of the people on your three mailing lists.

THREE WEEKS BEFORE THE PERFORMANCE

► Send a press release announcing the concert and a black and white photograph with caption to all the people on the media list.

► Phone the people on the priority media list to make sure they received the press release. Ask them again to announce the performance and tell them an invitation is forthcoming.

► Send a press release and/or a promotional flyer announcing the concert to all names on your mailing lists. If there is time, write on each press release intended for fans the words, "Hope you can come."

TWO AND A HALF WEEKS BEFORE THE PERFORMANCE

► Send a press release telling *where* the record can be bought to everyone on your three mailing lists. If any early reviews have appeared, make copies of them and include them in this mailing.

TWO WEEKS BEFORE THE PERFORMANCE

► Mail invitations to the performance (two guest passes per person) to key reviewers, DJs, and program directors. Include a letter telling them that they will be personal guests and that additional records and press kits will be on hand for them.

► Mail invitations and personal letters to others who might help sales of your record: club owners, store owners, promoters, booking agents, and potential record distributors.

ONE WEEK BEFORE THE PERFORMANCE

► Call everyone invited to the performance and personally invite them again. (An alternative is to send out a mailgram.) Let them know that this is a big performance and that you need reviews, airplay, and additional bookings. Let them know your record is a dark horse and needs its chance along with the many major label records released.

AFTER THE PERFORMANCE

► Telephone or write thank-you notes to people who were sent invitations and showed up.

► Send off any printed reviews that resulted to all the people on the media and industry mailing list.

► Start another series of staggered mailings for an upcoming performance.

TIME AND MONEY

If you are going to take the time to finance, produce, and manufacture your record, not doing the follow-through promotion to let people know about it is just plain crazy. You are the person who should direct the energy that creates airplay, reviews, and, finally, sales, because you are the person who cares the most. Although you can hire people to do some specific tasks of promotion, the main responsiblity of the job rests with you. Remember, it is your time, your efforts, and your music which reap you the benefits you deserve!

Your greatest promotional investment will be time; it will also be your greatest ally. Success with promotion happens over the long haul, not with a one-time, one-stamp effort. It will take a great deal of perseverance before you can expect to see tangible results from your efforts—as long as two months to convince an influential reviewer to come and hear you perform; three months to book some good college dates that will happen six months down the road; six months to convince two or three radio stations to play your record. It may take years and perhaps two albums to build an audience that will prove to a major record company that you are worth signing to their label.

Meanwhile, you will be doing the tedious, unexciting, and seemingly endless work of mailing out press release after press release, making phone calls, and updating mailing lists. Just as learning an instrument didn't happen overnight, neither will you achieve instant success in promoting your music. You will need many of the same qualities: perseverance, enthusiasm, confidence, and a strong desire to succeed. You will, however, be able to look back over each block of three months and see progress in all areas: in reviews and airplay, in better gigs, in more record sales.

The time needed for promotion *will* cut into the time you spend creating your music and rehearsing with other musicians. Once again, if you are committed to furthering your career, it is no longer realistic to set aside business responsibilities for the mythical manager, promoter, or P.R. person.

As for money, your greatest expense will be your initial outlay for good promotional materials that you will use repeatedly in the year following the release of your record. To economize, as well as to better publicize your record, you should make use of the elements from your album cover for most of your promotional materials. (The cost of album cover design and production is discussed at length in the 'Time and Money' section of the chapter on Graphics.) Press releases can be duplicated at an instant print facility for about $11 per 500.

A professional photographer will charge from $35 to $100 for a shooting fee and from $15 to $40 per

print ordered to be duplicated for promotional purposes. In order to save money, you should try to combine the photo session needed for promotion with that needed for your album cover. Reproductions of black and white glossy photographs at a multiple photo facility range from $30 to $40 per 100.

An initial, one-time expense you will have is a bulk mail permit. While this will cost a little extra at the start, it will cut down your postage costs considerably as you proceed with your promotional mailings. (See the chapter on Business for details.)

After you get started, your ongoing expenses will be your phone bill ($150 a month is not unreasonable), postage, reprints of reviews, additional press releases, extra stationery and envelopes as needed, transportation, and wear and tear on your shoes and your soul. You might expect to set aside from $300 to $500 a month for promotional expenses.

Peter Mintun, Cue Records, placed this 2¼" x 2¾" ad in The New Yorker. *His postcard handout lists the contents of his second album.*

Mail orders from Hawaii were jamming my post office box and I didn't have sense enough to realize that letter reaction like that must have meant I was getting monster airplay on KPOI. The truth hurts. A full year later I ran into John Selby from KPOI and he said, 'Wow, man, you were red hot over there. You could have dumped an easy 5000 records and gigged your ass off'. You know that expression Mr. Natural makes when he falls over backwards after witnessing Flakey Foont do something dumb? That's how I felt.

JEF JAISUN
Virgin Vinyl Records

As your record sales increase, you may choose to hire a P.R. firm or an independent promotion firm. An average monthly fee for a P.R. firm working on a national basis is $800 to $1200. Fees may be lower for a firm hired to publicize one key performance. The P.R. firm will also charge you for every phone call they make on your behalf and every stamp they lick. The fee for an independent record promoter usually starts at $1000 a month, but can be higher depending on the kind of stations covered and the difficulty of the job for which they are hired. The independent record promoters seldom charge you for their phone calls. In both cases, if you hire these firms, find out what additional expenses you will be paying for and ask for an estimate.

Tight Budgets. To best decide how to save money, list your needs in order of priority. Here are some tips:

► Researching your audience, assembling a media list, writing press releases, and putting together a plan cost little more than time. Spend it liberally. Do these steps in advance of recording so that you aren't dividing your energy while recording, or cutting into time you will need to rehearse for performances scheduled after your record is released.

► Your indispensable promotional materials are your record, press releases, and photographs. Their design, wording, and clear reproduction are crucial. This is not the place to save money.

► If you need to be stingy, hone down your priority media list and mail fewer photographs, since they are more expensive to duplicate. One of the main reasons for having two categories for your media and industry mailing lists is so that you know how to decrease the amount of promotional mailings, if necessary. Even when you have a bulk mail permit, multiple mailings can overextend your monthly budget.

► Flyers, posters, banners, and other extras are luxury items. However, if you remember to order extra cover slicks at the time your record is printed, you can use them to make inexpensive, effective posters by mounting them onto larger pieces of paper. (For more information, see the chapter on Graphics.)

► If you're almost broke when your record is released, put a few boxes of records together with some press releases in the back seat of your car and personally deliver them to local press and radio stations on your priority media list and local booking agents, club owners, and promoters. Include personal letters. Make follow-up phone calls a week later.

Chapter 2
Sales

AT SOME POINT, YOUR EFFORTS AT PROMOTION WILL BE successful enough to convince people to buy your record. Your main sales job is to make it available.

Although you will not be able to make your record as accessible and as visible as a Stevie Wonder album, you will be able to persuade most small stores and some major ones in your community to carry it. You can also sell it through mail order and at your performances. As sales increase, through your efforts at booking and promotion, you might also be able to persuade a record distributor to help give your record wider distribution.

Initially, you will have to do most of the sales work yourself. You will very likely confront the same challenge as people learning to juggle: trying to set many different elements into motion at the same time. Reviewers will prefer to review your record or DJs to give it airplay after they know it is being sold in record stores. Most stores and record distributors want to be assured that both performances and promotional support are forthcoming before they agree to handle your record; and, of course, people won't buy your record until they've seen you perform, read about your album, or heard your music played on the radio.

Coordinating all of these elements takes months of hard work. You'll wish you could make everything happen at once. In the meantime, set reasonable, modest, and specific sales goals and try hard to accomplish them. Many independents take a year to sell 5,000 records. Remember: performing is the most effective method for giving people a taste of your music and letting them know your record is available.

FORMAT AND PRICING

Today's recordings are available as long playing records, compact discs and cassettes. The '45' single, which has become increasingly rare, may be replaced by the CD single. Other formats include a 7" record to be played at 33⅓ RPM; and 12" 45s.

Since many recording labels release music in different formats, where and how you intend to reach your audience and where your music will be sold are important factors in determining the format and quantity appropriate for your project.

The recording company decides on the retail list price of records, cassettes and compact discs. Most set the retail list price at $8.98 or $9.98 for long playing records and cassettes and $15.98 or $16.98 for compact discs. Lower retail prices (between $12.98 and $14.98) for compact discs are anticipated by late 1988. The retail price of the compact disc single is expected to be just below $5.00, the retail price common for the 12" 45. 45" singles are $1.98. The retail price determines the following discount prices:

► A discount price at which stores frequently sell to customers (set by the store).

► The wholesale price at which record distributors buy from recording companies (distributor wholesale price).

► The wholesale price at which stores buy from a record company or from record distributors (store wholesale price).

Here is the range of figures you will most likely be dealing with.

Distributor wholesale price	Store wholesale price	Retail list price
LPs or Cassettes		
$3.75–4.49	$5.38–5.83	$8.98
$4.00–5.48	$5.98–6.18	$9.98
Compact discs		
$8.35–10.00	$11.15–11.75	$15.98
$8.80–10.70	$11.80–12.50	$16.98
CD singles or 12" 45s		
$2.00–2.49	$2.98–3.23	$4.98
7" 45s		
$.89–1.00	$1.18–1.28	$4.98

The lower wholesale prices are given as incentives for large volume buys. Frequently, major record labels include a bonus of 15 free records per 100 sold, which means an even lower distributor wholesale price.

As an independent, you must set prices that work for you. Do not be afraid to be innovative or to offer retail or wholesale prices different from the ranges quoted above.

You determine your store and distributor wholesale price schedule in much the same way that you determine how much money you will perform for in any given situation.

You ask yourself what is the nature of your competition and what is your popularity (or draw). Specifically, you must ask yourself these questions:

► Is my record packaged and recorded well enough to compete with comparable records available at the price I have set?

► What will my total expenses be?

► How many records must I sell to break even?

► How long can I wait for my money?

As you read the rest of this book, keep these questions in mind. In addition to helping you determine your pricing policies, they will help you decide how much money to spend on recording and album cover design, how many records to press, and what promotional materials to order initially.

SELLING AT PERFORMANCES

Many people buy records as a direct result of hearing performers at clubs, concerts, or festivals. A live concert is so powerful an introduction to a record that many labels, both large and small, won't sign artists who are not willing to perform on a regular basis.

One of the greatest advantages of making records yourself is that you can sell them at performances. This is virtually impossible if you sign with one of the major labels, as they feel it undercuts the efforts of distributors and stores in the area. (If you have signed with a small label, arrangements for having large quantities of albums supplied to you for sales at performances should be negotiated at the time of your contract. Otherwise, once you have received the free ones you are entitled to, you will have to buy them at the same cost as the distributors.)

Selling at performances is good business. It's the most direct way for people to buy your record when your music is fresh in their minds. Sales can be as high as 50% of the audience.

Selling at performances is a quick way to start making back some of the money you invested in producing your album. You don't have to give a store or distributor a cut or wait to be paid. In the first few months, you should be able to count on direct sales to at least meet your monthly promotional and sales expenses, such as transportation costs and phone bills.

Finally, selling your record at performances starts a bandwagon of fans who will often go to astonishing lengths to support you. They will buy your record and play it for friends. They will call radio stations with requests. They will look for extra copies in record stores near them. The demand created by these fans can be used to persuade stores or distributors to handle your record and reviewers and DJs to give it attention.

Special Prices. Some artists sell their records, cassettes and compact discs at performances for the full retail price. Others like to offer fans a special discount. Although opinion varies as to whether this will decrease store sales, most artists agree that, unless you are selling thousands of records at performances, all sales help generate others.

If you take advantage of your performances to offer a special price, display that fact prominently on your poster: "Special Performance Price." Round off your price so that you can make change easily—like $5.00 or $6.00. Most states require that sales tax be collected for record sales, so you should build the correct sum into your price.

Club Performances. Club owners are generally receptive to having records sold at a performance, as it adds excitement to the event. Sometimes club owners will go out of their way to be helpful, particularly if the artist has taken the time to involve them in the overall plans. If you want to sell at a club, try to make arrangements in advance of the performance.

At concerts people started to request recordings of the songs I'd written so I decided to make a record. It began to sell well and Folkways, a New York City–based record company, became interested in what I was doing. *A Pilgrim Son* continues to sell and due to the venture of having produced my own record I now have another album out on a well-respected label.

MARCUS UZILEVSKY
Oaksprings Workshop

George Thorogood's second album, Move It On Over, *on Rounder Records, has now sold over 450,000 copies and topped number 75 on all three trade magazine record charts. Its success was greatly due to large-scale FM airplay and subsequent AM airplay, gained mainly through prolonged efforts and hard work by such independent promotors as Augie Blume and Associates, coupled with performances that made fanatics of attendees.*

Only in rare cases will club owners ask that a portion of the money be turned over to the club.

Concerts. Some promoters of concerts and festivals allow records or other promotional items to be sold at their events. If you make inquiries well in advance, your chances for acceptance will be greater.

Soon after you have made final arrangements for performing, ask about auditorium or union regulations on consignment sales, whether there is a convenient space for you to set up a display or sales booth, and whether there are special fees, insurance requirements, or other red tape. Make sure you let the promoters know that you are willing to do most of the work involved and that you do not intend to add to their burdens.

In general, you will find that outdoor concerts, in almost all musical categories, include some provision for sales of albums and promotional items. Promoters of these concerts understand that a festival often introduces unusual or unknown artists, and that records made by them are seldom available in the stores. They also appreciate that income from record sales at the concert supplements the musicians' pay.

Nevertheless, even when promoters are receptive, sales arrangements vary. A common arrangement is for the promoter to provide a space where records can be sold and to take responsibility for handling the sales. The artist consigns the records to the promoter and the promoter takes a percentage of the actual sales.

Sometimes local record distributors arrange for special booths to sell all the records they carry, including yours. They pay the promoter either a percentage of sales or a rental fee for the booth. The drawback to this arrangement is that artists do not see the cash immediately from these sales but must wait for payment from the distributor. Occasionally the distributor will agree to pay directly following the concert, but it is rare.

In other cases, the artists themselves set up a card table or booth to handle sales, either without charge, for a small fee, or for a percentage of the sales. If you do this, don't depend on volunteer help to staff your booth. It can be frustrating, inefficient, and an unwelcome burden on friends. Sitting in a booth away from the main area of the concert, and dealing with sales and money, is hard work. It is a job that involves responsibility, time, and energy, and you would do better to pay whomever helps you.

Increasing Sales. It is not enough simply to make arrangements to sell your records at performances. You must take advantage of this sales opportunity. Here are some suggestions:

► Perform songs from your record; it is a good way to interest the audience in buying it. This might seem obvious, but many performers become so carried away with new material, and so tired of performing old songs, that they neglect doing this. When you do perform those songs, be sure to tell the audience that they are on your record.

► Announce at least once during each set, preferably right before your last song, that your record is available for sale and where it can be purchased. The announcement should be simple and short, with no added hype: "Many of you know that we recently released a record called _____. For those of you who would like to buy a copy, we have some on sale here in the main lobby for $_____. It's also on sale at (name local record stores where it can be found)."

► Reinforce your announcements with a display near the front of the stage or in the lobby that shows your album cover and the words, "On Sale Here."

► Consider giving away some small promotional items which will help people remember the name of the record and where to buy it when they leave the concert. These can be postcards, matchbooks, posters, bumper stickers—whatever you dream up and can afford.

► Add each buyer's name and address to your fan list. (See the chapter on Promotion.) Someone who has just bought your record will usually appreciate being notified of future performances you have in the area, new records which you intend to produce, or other relevant news. Be careful to keep accurate sales records; you will need them for tax purposes.

SELLING IN STORES

Placing your record for sale in record stores should be one of your main sales goals. Once you have persuaded an audience that your record is worth buying, it will be important that stores in the area carry it.

Obtaining Accounts. Long before you start recording your album or designing the cover, you should visit all the record stores in your area to see which records they carry and how they are priced. See whether they specialize in any particular kind of music. Check their stock to see what other records from independent labels they carry and how they are displayed, as well as what their selection is of your type of music. Explain your project to the owners and ask what volume of sales might be expected. This will give you an initial feeling of how easy it will be to go back to them when you receive your records from the manufacturer.

Before you make your visits, keep in mind the following two points. First, success at getting your records into a store does not guarantee sales. No matter how good your records are, they won't sell until you create a demand for them. Customers generally know what they are looking for when they go to a store; they are unlikely to find and buy your record by some happy accident. Even the smallest record stores carry as many as 500 titles; the largest 'super stores', up to 16,000.

Second, initial sales in stores will be slow. It can take up to six months of steady work in both promotion and performances to convince interested fans to spend money on your record rather than on one of the top hits attracting their attention as they enter a store. Recognizing this early will spare you the frustration which often follows unrealistic expectations. In smaller stores, sales may average only a few records a month; in the larger ones, perhaps as many as five a month.

Your awareness of these points will help you understand the perspective of the store owners. They make their money on the biggest-selling albums of any genre. They will carry your record if there is a demand

for it, to complement the records they offer in a particular category (electronic music, for example), or, in exceptional cases, to do you a favor.

You will probably find that the most receptive stores are the small, individually owned ones, especially those specializing in particular kinds of music, such as jazz, bluegrass, or reggae. The owners of these stores are often sympathetic to individual business efforts, which in many ways resemble their own. Like independent labels, they are attempting to provide customers with records they might not find in the larger chain stores.

The next stores to visit are the large discount record stores which depend on huge volumes of business for their success. In some instances, they price the records so low as to net them less than twenty cents an album. Records that sell in two's and three's are not going to interest them, nor will dealing with an individual rather than a distributor. Not only does it complicate their bookkeeping, but past experience has led them to believe that individuals won't service the account regularly or keep the records in stock. What is encouraging is to realize that at *some* point they will want to carry your record.

Once your record is out, you should persist in going back again and again with news of reviews and

One of the most tedious jobs of being a record company is setting up and maintaining distribution accounts. The painstaking work we did on the distribution end helped land our CBS contract and put us in the position of not having to do it anymore.

STEVEN SEID
415 Records

airplay and reports of sales in other places. Your perseverance will indicate that you are serious and that you can responsibly service the account. When the discount stores think that you are going to bring in customers, they will stock your record.

You might want to browse through a few of the 'rack' stores that carry records as only part of their total inventory, such as supermarkets, department stores, and drugstores. These racks are traditionally stocked with the top twenty albums in the country. Trying to gain access to these stores is usually a waste of time.

You need not confine your sales efforts to record stores. Depending on the style of your music, you might think of placing your record in health food stores, bookstores, small craft shops, or religious or ethnic shops. Direct-to-disc records (see the chapter on Recording Options) and other exceptionally well-recorded albums are sometimes sold in stereo or audiophile stores and are occasionally played to help demonstrate the equipment.

When your record is out, go back to the stores which were most receptive. Save returning to the more reluctant ones until you have proven sales at performances or other stores. You should, however, drop off a copy of your record and press kit at all the stores that might carry your record and tell them that you would appreciate hearing their response. Make a point of revisiting the stores within a week of leaving off promotional copies. If you perform in the area, invite store managers to attend. They will probably refuse, but at least they will be aware of your efforts to help promote your record. Send stores all your press releases.

As was stated in the previous chapter, reserve making your greatest promotional push until after you have set up distribution in enough record stores so that people can locate your record easily. There is nothing more frustrating than to read a review or to hear a record played on the air and to not be able to find it. Even the DJ will be discouraged if listeners call and complain that no store carries your record.

Discounts and Consignments. Stores normally buy records from distributors at approximately half the retail selling price. Variations of as much as fifty cents below or above that figure have been reported. In some cases, independents offer records to stores at close to a distributor's discount so as to induce the stores to carry them. Bear in mind that, as the owner of your record label, you determine the pricing and payment policies. Mixed pricing policies make store owners uncomfortable. Work out payment arrangements before visiting stores and keep them consistent.

One way to encourage stores to carry your record is to offer it to them on consignment, which means they pay only for records sold. You might also decide to sell your record to the stores at one price on consignment and at another, lower price for outright sale. In either case, the record label always agrees to take back records which are found to be defective upon opening.

A sample consignment form is shown on page 26. Whatever form you use, make a carbon so that both you and the store can have a copy. Every time you check with the store and discover that they have sold records and need more, collect for the ones they have sold, and make out a new consignment form. One easy way to keep track is to use the sales record form on page 28 and keep that form and the separate consignment forms in a notebook. The consignment form acts as both receipt and order form; the sales form keeps track of total sales and consignments.

As long as you service the stores personally, they will usually pay cash each time you consign more records. This method helps eliminate delays in payments, something you will appreciate more once you start working with distributors and pricing and billing policies become more complicated.

Servicing Accounts. Once you have put records in a store, it is your job to keep track of them.

Most of what we do is musical comedy and New Wave. We're very big into irreverence—we just released a lampoon album of the Village People. Novelty records used to be released fifteen to twenty years ago by major labels, but nowadays they're very secular, very conservative. Our best market is New York; there are crazier people in New York.

HAROLD BRONSON
Owner, Rhino Records

CONSIGNMENT CONTRACT

Date _____

Consigned to _____
               name of store

_____
address   phone

_____ copies of the album called _____,

_____.
name of label   catalog number

Suggested retail price _____

Price to Consignee   _____

Payment:

_____ days after billing for records sold. Full returns accepted.

Records are property of _____
                         name of label

and may be removed at their discretion.

Thank you.

_____
signature of consigner

_____
signature of consignee

Sample consignment form. You can have printed forms prepared with your company's logo.

Only in the case of incredible demand will store managers call you when they run out of copies of your record. The first time you go to a store, be sure to let owners and managers know that you are aware of your responsibility to service the store personally. You must make it as easy as possible for the stores to carry your record. Regular servicing of accounts and extreme courtesy on your part are essential to setting up a good working relationship.

To start, consign only a couple of albums at a time to the stores, even if you have to go back as often as every two weeks. Psychologically, it's better for them to sell out a few copies than to have unsold stock collecting dust on the shelves. If you find that your record is not 'moving' in a store, either reduce the number consigned (even if you are reducing the number from five records to two) or take them out altogether and reallocate them to stores where they are selling.

When stores do agree to sell your record, give them one of your posters to put up—or ask if they would like you to do it. You might also make your own 'bin' card to save your record from being filed in either the 'miscellaneous' section or one of the other alphabetized bin sections. Another old sales trick is to move your record up to the front of the section (not while the owner is watching!).

When sales pick up in any particular store, you can ask for more advantageous placing of your record, in-store play, and window display. The store manager will not do any of this automatically; you will have to ask. At the start, however, when you don't know what the volume of sales is going to be, keep your requests simple. Your priority is establishing a good working relationship.

Having Friends Help. Friends may offer to urge the stores near them to carry your record or even to sell records for you. However, relying on friends to do this is often more trouble than doing it yourself, especially as the number of stores carrying your records starts to increase. The store owner needs one person to assume responsibility for the account. Your friend may get the records into the store, but who is going to reconsign and collect money? If your friend collects money and doesn't see you immediately afterwards, he or she may owe you that amount indefinitely. The payment might not seem large in itself (ten dollars or less perhaps), but small sums from many friends add up fast.

The best way to handle offers of help is to ask your friend to make a list of the names and addresses of stores and to visit them either alone or with your friend. Explain that you need to keep careful track of all the store business for tax purposes and that, as much as you appreciate the favors, you need to do the work involved yourself.

The other possibility is to hire your friend (or someone else) to handle *all* the accounts as a job paid hourly with a commission on sales as added incentive.

RECORD DISTRIBUTORS

Consigning records to stores and selling them at performances and through the mail is hard work. From the beginning, you will wish that someone would do it for you. That is the business of a record distributor. A record distributor's job is similar to your own solitary efforts to put your records into stores where they can be sold, except that it is done on a grander scale.

Record distributors make money by carrying records from many different labels and servicing as many stores as they can manage. The range is from small, regional distributors, such as City Hall in San Francisco, which handles mostly jazz records from independent labels, to large distributors, such as Record People on the East Coast.

We have consciously set up Village Music to serve as a large 'specialty' record store. We carry over 1000 independent and import labels, accounting for as many as 17,000 titles in the store, approximately half our stock. Local independent artists sell especially well here.

JOHN GODDARD
*Owner, Village Music,
Mill Valley, California*

Record Store Inventory

Store _____ Date _____ Salesman _____

ARTIST/RECORD	1 BEGINNING INVENTORY	2 RECORD COUNT	3 (1−2) RECORDS SOLD	4 RECORDS DELIVERED	5 RECORDS RETURNED	6 (2+4−5) ENDING INVENTORY
_____						
_____						
_____						
_____						
_____						
_____						
_____						
_____						
_____						
_____						
_____						
_____						
_____						
_____						
_____						
_____						
_____						
_____						
_____						
_____						
_____						
_____						
_____						
_____						
_____						
_____						
_____						
_____						
_____						
_____						
_____						
_____						
_____						
_____						
_____						
_____						
_____						
_____						
_____						
_____						
_____						
_____						
TOTALS						

A sales record form keeps track of inventory at each store.

Record purchases from mail order catalogs are increasing. This catalog from the New Music Distribution Service lists more than 2300 records from more than 420 independent record labels.

A decade ago, independent record distributors served many major labels. Since their volume sales and steady output insured profits and cash flow, these distributors could risk carrying new and untried music from smaller record labels. When the major labels withdrew distribution from these independent distributors, many shut down. As a result, small label distributors are experiencing changes, shrinking pains and cash flow problems, which often translate into collection difficulties for labels supplying them with product.

Keep these facts in mind as you look around for a distributor. It will help you understand why they will not take on your record until they believe it will sell. When you can prove sales through your own distribution system, and can show some success with promotional and/or touring efforts outside your region, distributors will want to talk with you.

Finding a Distributor. With few exceptions, independent record labels are handled by entirely different distributors than the ones servicing major labels. In fact, there are two different trade organizations of record distributors: the National Association of Recording Merchandisers (NARM), whose members are mainly distributors of major labels, and the National Association of Independent Record Distributors (NAIRD),

which is an organization of distributors of records from small labels and independents.

Most independent distributors cover specific geographical territories and, often, specific types of records, such as country or jazz. Many started their businesses within large cities and branched out to cover adjacent areas. Generally speaking, you have to seek out the independent distributor region by region, sometimes using as many as three per state to be assured of total coverage. You can investigate the regions served and the labels handled by independent distributors by referring to *The Billboard International Buyers' Guide* under the heading 'Wholesalers—Distributors'.

In general, you are better off starting with a distributor in your area who specializes in records similar to yours. When your own distribution system becomes too unwieldy for you to handle, or takes too much of your time, *and* you are showing good sales, ask the owners of the stores carrying your record for the names of their distributors. It won't be hard to convince these distributors to take over your accounts; you have leverage for a good deal since you can guarantee a certain number of sales.

If you think that there might be a demand for your record outside of your region (either because you are touring or getting airplay there), you may need to find a distributor in that area. Seek the smaller distributors first, because they will be much more willing to take you on and can give your record more personal service and attention than a large distributor. Sometimes you can find another independent record manufacturer, such as Flying Fish in Chicago or Takoma Records in Los Angeles, to outlet your record through their distributors and thus save your having to locate and deal with all of them yourself.

To learn about different distributors and their reputations, you can join NAIRD (whose members also include record manufacturers) and attend its annual convention. Almost all the distributors who handle independent labels attend because it's a good place for them to learn about new records. There you can meet the distributors personally, play your album for them, acquaint them with your promotional and performance plans, and ask questions. At the same time, you can speak with the owners of labels that use various independent distributors. It's in your interest to find out about different distributors' reputations for service and payment if you are going to be trusting them with your record and dollars. By the time the convention is over, you should know which distributors are appropriate for you. (More information on NAIRD and its annual conventions is provided in the chapter on Business.)

If you are unable to attend the NAIRD convention, write to distributors listed in the *The Billboard International Buyers' Guide* that handle labels similar to yours. Enclose your album, your press kit, and a letter outlining your promotional and performance plans. If you have enough money budgeted, follow up your letter with a phone call. The kind of response you get from them will tell you whether they are interested as well as whether you and they can work well together.

You might also write to other independent labels that have released records similar to yours. Ask not only what distributors they use, but also which ones have good reputations.

Chris Strachwitz, who owns Arhoolie Records, an independent label specializing in rural American music, claims he has found it best to wait until distributors contact him. In his experience, if he has to convince a distributor to carry his records, it almost always ends up being more trouble than it's worth.

Pricing and Payment. Distributors buy records from record labels with an agreement to pay within a specified time period, usually thirty, sixty, or ninety days. The label agrees to take back unsold and/or defective records. The usual price is roughly between 35% to 45% of the retail list selling price. For a $7.98 record, your price to a distributor would vary between $3.00 and $3.60; for an $8.98 album, between $3.60 and $4.25. Variations would be due to your discounting policies, your leverage in the marketplace, and the volume of your records sold.

There are some additional discounts often given to distributors as quick pay inducements:

▶ A 10% or 15% discount for C.O.D. (cash on delivery) payment.

▶ A sliding scale discount. For example: 10% discount for payment within thirty days; 5% for payment within sixty days; 2% for payment within ninety days.

▶ A one-for-ten policy. The label gives the distributor one free record for every ten records bought

and paid for within a specified time period, usually thirty days.

There are further variations on all these discounting policies. Work out your pricing and payment policies in advance of negotiating with distributors and keep them consistent to avoid any unnecessary conflicts.

Once you have received an order from a distributor, you must arrange for shipping or delivering the records. Normally the distributor specifies the method of shipping and payment. Include an invoice stating the terms of sale with each delivery.

Collection. The biggest headache that any label, major or independent, faces in dealing with distributors is the long wait for payment. Even when distributors agree to pay within thirty to ninety days, in practice it often turns out to be longer, particularly for the newer labels, who have the least leverage. The excuse the distributors most often give is that they are waiting for stores to pay them.

At some point, you will have to decide what's more important: the quantity of records that the distributors may be able to sell for you and the new sales area outside of your community they might open up—or getting your money fast.

The only time you have *real* leverage is when your records are selling quickly and your distributor needs to reorder, or when you put out a second record. Otherwise, you may find that distributors ignore you. For this reason, it's all the more important to find out

Ralph Records' price schedule was sent to retailers and distributors with an informal letter encouraging continued support. The mailing helped stimulate interest in a then-fledgling company—now a major independent label.

A store will generally pay a few cents more for real service: good fill on their orders, in-store play copies, visits from the salesman now and then, somebody who will listen to them. Some stores buy just pennies; others buy service. A good distributor will offer both good price and good service. That's his business.

BRUCE IGLAUER
Owner, Alligator Records

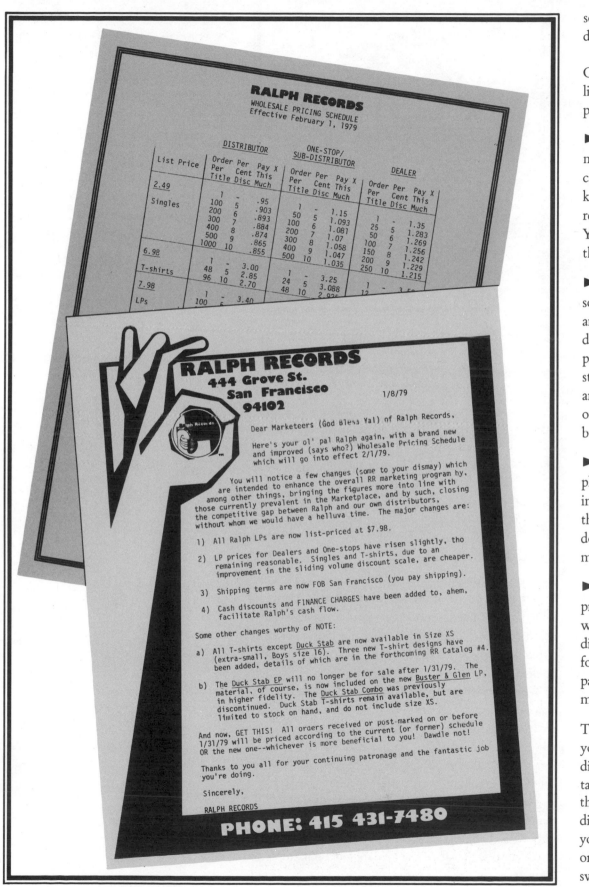

RALPH RECORDS
WHOLESALE PRICING SCHEDULE
Effective February 1, 1979

List Price	DISTRIBUTOR			ONE-STOP/ SUB-DISTRIBUTOR			DEALER		
	Order Per Per Title	Per Cent Disc	Pay X This Much	Order Per Per Title	Per Cent Disc	Pay X This Much	Order Per Per Title	Per Cent Disc	Pay X This Much
2.49	1	-	.95						
Singles	100	5	.95	1	-	1.15	1	-	1.35
	200	6	.903	50	5	1.093	25	5	1.283
	300	7	.893	100	6	1.081	50	6	1.269
	400	8	.884	200	7	1.07	100	7	1.256
	500	9	.874	300	8	1.058	150	8	1.242
	1000	10	.865	400	9	1.047	200	9	1.229
6.98			.855	500	10	1.035	250	10	1.215
T-shirts	1	-	3.00						
	48	5	2.85	1	-	3.25			
	96	10	2.70	24	5	3.088	1	-	3.50
7.98				48	10	2.935	12		
LPs	1	-	3.40						
	100	5							

RALPH RECORDS
444 Grove St.
San Francisco
94102
1/8/79

Dear Marketeers (God Bless Ya!) of Ralph Records,

Here's your ol' pal Ralph again, with a brand new and improved (says who?) Wholesale Pricing Schedule which will go into effect 2/1/79.

You will notice a few changes (some to your dismay) which are intended to enhance the overall RR marketing program by, among other things, bringing the figures more into line with those currently prevalent in the Marketplace, and by such, closing the competitive gap between Ralph and our own distributors, without whom we would have a helluva time. The major changes are:

1) All Ralph LPs are now list-priced at $7.98.

2) LP prices for Dealers and One-stops have risen slightly, tho remaining reasonable. Singles and T-shirts, due to an improvement in the sliding volume discount scale, are cheaper.

3) Shipping terms are now FOB San Francisco (you pay shipping).

4) Cash discounts and FINANCE CHARGES have been added to, ahem, facilitate Ralph's cash flow.

Some other changes worthy of NOTE:

a) All T-shirts except <u>Duck Stab</u> are now available in Size XS (extra-small, Boys size 16). Three new T-shirt designs have been added, details of which are in the forthcoming RR Catalog #4.

b) The <u>Duck Stab</u> EP will no longer be for sale after 1/31/79. The material, of course, is now included on the new <u>Buster & Glen</u> LP, in higher fidelity. The <u>Duck Stab</u> Combo was previously discontinued. Duck Stab T-shirts remain available, but are limited to stock on hand, and do not include size XS.

And now, GET THIS! All orders received or post-marked on or before 1/31/79 will be priced according to the current (or former) schedule OR the new one--whichever is more beneficial to you! Dawdle not!

Thanks to you all for your continuing patronage and the fantastic job you're doing.

Sincerely,

RALPH RECORDS

PHONE: 415 431-7480

something about their payment reputations before you deal with them.

Can you speed up the collection process at all? Only through continued diligence and then, only by a little. The following methods have been used by independents with varying degrees of success:

► Sell or consign records to distributors in small numbers at first, so that if sales begin to increase radically and a distributor actually needs more records to keep up with demand, you can refuse to provide more records until the last amount consigned is paid for. Your chances of getting paid are better anyway, since the amount of cash involved is smaller.

► Be extremely diligent in billing and invoicing. As soon as thirty days have gone by, send the distributor an invoice and personal letter. Send another one in sixty days and another again in ninety days, until you are paid. If ninety days go by and you have not been paid, start phoning and ask to talk to the bookkeeper. If you are told repeatedly that the bookkeeper is 'out of the office', complain to the person on the phone. Keep bothering them until you are paid.

► Sometimes the only way to collect is to be unpleasant; it's one of the least appealing aspects of selling. If you are not persistent in billing and invoicing, the distributors will think (and rightly so) that you don't care when you are paid. The labels that are the most aggressive are paid first.

► An alternative to trying to speed up the collection process is to simply accept the fact that you have to wait to be paid. As one independent label owner candidly said, "You have to realize that you are a bankroller for the distributor—a lender of money. Not getting paid on time means that they are using your money for maintaining their own cash flow."

The foregoing warnings are not meant to discourage you from attempting to sell your record through distributors, but simply to inform you that it often takes awhile for money to get back into your hands and that you should plan accordingly. When you do find distributors who pay on time and also sell records for you, graciously acknowledge them. When your records sell in larger quantities, you will be tempted to switch to a bigger distributor who may promise to sell more records. Try to work it out so that the smaller distributor services the smaller stores and the larger one deals with the major chains. Consider the new move very carefully, weighing possible profits against the loyalty and hard work of the smaller distributor.

Distributors and Promotion. Now that you have found a record distributor to help you sell records, don't think you can go home and relax. You need to participate actively in keeping that distributor interested in your records and working on your behalf, especially if you don't yet have a proven volume of sales. Think of the distributor as a business partner working with you to achieve a mutual goal: selling records.

When you talk with distributors about handling your record, ask what extra services they provide, such as promotion or help with setting up performances in their regions. In the last few years, several independent record distributors have increased their services to supplement the promotional efforts of the labels. Even when distributors do provide promotional services, you should continue to book and promote on your own. In this way you can double your chances for success.

Your distributor will need supplies of promotional materials, such as posters, for use inside the stores and press kits that their salespeople can use to convince stores to carry your record. Offer to supply copy for any promotional brochures used by the distributor. If you have included a short description of your music either on the back of your album cover or in your first press release, use this on your brochures. It's good to be consistent about the wording used in reference to your record.

The distributors will also need free records, depending on what extra services they provide. Usually they will want to make at least one copy available to each store they service, either as a way of introducing your music or for in-store play. To make sure that records supplied to the distributor are used for promotional purposes and not sold, clip the corners or punch holes in them.

When you are touring in an area serviced by a distributor, let the distributor know so that the stores can be persuaded to take extra stock or put up special displays. You can also offer to meet some of the bigger store owners or salespeople personally or even give an in-store promotional performance. Let the distributor know about your own plans for getting reviews or airplay and ask for additional suggestions. Even if you are not tour-

With Kaleidoscope Records, an independent label, I could do the music the way I felt it. When we started negotiating with A&M, we asked for complete control over the music—what material was to go on the album, how it was to be arranged, the instrumentation, and how the music should be produced and mixed. We even specified that we wanted a Class A pressing—the same as they use for classical recording.

DAVID GRISMAN
Horizon Records (A&M)

ing, send all your distributors all your press releases and favorable reviews to inform them of your progress.

Sometimes it is worthwhile finding out who the salespeople working for each distributor are and dealing with them personally, either by adding them to your mailing list, phoning them occasionally, or visiting them when you are in the vicinity. When you are dealing with distributors handling many different labels, the salespeople will not always be personally acquainted with all the records they are selling. Any input from you is bound to give your record an extra push.

CATALOGS

When you offer your record for sale, you qualify for listing in one or more record catalogs. It is important that you get listed so that people who may have heard of your record second-hand can locate you and either order the record directly, or though record stores or distributors.

Schwann and Phonolog. *The Schwann Record and Tape Guide,* published biannually and sold in most record stores, lists records over two years old that are for sale in the United States, by artist or group, and by category, such as classical, popular, or jazz. A monthly supplement includes information on new releases. Listings are free if a record is distributed nationally and is generally available in record stores. Records sold by direct mail or in stores in which retail records sales are not the primary business, such as religious book stores or craft shops, will not be listed.

Phonolog Reporter is a comprehensive, loose-leaf catalog, available by subscription only, that lists currently available records, cross-referenced by label, title, artist, and category. Listings are updated weekly in a supplement, *The Weekly Reporter.* Listings in *Phonolog* are free and, unlike those in the *Schwann* catalogs, are not limited to records that are sold and distributed nationally.

To obtain a listing for your record in either of these catalogs, write to the addresses listed in the Directory of this book. Include the names and addresses of distributors who service your record.

Both *Schwann* and *Phonolog* need the following information:

► record label name, address, and phone number

► title of album

► name of artist or group

► catalog order number

► 45, EP, or LP indication

► Stereo, Mono, or Quad indication

► whether the recording is available as a record, cassette, or eight-track tape

In addition, *Phonolog* needs the following information:

► titles of songs

► names of composers

► ASCAP or BMI affiliation (see the chapter on Song Rights)

► lengths of songs

Remember to list the information in the order shown on your record label, the 'A' side first.

Library of Congress. The Library of Congress in Washington, D.C. assigns numbers to recordings which local libraries are likely to order. These numbers are printed on catalog cards which the libraries order from the Library of Congress. The catalog number is normally given to a recording before its release so that it can be printed on the album cover or tape container.

Decisions as to whether the recordings qualify for Library of Congress numbers are usually made on the basis of the recordings' historical or sociological significance. For example, traditional, ethnic, and folk music, as well as new releases of jazz from the 20s and 30s often qualify, whereas card numbers are seldom assigned to current popular, jazz, and rock recordings; humorous recordings; movie or theatrical soundtracks; instructional recordings; teacher's manual records; or home study courses (such as those produced by business and professional associations).

If you think your recording would qualify for a Library of Congress number, send a request and a copy of your tape to the Library of Congress. (The address is listed in the Directory.) Include the following information:

► title of the recording

► name of the artist or group

► list of songs

► names of composers

► lengths of the songs

► Stereo, Mono, or Quad indication

► 45, EP, or LP indication

► whether it will be available as a record, cassette, or tape

The Schwann Record and Tape Guide *and* Phonolog Reporter *are the standard reference sources for locating and ordering albums.*

There is no charge for obtaining catalog numbers. However, you must send your application in at least eight weeks before you need the final copy for your album cover. You will also need to send two copies of your album to the Library of Congress as soon as you receive your records from the manufacturer.

MAIL ORDER SALES

The assumption behind selling records by mail order is that an easily identifiable group of people already exists who like your music and that they can be reached by mail and informed of your album. The more specialized the tastes of that group, the greater are your chances of success in selling by mail.

Success in selling through mail order depends on 1) accurately assessing your audience (see the chapter on Promotion), 2) researching and obtaining mailing lists aimed at that audience, and 3) sending out advertising packages that effectively communicate your message to them.

Audience. The easiest market for mail order is your fan list, the people who have been coming to your performances for many months, whose names and addresses you have been collecting.

The next most likely buyers by mail are devotees of a certain category of music, such as jazz buffs who collect hard-to-find albums, opera lovers interested in LP reissues of old 78s, banjo enthusiasts, or electronic music composers. If your music fits into such a specialized category, you have a good opportunity to seek out your audience and to sell to it by mail. Successful mail order sales have also been reported of records appealing to people interested in specific subjects, such as music to meditate to or grow plants by, songs aimed at women's groups, ethnic tunes, and 'bikers' music. One ingenious idea for marketing a Greek folk music record was to go through the phone book and pick out all the Greek names.

Mailing Lists. As mentioned in the chapter on Promotion, a good way to start a mailing list is to borrow lists from other performing groups or small labels that have followings similar to yours. It's surprising how many artists and small labels don't feel competitive or closed about sharing lists. In fact, many independent labels started their companies with lists borrowed from an already successful one. Borrowing or sharing implies an exchange; the spirit of both parties is important.

Cooperation, goodwill, trust, generosity, and grace are important to people willing to share in this way, and you should respond in kind.

Specialized mailing lists can be rented for about $40 per 1,000 names, often in the form of self-adhesive addressed labels. The varieties of mailing lists available will astonish you. To rent lists, look in the Yellow Pages of the major city nearest to you under 'Mailing Lists'. Write or phone for catalogs of the lists the rental company carries. For a larger fee, these companies can also research specialized lists for you, such as all the banjo teachers in America. The reason these companies prosper is obvious: mail order works.

Some mailing list companies also offer such extra services as computerizing and collating various mailing lists for your use at regular intervals, preparing your advertising and graphics, handling the actual mailing, and even filling the orders. What services you use depends entirely on the number of people you want to reach and the limits of your mail order budget.

Mail Order Package. The package that arrives in people's mailboxes telling them about your record is an advertisement, along with the many others they receive. If you want to capture their attention, you need exciting graphics. Don't scrimp on amateurish artwork or poor copy. This does not mean that your mailing package has to be 'slick'; good advertising should reflect the image and consciousness of its source and should be suited to its audience.

If your mail order goal is just to sell to fans who are already interested in your music, you may need only an inexpensively printed personal letter and mail order form.

If, on the other hand, you are trying to interest 5,000 strangers whose names appear on a mailing list, you should have your graphic designer prepare a special mailing package for you, using the graphic elements from your cover and other promotional materials. A mailing package usually contains a picture of the cover, a description of the music on the record, a personalized letter explaining why you are offering the record through mail order, an order blank, and, if you can afford it, a return envelope. In general, the number of responses you receive is frequently related to how easy you make it for people to order and send their money.

Independent labels have also found that response to mail order is higher when more than one record is

Pre-tour promotion and sales for Ralph Records' Rhythm and Noise *were stimulated by concert flyers using the same graphic as on the album cover. Concerts in San Francisco drew up to 150 fans.*

offered. You might save money and increase effectiveness by doing a cooperative mailing with other independent labels whose music appeals to a similar audience as yours.

Advertising. Another way to stimulate mail orders is to advertise your record in publications that reach your target audience—either in the classified sections, which are cheap and often effective (especially for specialized music), or with a larger 'display' ad, which may or may not include a coupon, in the body of the publication. When advertising in this way, you will need to conform to federal regulations regarding mail order sales (see below). It is also wise to offer a free brochure with further information.

In the opinion of many small labels, advertisements are not worthwhile until your sales have reached a total of 15,000 to 20,000 albums and you know the publication reaches your audience. Don't forget that sales generated by advertising may show up in the stores and not in mail orders.

If you want to test the value of mail order on a small scale, you can do a trial run with the fans on your mailing list. You can judge by their response if a more general mailing to people who might never have heard your music is likely to be worth the effort. If the response to your mailing is between five and ten percent of your fan list, you might try putting some inexpensive classified ads in magazines or newspapers which appeal to your audience.

Federal Mail Order Regulations. In 1976, the Federal Trade Commission issued a Trade Regulation Rule on Mail Order Merchandise imposing certain obligations on sellers who market their products by mail order sales. Apparently, the FTC had received numerous complaints from customers who had submitted their checks for products from mail order merchants but never received the product or else experienced a long delay in receiving the product. The purpose of the Rule is to protect mail order customers from abuses by the mail order merchants.

In any advertisement for mail order sales, the Rule requires the seller to state just when the seller expects to ship the product, for example, "please allow four to six weeks for delivery of the album." If no time is mentioned, it is assumed that the product will be shipped within thirty days of the buyer's order. If the seller is not able to meet the delivery date, the buyer must be advised of the new shipping date or told why a revised date cannot be set and then given a chance to consent to the delayed date or to cancel the order. A refund of the buyer's payment must be made in no more than seven days.

If the new shipping date is no more than thirty days from the original shipping date, the buyer is automatically deemed to have accepted that date unless the buyer notifies the seller otherwise. If the new date is greater than thirty days or a new date cannot be set, then the seller must notify the buyer that the order is cancelled unless the seller receives notice from the buyer in thirty days consenting to the delay or the seller actually ships the product within thirty days.

All notices to the buyer must be by first class mail and must provide the buyer with an opportunity to respond, for example, by enclosing a business reply card or a postage prepaid envelope. Of course, if the seller decides the order cannot be filled, the buyer must be notified and refunded the money in no more than seven days.

Finally, the seller is required to maintain records of compliance with the Rule. If the seller does not, there is a rebuttable presumption that the seller has failed to comply with the Rule. In other words, the sellers should keep records of their notices to buyers and any evidence of shipment of the product or refund. If there is ever a dispute between the seller and buyer, then the better the seller has documented the transactions, the stronger the defense against the buyer's claims.

SAMPLE SALES PLAN

Setting specific and reasonable goals, as suggested in the introduction to this chapter, means outlining a plan. The following schedule is an example of a modest three-month sales plan for an artist who has been playing regularly at clubs in a large metropolitan area and doing an occasional concert. The goal is to sell a total of 500 records in stores, at performances, and by mail order.

FIRST MONTH

► Set up distribution in 15 small specialty record stores. Sales expectation: 2 records a month in each store (30 records).

► Sell 50 records at performances.

► Sell 20 records through the mail.

► Total month's sales: 100 records.

SECOND MONTH

► Add 10 new stores to the original 15. Sales expectation: 2 records a month in each store (50 records).

► Sell 75 records at performances.

► Sell 30 records through the mail.

► Total month's sales: 155 records.

THIRD MONTH

► Add 10 stores in adjacent counties. Sales expectation: 2 records a month in each new store (20 records).

► Use promotion to increase sales in the first 25 stores to 3 records a month in each store (75 records).

► Sell 100 records at performances.

► Sell 50 records through the mail.

► Total month's sales: 245 records.

The above plan nets a total of sale of 500 records in the first three months.

TIME AND MONEY

Once you have spent money on sales materials, such as invoice forms or sales books, or, in the case of mail order, on a mailing package, your most common sales expenses will be shipping and mailing, additional printing and stationery, phone, transportation (gas, tolls), and lunches and refreshments while driving around. Many of these expenses will be paid for with cash out of your pocket, because they won't seem like much at the time. However, you will find that these small amounts add up quickly and can total somewhere between $150 and $400 a month.

Selling costs time. Just persuading fifteen of the smaller record stores in your area to sell your album may take up to two solid weeks. You will have to budget your time carefully in order to balance the time spent in selling with other activities, such as promotion, booking, performing, or composing.

In the first few months, your expenses will almost always exceed your income from the sales of records. You will be spending extra money for promotion and sales efforts. If you are consigning your records to stores or to distributors, income from sales from those sources will likely be deferred from one to six months. Your greatest challenge will be keeping enough money on hand to meet monthly expenses. One way to do this is to sell records at performances, which will net you immediate cash.

Tight Budgets. The following suggestions will help you keep costs to a minimum:

► Ask your pressing plant whether they will ship records for you directly to distributors. They will bill you for the actual freight charges, but not for the time 'making up' the shipment to be mailed.

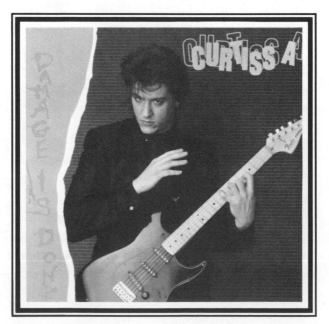

Twin Tone took out a series of ads in such underground magazines as Op, Trouser Press, Matter, NY Rocker, Boston Rock, *and the* Unicorn Times. *They featured four Twin Tone records, including the one by Curtis A, with the headline "Hooked on Profit" and included mail order information. Lots of mail orders resulted.*

► Send your records by special fourth class mail, which is reserved for books, records, and tapes. It's far cheaper than first class, and, except during a peak season (like Christmas), it will take only a few extra days. The cost is 63¢ for the first pound and 23¢ for each additional pound up to seven pounds. If you need to ship your records fast, consider using the United Parcel Service.

► Mailing records C.O.D. adds about $1.20 to the total cost. It also takes about five to seven minutes to fill out the paperwork needed by the post office.

► Buy record mailers in bulk. They cost about 25¢ each if you buy them in small quantities; about 20¢ each in bulk. You might also find one or two other independent labels to share a large order and save you all money.

► If you have not already done so, get a bulk mail permit, which allows you to mail 200 or more pieces of identical mail for an astonishingly low cost. (See 'Postal Services' in the chapter on Business).

► Keep returns for warped or damaged records to a minimum by storing your records properly and by packing them carefully for mailing and shipping. Leaving them in a car or car trunk almost always causes warping. (See advice for storing records in the chapter on Manufacturing.)

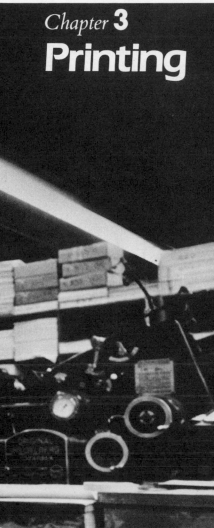

Chapter **3**
Printing

MOST INDEPENDENTS ARE MOTIVATED BY THEIR MUSIC to make their own records. Their goal is to preserve their creations in a form which can be heard and shared by others. Perhaps that is why they so often overlook the visual aspect of a record, the cover. As will be stressed repeatedly in this book, an eye-catching, well-designed and printed cover is crucial to the commercial success of an album.

This chapter on Printing, and the following one on Graphics, will outline the steps involved in producing album covers. Unlike promoting and selling your record, much of which you can do yourself, none of the processes described in this chapter can be done by amateurs. They require complex machinery, operated by professionals, in plants geared for mass production. These firms are scattered across the country, and you probably will not be able to oversee the work personally. What you can do is to become familiar with the steps involved and their relative costs so that you can select the firms and choose the options appropriate to your project and budget.

This chapter will occasionally make reference to your graphic designer. The role of a designer and the subject of design will be discussed at length in the chapter on Graphics.

THE PRINTING PROCESS

Before you select a printer for your album cover, you should have some understanding of the basic processes and the options available to you. The following description includes most of the terminology you will encounter when reviewing printers' brochures and determining the specifications for the printing of your cover. The procedures described all refer to 'offset' printing, which involves a number of photographic steps from artwork to finished piece. Almost all printing related to record production is done by this method. While we consistently refer to 'album covers', some printers use the term 'record jacket' instead.

Color. The first basic decision in the printing process is the number of inks to be used—one-color, multiple flat colors, or four-color (full-color) process. The one-color method involves printing white or colored paper with black or another color of ink. A common economical design involves using type with a black and white photograph or a line drawing, with many variations possible. By using more than one

color of ink, a broad range of effects can be achieved, depending on how the colors are combined.

Four-color, or full-color, printing involves three primary colors—red, yellow, and blue—plus black, generally on white paper. The proper combination of these four colors allows for the reproduction of color artwork or photography, with solid areas of any color or shade. Many album covers are printed four-color on the front, with the back cover one-color, usually black on white.

Halftones. In order to print continuous-tone black and white photographs, they must first be converted into 'halftones'. This process breaks up each photograph with a dot-patterned screen. If you examine the printed photographs in this book with a magnifying glass, you will see the tiny dots. When viewed at normal distance, they produce the illusion of a full range of tones from black through grays to white.

Color Separations. Color photographs must also be converted with a complex halftone process known as making 'color separations'. Four halftones are made of the print or slide, each through a different filter, the result being a separate halftone for each of the three primary colors (red, yellow, and blue) plus black. When these four halftones are printed over each other, they combine to reproduce all of the colors of the original photograph. If you closely examine the printed color photographs on the covers of this book, you will see that they are made up entirely of red, yellow, blue, and black dots. Full-color artwork requires color separations.

Mechanicals. The process of printing starts when you deliver camera-ready artwork (also referred to as 'mechanicals') to the printer. This will consist of all the line art (type or lettering, borders and rules, black and white drawings) assembled on 'boards' (also referred to as 'flats'), correctly sized and placed in exact position. The finished mechanicals may also consist of overlays on transparent acetate for overlapping areas, and a top sheet of tissue indicating to the printer which areas are to be printed with which color ink. Photographs and full-color artwork are furnished separately, with their size and position indicated on the boards. (The process of preparing camera-ready artwork will be described in detail in the chapter on Graphics).

Negatives, Stripping, and Proofs. The people in the printer's 'camera department' photograph each layer of the mechanicals to produce negatives.

Any special design elements, such as reversed areas (having the title in white on the dark area of a photograph) are separately prepared photographically. All photographs are converted into halftones. All the negatives—line art, each overlay, special bits of film, halftones—are then combined to produce one or more final negative for each color ink. In four-color printing, there will be one final negative each for red, yellow, blue, and black.

Once this process, called 'stripping', is completed, the printer will prepare optional (but very necessary) proofs to enable you to check the work. These can take a number of forms, depending on the method of printing used. For a one-color or simple two- or three-color job, you will be furnished with a composite photographic print of the final negatives, called a 'blueline' or 'brownline' according to the proofing material used. If you are using a complex multiple-color or four-color process, you will usually be furnished with a 'color key', consisting of one layer of acetate for each color.

Checking Proofs. The single most important role that you can play in the printing process is to make sure that you order proofs and that you and your graphic designer carefully check them. This is the point of no return before thousands of copies of your record will be printed. It is your responsibility if errors are not caught, no matter how much at fault the printer or separator may be. Make sure that both you and your graphic designer are satisfied that the proofs are correct before giving your printer the go-ahead.

First check for mechanical errors. You'll be amazed at the mistakes that can occur in the process of converting your mechanicals into final negatives: broken lines, improperly sized photographs, or a line of type simply missing because it fell off the flats.

In the blue- or brownline, it is difficult to check the actual color, but an experienced eye can determine if a halftone will reproduce the original with fidelity.

Color keys will fairly accurately represent how the colors will look when printed. The word 'fairly' is used because it is impossible to match exactly the inks as they will run on the press. Your graphic designer will be the best judge of whether the colors are right and will know what changes to request if they are not. If the colors are off, the separator should redo the work at no extra cost.

This Residents album featured computer cover art drawn and separated by Pore Know Graphics on a Commodore 64 computer with Koala Industries and Data Transforms software.

Printing. Upon acceptance of the proofs, the negatives are exposed onto metal plates which have been coated with photographic emulsion. After processing, one or more plates are mounted on the press. Each plate picks up its designated color ink and deposits it on a rubber roller, which in turn transfers the ink onto the paper. A quantity of paper must always be run through the press until all the inks are registering properly and the color is even. This is referred to in the trade as 'making ready'.

The fronts of album covers are usually printed on white, seventy-pound, gloss-coated paper, which gives them a slippery, or slick, feeling (the results are termed 'slicks'). Album cover backs are generally printed on cheaper, uncoated stock. You could request a glossy stock for the back, or perhaps a dull-coated paper for the entire album. 'Shore-pak' covers are printed directly onto cardboard. These are sometimes thinner and less protective than slicks which are printed separately and glued onto heavier cardboard.

For economy and efficiency, full-color covers (and/or backs) are usually printed, or 'gang run', on presses that accommodate six, twelve, or twenty-four album covers. As color separations vary slightly from one to the next, the inks on the press will be adjusted to match exactly the colors for only one set of separations. Hence, all the other album covers being simultaneously printed will come out similar but not necessarily identical to the colors indicated on the proof. In the experience of most major and independent label artists and their designers, the color is almost always adequate.

If you want the colors absolutely identical, you can ask the printer for an exact 'color match'. To obtain this, the printer will either run your job separately or adjust the inks on a gang run to your set of color separations.

One-, two-, and three-color printing is not gang run. These jobs are usually done on smaller presses, often requiring a separate run for each ink.

If the cover is complex and exact color and/or registration is essential, a 'press proof' will sometimes be requested. This is made after the press and inks are set up, but before the quantity run is actually made, to check how the final piece will look printed on the actual paper. Press proofs should not be confused with color keys or other proofs with which you will be furnished when color separations have been completed.

Fabrication. When the ink on the slicks or cardboard is dry, the covers are usually coated with varnish for further protection against scratches, as well as for a richer, glossier look. Some firms offer a more expensive form of coating, called lamination, which is shinier but requires different machinery, takes slightly longer, and costs more. Other firms omit varnishing entirely, stating that the paper they use doesn't need it. The ink may scuff easily, however. Always ask whether varnishing is included in the printing; if it is not, ask to see samples of unvarnished, printed paper.

After varnishing, the slicks are trimmed, glued onto cardboard stock, and then folded into covers. Printing firms often refer to these latter processes, including varnishing, as 'fabrication'.

When the covers have been fabricated, they will be shipped to the pressing plant and collated with your records. Because records should be boxed immediately after they have been pressed, the plant will wait to press records until receiving the covers and any inserts that are being printed.

Labels and Special Inserts. The printing of labels is usually done by the pressing plants, not by the cover printer (unless they are located in the same firm), so that they can be pressed directly onto the vinyl at the moment the records are formed.

Special inserts, such as lyric sheets or postcards, can be done by a local printer, by the printer who does your covers, or sometimes at the pressing plant. If you use a separate printer, be sure to have the inserts delivered to the pressing plant in plenty of time for collating. Manufacturers will not press your records until everything is there and ready to be packaged.

CHOOSING A PRINTER

Always choose a printer that specializes in printing album covers. Their procedures are geared for gang runs; they have separate machinery for varnishing (which saves cleaning it off the printing presses); they buy paper and cardboard in huge quantities (which helps keep costs down); they understand the special requirements of graphic designers as well as the timing and scheduling needs of pressing plants. For all these reasons, you'll find them cheaper and more efficient than other commercial printers. Virtually everyone who manufactures records, major labels as well as independents, uses these printers.

Some of these printers are affiliated with firms that manufacture records; some are separate facilities entirely. All are listed in *The Billboard International Buyer's Guide* under the heading 'Design, Artwork, Printing and Lithographing'. The quality of work at most of these printers is good to excellent; therefore, in researching them, you will be shopping mainly for price and service.

A portion of a halftone enlarged 600 times shows how the screening process breaks a continuous tone photograph or drawing into a series of tiny dots, making it suitable for offset printing.

Before you interview graphic designers, write to some printers and ask for their price brochures and samples of their one-, two-, three-, and full-color album covers. Since much of your printing cost depends on the design of your cover, you will need to be conversant with comparable costs from various firms when discussing artwork with your designer.

Final choice of a printer will probably be made with your designer. Since his or her artwork is at stake, it will be important to work with a firm in which your designer has confidence. If the firm is unfamiliar to you, or if your designer has not worked with a variety of album cover printers, you will both be making your decision based what the sales representative tells you. He or she should help you make choices appropriate to your budget and should try to resolve problems which occur during the printing process.

When you place your printing order, you will be asked for an advance deposit, with payment in full before your covers are shipped to the pressing plant. Usually, first-time customers will not be granted other terms. Once you have used a printer several times, you can establish credit and expect some reduction in price.

TIME AND MONEY

It takes four to six weeks from the time your graphic designer ships the mechanicals to the printer to complete fabrication of your album cover. Mechanicals for your labels should be shipped at the same time as album cover mechanicals, since they will also take four to six weeks to be printed, particularly if color work is involved. Usually you would begin processing your master tape at this time as well. (See the chapter on Recording Procedures.) If you are having special inserts printed separately, make sure they are finished and shipped at the same time as fabricated covers so as not to hold up pressing records.

Price comparisons are difficult to work out in advance of knowing what your cover design will be. However, you can make rough estimates so that you and your graphic designer can decide on a method of printing, as well as what extras you can afford.

Most of the processes described in the preceding pages are considered individually by printers when estimating costs. The most commonly requested and most often used 'extra' elements are halftones or color separations, proofs (color keys and/or brown- or bluelines),

The stripping process involves preparing a separate sheet of film, the full size of the cover, for each color ink to be run on the printing press. KM Records, Burbank, California.

This piece of machinery fabricates the covers by pasting the front and back cover slicks on blank cardboard jackets. KM Records.

different color inks, extra slicks, and varnishing. Optional, more expensive, and less commonly requested extras are press proofs, color match printing, non-standard papers, lamination, full-color labels, specially printed inserts, and double-fold covers. Stripping, which all jobs require, is also considered individually by printers.

Depending on your final cover design, these elements can add up to quite a bit of money. Detailed bids should be sought in writing from various printers by you or your graphic designer when the cover design is finalized; agreements made by phone should be confirmed in writing. Some printers combine costs for various processes and offer them at a package price; for example, some quote special prices for one-, two-, three-, and full-color printing with the cost of

halftones, color separations, printing, and fabrication included in the price.

Often, package prices don't include charges for important items, such as extra stripping, color keys, or varnishing. Prices seldom indicate whether the printing is onto slicks or cardboard. If you are considering package prices, make sure your final estimate from the printer details costs based on your final design. If you are also considering omitting a process offered in the package price—for example, color separations—ask for an appropriate reduction in the final bid.

Because the process of making separations is delicate, your graphic designer may request that they be made in a color lab whose work he or she knows and trusts. Unless you are choosing a special package plan priced for economy and efficiency, costs of separations at color labs will be roughly comparable to those at most printers.

The following outlines average charges or methods of figuring charges for the various printing processes. It will give you a rough idea of what printing is likely to cost.

► The cost of converting black and white photographs to halftones varies from $3.50 to $15.50 per photograph, according to its size.

► The cost of color separations varies from $300 to $750, depending on the size of the artwork, the reputation of the lab, and the nature of the artwork itself. For example, artwork containing both pastel tones and bold color is more difficult to separate than artwork containing only broad areas of bold color.

► Stripping charges are usually figured at an hourly rate, depending on how many photographs (or other film work, such as reverses) are used, and whether the printing will be in one, two, three, or four colors. The process of stripping photographs and other elements for a two- or three-color printing job can be as complex and delicate as assembling color separations, and costs should be carefully estimated and compared when initially discussing graphics with your designer. Occasionally the cost of halftones and stripping are estimated together, particularly for a one-color photographic cover or back, but it is always wise to ask.

► Brown- or blueline proofs are sometimes supplied automatically, but often at an extra charge of no higher than $20. You should *always* request them.

► The price of separations usually includes a set of color keys or other proofs. If they do not, be sure to request them. The additional cost is usually no higher than $50 a set.

► Printing costs are usually based on using a seventy-pound coated paper for the front, and a cheaper, uncoated stock for the back. Requests for different papers will always increase costs, sometimes by as much as one-third. The printing costs do not include the costs of fabrication or pasting the slicks onto cardboard.

► The cheapest method of printing is the one-color process with black ink for both the front and back cover. It is cheapest because it uses standard ink and

paper, only one metal plate is involved, and the flow of ink can be more easily adjusted in the presses, thus wasting less paper in make-ready. A substitution of ink color rarely costs more than $20.

► After this one-color method, a two-, three-, or full-color front with a one-color back costs the least. Printing costs for 1000 back- and front-cover slicks average $300. The biggest surprise is that, if you discount the cost of color separations and/or stripping, printing costs for two- or three-color are roughly the same as for full-color. This is because most album cover printers consider two- and three-color printing a specialty job, to be run separately on different presses; the cost is comparable to gang running full-color with six, twelve, or twenty-four other covers.

► Today, printing covers directly on cardboard is cheaper than printing slicks and fabricating them onto cardboard. The major difference is that both the front and back cover must have the same color or colors—i.e., all full color, or all two-color, etc. For black-and-white covers front and back, costs average $325 for 1000 and $1050 for 5000. For full color, costs average $460 for 1000 and $1250 for 5000.

► An advantage to printing slicks is that no matter how many ink colors are used in the final printing, the

You'd be amazed how often we are furnished pre-separated cover art that's the wrong size. Many people don't realize that the front cover slick has to wrap around the jacket and that the front and back slicks are therefore of different sizes. You should always check with your printer and fabricator for the correct dimensions before preparing final mechanicals.

MIKE MALAN
Vice-president, production, KM Records

Communication between us and Rounder got confused. The upshot was that the wrong photo was used on the cover. If you look closely you'll see that the tuning pegs were left off the guitar. It wasn't until after the separations were made that we caught it, and by then it would cost both time and money. It was more important to get the record out. You just can't be too careful.

TONY RICE
Rounder Records

costs for printing covers drops radically as you order inceased quantities. For example, one printer offers 1000 full-color slicks for the front cover including varnishing for $225, but 5000 of them cost only $365. This means that it's much less expensive to print extra slicks initially than to pay for reruns. A good number to run initially is 5000–6000, even if you only need 2500 collated with records. The printer will usually be happy to store extra slicks until you are ready to fabricate them into covers. The printer will not, however, store fabricated covers, since 300 covers take up about as much space as 5000 slicks. You can request that some of the slicks be shipped to you for promotional purposes.

▶ Fabrication of slicks onto cardboard averages $165 for 1000 covers and $800 for 5000 covers. Note that there is no significant cost savings with the increased quantity. For this reason, you should fabricate only as many covers as you can use.

▶ Seven-inch record covers can be printed on coated, glossy cardboard similar to an album cover, or on thinner paper, similar to the quality of an album dust sleeve. As with slicks, the printing price drops radically as you order increased quantities. For example, 1000 four-color covers printed on cardboard cost $425, while 5000 covers cost only $610.

▶ Label costs are estimated in a manner similar to estimating album covers. The most common and cheapest prices are for one-color labels, with a choice from six to ten colored papers and either black or silver ink. The average price for one-color labels for 5000 records is $110. Costs for additional elements are extra, although they are scaled lower because of the label's small size. Separations for full-color labels, for example, average under $100.

▶ Design, typesetting, and layout charges for labels tend to be reasonable, since some of the copy and artwork on the album cover will be repeated on the label. Although printers offer these services, it's best to supply camera-ready artwork—it keeps the look of the label consistent with the rest of the album package design. All manufacturers will supply explicit information about label sizing and proper preparation of artwork.

▶ Some printers offer package prices for both the design *and* the manufacturing of covers (called 'stock' or 'economy' album covers). A discussion of them is included in the chapter on Graphics.

Remember: any special requirements, even ones that might seem minor to you, can result in an astronomical rise in costs, as can *any* changes in the original artwork once the processes have been initiated. A graphic designer experienced in album cover design can steer you away from costly extras and last-minute changes.

Tight Budgets. Once your album cover is designed, it is very difficult to trim actual printing costs, as they are directly related to the design. However, you can cut some of the luxuries to fit a tighter budget.

You might decide on an economy package plan and avoid having separations made at a different lab; you might omit printing a lyric insert until a second pressing; you can choose to have your labels printed in one color.

There are also things you should *not* omit. Don't decide against ordering proofs—they are your only check against error; don't run smaller quantities of your cover, as costs for much larger runs are negligible. Finally, last-minute, panicked changes in the original artwork are almost always a disaster.

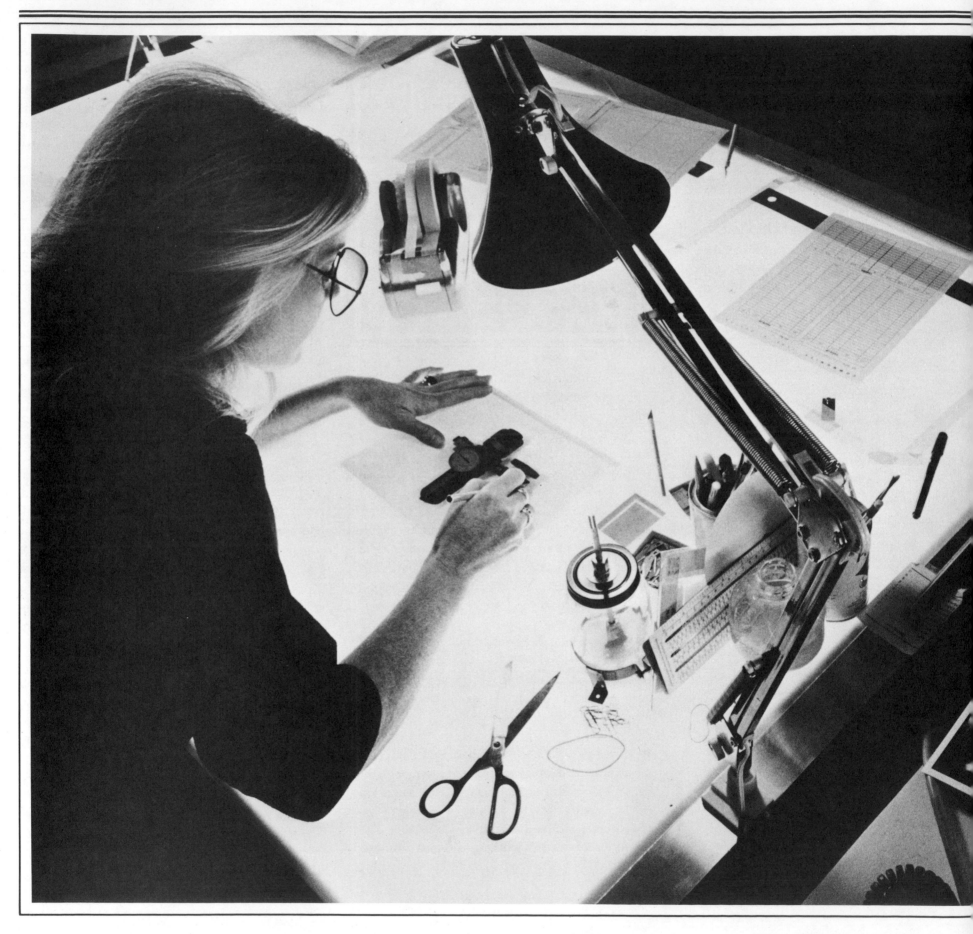

Chapter 4
Graphics

THE ALBUM COVER HAS BECOME AN ART FORM IN ITSELF. One of the best-selling gift books of 1977 was an anthology of album cover art. A number of art galleries have held exhibitions of paintings and drawings used on album covers. The music industry has even recognized the importance of the album cover with a Grammy Award for art direction.

The album cover's value can not be over-emphasized. In the competitive business of music, where 6000 albums are cut each year, your album cover is a vital sales and promotional tool. Like a good poster, television commercial, or magazine advertisement, an effective album cover attracts attention and helps sell the record. A well-designed album cover can make a DJ curious enough to listen to your music. It can make a reviewer or program director remember your name. It affects the store buyer's initial response. Thus, the graphics often determine if the record will have a chance to be sold. The old cliché about making a good first impression strongly applies to independent recording artists. Amateurish graphics arouse suspicion that music from independents may not be up to professional standards.

You are competing not only with the thousands of albums released by major labels, but with other independents trying to attract audiences. Your chances of enticing people into opening up your album and listening to your music will be greatly increased by taking the time, money, and energy needed to see that the music you spent so much love and care on is attractively packaged.

THE GRAPHIC DESIGNER

In spite of the importance of the album cover to a record's success, many independents often leave the cover to the last minute, after all the recording sessions have ended and the money is used up. A friend who is an artist or photographer is called in to help improvise —a gesture which may flatter the friend but rarely results in anything but a poor cover. This is similar to trusting a musician who is just learning to play an instrument to record a lead solo in what is to be your hit single.

Good cover design appears almost artless. Some designs look so deceptively simple that many people think they were easily, quickly, and inexpensively achieved. However, there's more to an album cover than a drawing or a good photograph. Like well-written and well-recorded music, good album covers depend on the skillful execution of ingenious ideas. You will do best to seek the assistance of a professional graphic designer who can translate the ideas and emotions you want to convey into a cover design that reflects your music and your personality.

In designing your cover, a graphic designer considers many elements—words and lettering, paper, photographs, drawings, colors, shapes, lines—and their relationship to each other. Like the song arrangements on your record, these elements of design can be simply or lavishly executed, depending on your budget and intent. A good designer, like a good producer, knows how to cut corners and save money when necessary. Moreover, he or she will deliver the work on time—something you will appreciate when there are deadlines to be met.

A graphic designer works with photographers, illustrators, typographers, printers, and others who might contribute to your project, just as other musicians may be called in to help you record. Finally, a designer coordinates all the elements that comprise the complex process of converting ideas into finished copy and artwork ready for the printer's camera. The more experienced your designer is, the more likely you are to wind up with a package that will please you and attract others.

A good working relationship with your designer is central to the production of a successful album cover design. You enter a partnership, much like that between musician and arranger, and each has specific areas of responsibility.

Your chief responsibilities are to set a budget for design and printing, to provide information that helps your designer create a cover concept, to write the words for the front and back cover, and to approve drawings, photographs, and preliminary sketches. Later on, you need to proofread carefully and approve all camera-ready artwork. You'll find that your input can have an encouraging and catalyzing effect on your designer.

Setting a Budget. The budget you set for producing your album cover determines not only whether it will be designed in one-, two-, three-, or full-color, but also how lavish the production will be, just as your budget determines whether you will record your music two-track or sixteen-track and will hire extra musicians to add elaborate orchestrations. You need to know what your budget is when you interview prospective designers so that they can decide whether to accept the job and, if so, how to execute it. In order to set that budget, read the rest of this chapter, which outlines the steps and average costs involved in the cover production process. Then reread the previous chapter on Printing. The design of your cover and the method of printing you select together determine your final cost. Set the budget for both simultaneously.

Cover Concept. To begin, your graphic designer will create a concept for your album cover and present it for your approval. The concept is a visual statement about the music and the musicians on the album. That statement can be concrete, such as a photograph showing the musicians with their instruments, or abstract, such as a cover which uses color and words to create a mood.

For this to happen, the designer needs to know about 1) your music and the key musicians who composed and/or recorded the music, 2) your potential audience and how you expect to reach them, 3) the image you want to project, and 4) your feelings about design. Often the failure of a designer to produce a cover that is pleasing to the client can be directly attributed to the failure of the client to communicate what is important in each of these areas.

You can present your music to your designer by playing two or three songs on a cassette recorder and then verbally describing the key musicians, the composers, the instrumentation, and how and where the music has been (or will be) recorded.

Information about your potential audience and how you plan to sell your album is essential. If you are planning to sell your album in stores, your designer should place your title in the upper third of the cover so that customers notice it when they are browsing through the record bins. If you plan to sell it mainly at your performances, your designer may want to use a picture of you or your group performing. If you plan to sell your album mostly to children, your cover will be designed very differently than if your audience is composed of truck drivers.

In thinking about the image you want to project, ask yourself, "What do I want my album cover to say about me and my music?" Think of the cover as a poster that helps sell your record. What atmosphere do you want to create? Is your group funky, elegant, unpretentious, rebellious, or religious? How do you come across in performance—costumed, casual, outrageous, sexy? Answers to these questions should describe the image you want to convey with your cover.

Some people object to the term 'image' because some performers (or their managers) have manipulated promotion to create concepts of themselves and their music that are false or misleading. A common term for this is 'hype'. The fact remains, however, that everything you do as a public person—how you appear on stage, what you say in interviews, and how you are represented graphically on your cover and other promotional materials—contributes to your public image. Your graphics should reflect an image consistent with who you are and where you want to go in the music industry.

You can communicate your feelings about design to your graphic designer by bringing in other album covers or posters that appeal to you (or do not). This will indicate your preferences for colors, photographs, artwork, line drawings, paintings, and styles of typeface or lettering. You'll find it effective to describe your taste with visual aids as well as verbally.

Supply the designer with a typewritten first draft of the words to appear on your album cover. Will the title feature the name of the musician or group, or a concept related to the music? Most first albums emphasize the group's name by using it as the title; second-album artists or more well-known groups often use other titles. What other copy will be included on the front and back cover? Words that highlight musicians and their accomplishments will be handled differently from titles and lyrics of songs.

Finally, if there are graphics that you or your group already use, such as a lettering style, a 'logo', performing photographs, or a banner or poster, bring them along. Sometimes they can suggest or produce a design concept. The cover illustration of this book came from a black and white photograph that had been previously published in a magazine; the designer felt that exaggerating the grain and hand tinting the photograph would give an abstracted feeling of the recording environment, as well as economically producing an original full-color image from existing black and white art.

I look at covers as true visual art. It's nice to be able to tell something about the music from the cover, but don't be blunt. Let the buyers use their imaginations. Put a sense of mystery there. Shock them if you like. Make them laugh. Avoid cliches.

RON CHRISLOCK
Silent Thunder Records

A 'logo' is a symbol or special lettering for your group's name or the name of your label. A logo creates instant identification. If you have no logo, commission your designer to invent one. You will use it not only on your album cover but also on most of your other promotional materials, such as letterheads, business cards, and posters.

Keep in mind that your cover introduces your relatively unknown name and talent. Be sure that beautiful artwork or a unique concept doesn't preempt necessary information, such as the kind of music you play or whether it is originally composed. (Later in this chapter is a discussion of copy content to help you decide on what information to include.)

Above all, it's *your* cover and *your* music. The more explicit you can be in this early stage, the more smoothly the production of your cover will progress. Don't rush these discussions; it may take two or three sessions before enough communication has occurred to come up with a concept for a cover that you will enjoy having represent you.

Other Promotional Materials. Towards the end of your discussions about cover concept, tell your designer what other promotional and business materials you need. Some of the elements of your cover

design—particularly your logo or the lettering for your title—should be repeated on stationery, business cards, press kit covers, posters, and the various other promotional items. It will keep their look consistent with the image projected by your album cover. You will also save money by having the artwork for these promotional materials prepared at the same time as your cover. After you see the designer's cost estimates for all the materials, you can adjust your list and put off ordering some of the less important items until you can afford them. (Priority items are listed in the 'Tight Budgets' section of the chapter on Promotion.)

THE PRODUCTION PROCESS

The person you hire as your graphic designer may do all of the production work single-handedly or may only create the concept and then coordinate and direct others to follow that concept through to completion; hence the term 'art director'.

Illustrators and Photographers. If photographs are needed, your designer may hire a photographer and arrange and direct a session with the camera, after which you will help select photographs from proof sheets. If original drawings or paintings are needed, your designer may ask an illustrator to prepare preliminary sketches for you both to review before ordering completed artwork.

If you have a particular photographer or illustrator you would like to use, let your designer know from the start. In general, however, once you have selected a designer, follow his or her advice—its what you're paying for.

Preliminary Design. Based on sketches and photographs you and your designer have chosen, your designer will prepare one or more rough facsimile covers. He or she will also give you final estimates on production costs, including typesetting, camerawork, and more unusual expenses, such as air-brushing of photographs. When you have talked over and approved a cover design and costs, your designer will then order completed work from the photographer and/or illustrator and begin to prepare camera-ready artwork for the printer.

Cover Copy. While your designer works on preliminary design ideas, you should prepare the final copy that will appear on your album cover and other promotional materials. This copy supplements the

Success with the basics: Margie Adam's
Songwriter is a fine example of
what can be accomplished with simple
type and black and white photography.
The design of this fold-out cover by
Barbara Balch established the use of a
series of close-up photographs by Holly
Hartman, which were used very
successfully and consistently for all
promotion and media regarding this
release on Pleiades Records.

Effective graphic translations from related art forms:
The jacket for Meg Christian's Face the Music on
Olivia Records is reproduced entirely as a four-color
separation from a batik by Sue Talbot. John Fahey's
Christmas album on Takoma Records is presented as
a two-color line reproduction from block cuts,
unusually printed on an ivory textured stock. A
repeated motif and simple type treatment, as designed
by Tom Weller, make for an effective black cover.

Well-balanced type and photography: These covers demonstrate the use of full-format photographs with dignified type treatments. Gregg Atwood effectively solved the problem of multi-language copy by duplicating his design on the front and back covers for Serenade's Oneg Shabbat (with photography by Ben Benet). Tom Copi and James McCaffrey used an on-the-street black and white photo plus a solid second color for David Hardiman's San Francisco All-Star Big Band on Theresa Records.

graphics; in combination, they convey who you are and what your music is about.

Words on the front cover are called 'cover copy'; words on the back are referred to as 'liner notes'. Information can also be printed on sheets that are inserted into the covers, called 'lyric sheets' or 'special inserts'. Liner notes and lyric sheets are especially important to independent recording artists because they provide concrete information about the music to people who may be completely unfamiliar with it. Lyric sheets are necessary if you are using your record to help sell your songs to other performers or publishers.

The primary function of your cover copy is to indicate what kind of music you offer. Sometimes you can do this through the graphics, as with a cover showing a banjo and fiddle player to indicate country music. Often, however, the graphics do not automatically imply what type of music is inside. Four people standing against a barn door may convey a wholesome, outdoor image, but the people could be a rock group or a string quartet. You may have to state your style in words.

Many artists resist including this information because they think it categorizes their music too narrowly. When asked what kind of music is on their album, they say something vague, like "Innovative" or "A mixture of all musical styles." If you are one of those people who gets uptight at answering this question and thinks that people should just listen to your music to find out what it's like, remember that program directors see as many as two hundred new titles a month, and store owners over five hundred. They need to know as quickly as possible what kind of music you are offering.

Moreover, if you don't define your style, others may do it for you in a totally unacceptable way. More than one musician has wept at the misleading descriptions critics, DJs, or even their fans have given their music. To avoid this, find words that do justice to your music and put them on your cover. Use the same words on your press releases or other promotional materials. If you are designing a fold-out cover, it is wise to provide some information on either the front or, more commonly, the back, so that reviewers, program directors, and distributors can tell something about the music without opening the album.

Copy Requirements. Here is a check list of information most often included on album covers. (On a fold-out cover, some of the information usually placed on the back cover may be printed inside the fold-out.)

FRONT COVER

► Album title

► Your name (or your group's) if different from title

► Logo (if different from group name)

► Stereo, mono, or quad indication

BACK COVER

► Names of musicians, together with instruments played

► Song titles

► Lengths of songs

► Names of composers

► Name of publishing company*

► ASCAP or BMI affiliation*

► Copyright notice for the songs*

► Copyright notice for the album*

► Copyright notice for the cover design*

► Credits for producer, engineer, arrangers, art director, photographers, illustrators, recording studio, mastering lab, and manufacturer

► Biographical material or information about the music, lyrics, or illustrators

► Album dedication or special thanks (optional)

► Name and mailing address for your label (this is *very* important)

► Mail order price (optional)

► Stereo, mono, or quad indication

SPINE

► Album title

► Label name

► Copyright notice for the album*

► Album number†

► Stereo, mono, or quad indication

LABEL

► Label name

► Album title

► Your name (or your group's name) if different from title

► Album number†

► The words 'Side One' and 'Side Two'

► Song titles

► Lengths of songs

► Names of composers

► Name of publishing company*

► ASCAP or BMI affiliation*

► Copyright notice for the songs*

► Copyright notice for the album*

► Producer credit (optional)

► Stereo, mono, or quad indication

► Speed (e.g. 33-1/3 rpm)

Preparing Copy for Typesetting. When you have decided what copy you want to use on your album cover and other promotional materials, you will give it to your graphic designer who will mark, or 'spec', the copy for typesetting.

Organize the copy for your designer by typing the words intended for each piece—album cover front, album cover back, label side A, label side B, letterhead—on a separate sheet of paper. Even if the words are the same (copy for press kit covers and album covers, for example), the type sizes and other treatments will vary.

Use a typewriter with a good black ribbon, double-space the copy, and leave two-inch side margins. Proof-

---

*Publishing and copyright are discussed in the chapter on Song Rights.

†The album number is an arbitrary number you select for quick reference to each album you issue under your label. Number future albums sequentially. Don't get tricky. #101 or #1001 are good starts. Numbers like 13068 or THS 627 are illogical and hard for dealers and distributors to deal with.

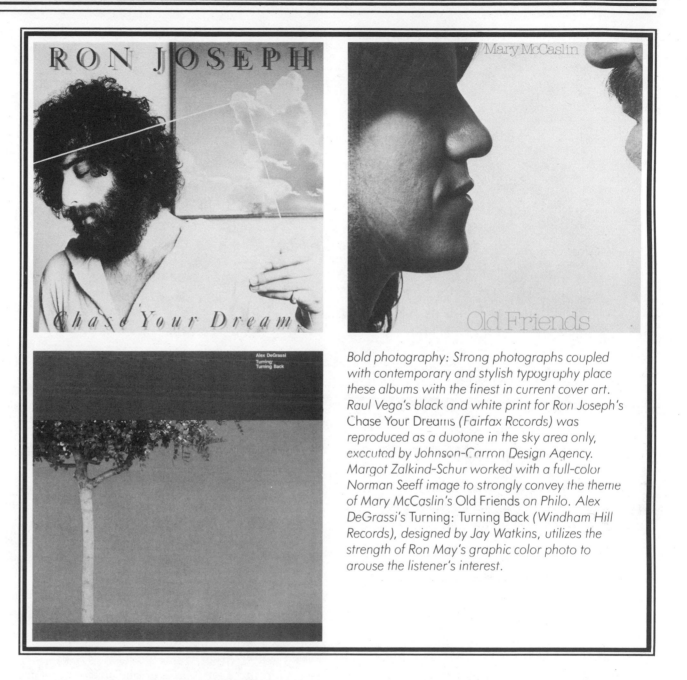

Bold photography: Strong photographs coupled with contemporary and stylish typography place these albums with the finest in current cover art. Raul Vega's black and white print for Ron Joseph's Chase Your Dreams (Fairfax Records) was reproduced as a duotone in the sky area only, executed by Johnson-Carron Design Agency. Margot Zalkind-Schur worked with a full-color Norman Seeff image to strongly convey the theme of Mary McCaslin's Old Friends on Philo. Alex DeGrassi's Turning: Turning Back (Windham Hill Records), designed by Jay Watkins, utilizes the strength of Ron May's graphic color photo to arouse the listener's interest.

read your copy. You will have to pay for all corrections in typesetting needed because of your mistakes. The neater the copy you give to your graphic designer, the more easily it can be marked with instructions to the typesetter, and the less likely you are to have errors in the typeset copy.

Before sending the copy off to the typesetter, your designer will very likely ask you to carefully check and proofread the copy once more for typographical errors. Make sure you have included all the information you want; errors you don't catch and last-minute changes will be expensive and time consuming to correct.

One error that occurs more often than you would imagine is incorrect matching of the songs on the record label and songs on the master tape. Double-check!

Galleys. After the type is set, 'proofs', or 'galleys', will be returned for you and your art director to proofread. Check carefully for errors in spelling, numbers, addresses, punctuation, grammar, and consistency of style. There are *always* errors, and they are not always obvious on the first proofing. Double-check everything with a suspicious eye and a clear head.

The galleys will then be returned to the typesetter for corrections and processed into final 'repro' copy.

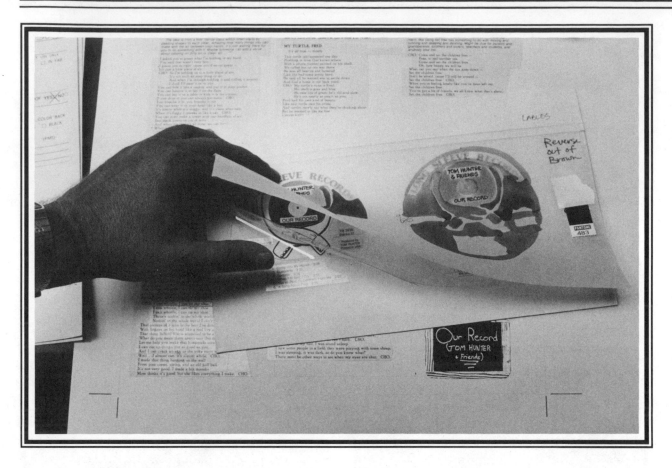

The mechanical for Tom Hunter's label on Long Sleeve records. The type is pasted on the board, with additional graphics and type to be run in another color pasted on an acetate overlay. The top tissue overlay shows a schematic of how the colors should appear on the final label.

Camera-ready Mechanicals. All completed typeset copy, illustrations, photographs, photostats, and borders will then be assembled for the meticulous job of pasteup.

The line art, lettering, copy, borders, and black and white illustrations will be pasted onto boards, or 'flats', correctly sized and positioned for each piece of artwork ordered: front cover, spine, back cover, label side A, label side B, letterhead, and any inserts. Photographs will be marked or cropped to indicate what portions are to be used, with their size and positioning shown on the flats. Color photographs will be ordered as either 4″ x 5″ or 2¼″ square transparencies (35 mm is usually unacceptable as it does not provide the appropriate quality). Their size and positioning will also be indicated on the flats. For a two- or three-color design, your designer may prepare overlays for various overlapping areas.

At this point, your designer will ask you to proof the flats, checking for errors or omissions, and to give your final approval. Written instructions will then be prepared for the printer regarding color separations, special screens, reverses, or anything else that might

not be clear from the instructions on the flats. Finally, your designer will carefully wrap the artwork for mailing to all the appropriate places: color lab (color artwork or photography), album cover printer (cover front and back), local printer (lyric sheets, stationery), and record manufacturer (label).

When color keys or brown- or bluelines are ready, you and your designer will (once again!) examine them meticulously, and, if they contain mistakes, instruct the printer on corrections.

Note: make sure that your label artwork contains a matrix number which matches its counterpart assigned to your master tape, so that your labels go on the right record and on the right side. (A convenient marking system is to end the matrix number for side 1 with '-1' or 'A' and side 2 with '-2' or 'B'. This helps avoid error or mismatching of labels and sides.)

CHOOSING A GRAPHIC DESIGNER

To insure good cover design, you should definitely hire a professional graphic designer, preferably one with experience in album cover work. Someone who has worked with a square format, all the printing processes, and record marketing requirements, can more easily prepare correct artwork. One printer in Nashville cited that over fifty percent of the color work from independents was improperly submitted. This often leads to expensive and unsatisfactory changes.

In the same way that you will preview different recording studios to find those suitable to your budget and needs, so should you spend the time interviewing graphic designers and looking through their portfolios. Don't assume that, because a designer is famous, he or she will be too expensive or inaccessible. In the same vein, no matter how famous or skilled a designer is, he or she may not be right for you. Designers are, above all, artists like yourself, with unique and special gifts as well as professional skills. You'll want to see samples of their work and judge it for yourself.

The best way to find a designer is to ask other recording artists. Don't hesitate to approach designers who have worked for major labels whose album covers you really like. If your music appeals to a special audience, see if there is a designer in your community whose style is attractive to this audience. Another possibility is to call local graphics cooperatives for recommendations. You can also look in the Yellow Pages of your phone book under 'Art: Commercial' or 'Advertising Agencies'.

Once you have several names and phone numbers of potential graphic designers, call and make appointments with them. Plan to spend at least an hour with each one. You should be aware that, as carefully as you will be interviewing them, they will be interviewing you. The relationship between you and a designer is a partnership; you have to be able to work together.

Designers will want some assurance that you understand their job well enough to communicate your needs and then to allow them the freedom to work creatively. People inexperienced in working with graphic designers are often afraid of relinquishing control and trusting that the job will be done well. As a result, they are continually worrying over the shoulders of their designers, trying to do the job for them. For this reason, many designers are reluctant to work with amateurs.

Be sure to communicate to these designers that you understand the rudiments of the printing process —enough to know the difference between one-, two-, three-, and four-color printing and how they are achieved. (These basics are outlined in the previous chapter on Printing.) You should also tell them that you are familiar with the production process and your responsibilities at various stages in it.

Finally, you should establish with the designer some of your priorities: your budget for design and printing, what other promotional materials you will be needing, some general ideas about what you want your cover to convey, and when you need the work completed. See how your designer reacts to your ideas and what suggestions he or she counters with. At the end of your interview, both of you should have a fair idea of whether your tastes are compatible and whether you can work together.

STOCK AND ECONOMY COVERS

If you are working within a tight budget, you can save a considerable amount of money by using 'instant album covers,' or 'stock covers'. Many printers who specialize in album covers offer a wide selection of instant covers. These covers are predesigned to fit different moods and subjects, with room left for the album title and, sometimes, for your photo to be overprinted. Many of the designs, however, are outdated and inappropriate. They are most suitable if you are dealing with a specific group of customers (for example, the members of a church) or you have presold your album. Costs are as low as $600 per thousand for covers with full-color fronts.

When I found the right graphic designer, we talked ideas just like we were in a band together. We were two artists working to express the same idea in two different mediums.

DAVE FRITZ
Wild Eye Records

Another alternative is to take advantage of the four-color 'budget', or 'economy', covers offered by some printers who include design services at low cost. Your cover will be designed by professional staff artists and designers, who work for the company. Choose a printer from among the biggest and the best, preferably one that works with major labels and turns out many covers.

If you do have your cover designed by the printer's staff artists, you can improve your chances of creating a cover you'll like by writing them a long letter describing your group, your music, and your aesthetic tastes. (Use as a guidelines the section of this chapter on 'Cover Concept'.) Submit clean, proofread copy for the front, back, and label, and indicate which information is the most essential, which is the least important, and what comes in between. If you have lettering for the title, a logo design, drawings, or photographs that you might want them to work with, by all means submit them. You might also include a cassette of three or four of your songs.

The final layout won't usually be presented to you for approval and changes, but you will see proofs for checking typographical errors, as well as a color key. The design will be simple, sometimes the covers will not be varnished, and you may be limited to a certain amount of copy. However, one large printer quotes a total price for design and printing of these economy covers at $495 per thousand—a considerable savings for a label interested in doing a pressing of only 1000 to 2500 albums. If your budget doesn't permit hiring your own professional designer, economy covers may provide you a with good alternative to using friends and amateur designers. Ask printers who specialize in this service to send you samples.

If you have to simplify further, at least hire a designer to create an effective logo for your group that can be used on your cover as well as on other promotional materials. Like a good melody, handsome lettering and striking symbols are memorable.

TIME AND MONEY

In the excitement of planning for recording sessions and selecting the music for an album, independents often overlook the fact that album covers require expenditures of a great deal of time and money. Yet your album cover affects the success of all your other

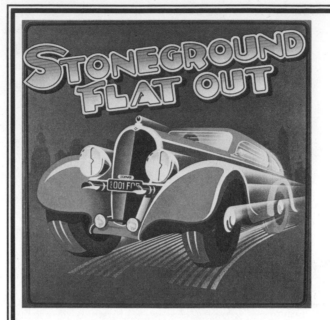

Period illustration and lettering: Stoneground's album on Flat Out Records, designed and illustrated by R. Tuten and D. Bread, and Peter Mintun's Grand Piano *on Cue, with a cover by Leslie Cabarga, are both exceptional examples of art deco–derived illustration and hand-lettering. Peter Mintun's back cover, produced by Good Times Graphics, complements this style with type and photography.*

efforts and should be planned accordingly. Don't wait until you've recorded your album to think about your album cover. Pressing plants will not press your record until the covers have been printed, so you will need to coordinate production of your cover with your recording and manufacturing schedule.

Once you have selected a graphic designer, it can take from six to eight weeks until camera-ready mechanicals can be shipped to the printer. Roughly four to six weeks of that time will be spent in design and production. Another two weeks or more will be spent assembling photo lab work and doing pasteup. (Remember: it takes *another* six to eight weeks after the mechanicals are delivered to the printer before covers are printed!)

If you have worked with a designer before, the entire process might be reduced to as little as four weeks, but seldom less. Scheduling enough time with your graphic designer in the preparatory stages is a must. Frequently the production process will be held up until you can submit copy or approve drawings, photographs, and preliminary sketches. Arrange to be available when you're needed for approvals and proofing.

Fees for album cover design from professionals start at $750 and usually include concept, rough drawings done by them, lettering, and pasteup. These fees will be based on the complexity of the production, additional promotional materials ordered, and the experience and reputation of the designer. Often a designer will charge amateurs more, not less, if he or she feels they will take up more time with explanations, aggravations, or undue changes of mind.

To the designer's basic fee will be added fees for photographers or illustrators. Professional photographers usually charge what is known as a 'day' fee for camera sessions and another fee for the photographs used. Day fees average $100–500 per day; $100 is an average price to pay for a photograph used on the cover and $25 for one to be duplicated for newspapers or magazines. These prices can be higher (or sometimes lower) depending on the reputation and skill of the photographer. Commissioned illustrations can run anywhere from $25 to $500 a drawing.

You will also be charged for such production expenses as typesetting, photostats, special art materials ordered for your project, and phone calls to printers or pressing plants. You should budget $100 to $250 for these expenses, the greatest of them being for typesetting. Ask your designer to estimate all extra expenses individually when you are negotiating fees and setting budgets.

Major and independent record companies seldom budget less than $2500 for the design and production of camera-ready mechanicals for an album cover.

Design fees usually do not discriminate between one-, two-, three-, or full-color work. It's as difficult to design in black and white as it is in color; some designers feel more so. However, color covers compete better in the marketplace and, if you can afford the printing costs, your best bet is a color cover and a one-color back. It's a successful standard format.

Good designers are literally worth their weight in gold. Save enough funds for a professionally designed album cover. Don't use up all your money recording.

Tight Budgets. Many independents have tried to cut costs by using their friends to design their covers. If your friends have the skills needed, you couldn't be luckier. If they do not, you will have problems. If you can't sell your record, you will have wasted the time and money you spent recording and producing it.

► If you have to start trimming your budget, begin by instructing your designer to work in one color. Although black and white covers can be more difficult to design effectively so as to compete with color ones, they are cheaper to produce and print. A strongly lettered title on a colored background or a striking black and white photograph, are good alternatives.

► You can also trim costs by ordering one-color labels or by omitting special inserts. These are far less important than your priority promotional materials.

► You can save a little money on production costs by submitting clean, proofread copy for typesetting. (Money is often wasted on changes in wording and careless mistakes.) You can also cut down the number of words.

► Typesetting can be bypassed entirely if you use a good calligrapher. Keep in mind, however, that hand lettering can look very amateurish if not *extremely* well done, and can be just as expensive.

Remember: saving money usually means spending more time—either in selecting companies or designers, or in preparation. In some cases, independents, particularly solo artists, spend as much money on the album cover as on recording. This is understandable given the close relationship of the cover design to an album's commercial success. Whatever your budget is, try to plan your project carefully so that you allocate a logical proportion of your time and money to each area of concentration. Save the time and money necessary to create a quality album cover that will help you achieve your goals.

Chapter 5
Manufac-
turing

As WITH PRINTING, YOU CANNOT DIRECTLY PARTICIPATE in the manufacturing of your record. Thus, it is to your advantage to know what processes are involved, so that you can research firms and negotiate intelligently with them. This chapter outlines record manufacturing step by step, discusses problems that may occur at each stage, and provides average costs. Suggestions are made throughout the chapter to help you obtain quality records that will sound as beautiful as your master tape.

THE MANUFACTURING PROCESS

Manufacturing records involves four processses that critically affect quality: 1) disc-mastering, or disc-cutting, 2) plating, or matrixing, 3) pressing, and 4) packaging, or collating albums and covers. Although some firms offer all processes as a package, many independents prefer to contract for several of these services separately. Pressing and packaging are always combined in one facility. During disc-mastering and pressing, you will have opportunities to check the work in progress. Although it will add to your costs, you should take advantage of these opportunities.

The manufacturing process begins when you or your recording engineer ships off your master tape for disc-mastering. (Proper preparation of the master tape is discussed in detail in the chapter on Recording Procedures.) Before you set this process into motion, be sure you are thoroughly satisfied with your master tape. It's far better to reject the recording work you have done already than to spend more money on manufacturing records which will disappoint you and which you will then have to promote and sell.

Disc-mastering. Disc-mastering, or disc-cutting, is the process of transforming the music on your master tape into grooves on an aluminum disc coated with lacquer. (A separate master lacquer is cut for the 'A' and 'B' side of your record.) Your tape is played through a disc-mastering console and converted by a lathe into the mechanical motion of a stylus. This stylus cuts the actual grooves, which physically represent the music on tape. In fact, some engineers can 'read' the lacquers and tell what kind of music is on them by the pitch, depth, and width of the grooves.

Before cutting the lacquers, the disc-masterer will adjust the controls on the disc-mastering console to match the alignment tones indicated at the beginning of your master tape, thus assuring the most accurate playback. He or she will also make adjustments for any noise reduction system used during recording, such as DBX or Dolby, since each system needs special decoding equipment to properly play back a master a tape.

Your recording engineer and/or producer may include special instructions to the disc-masterer as to how to cut the lacquers. They may request that the lacquers be cut as is ('flat') or that equalization be added to make certain cuts 'hotter'. They may request that the amount of stereo separation be adjusted or that the speed be increased or decreased. Sometimes they may request that monaural lacquers for singles be cut from one or two songs on your stereo tape. If an injection method of pressing your singles is anticipated, the disc-masterer may be asked to provide more 'land'—more space between the grooves—to help compensate for the inherent deficiencies of that method (See the section on 'Pressing' later in this chapter.)

With or without special instructions, the disc-masterer will listen to each tape individually and note any adjustments that need to be made while cutting the lacquers. The songs will be cut in the order in which they are sequenced on the tape.

Disc-mastering calls for skill and precision, as well as sensitivity, care, and good taste. Although people can learn to physically operate the machinery in about two weeks, they will spend from one to three years apprenticing before calling themselves professional disc-masterers.

However skilled a disc-masterer is, no adjustments in the mastering room will magically improve a poorly engineered tape or mediocre music. The limits of what can be done to make good lacquers are inherent in the tape itself.

Reference Lacquers. To make sure that the disc-masterer will make a disc-transfer acceptable to you and your engineer and/or producer, you should request that reference lacquers, or 'acetates', be cut before your master lacquers. Listen to the reference lacquers with your recording engineer or producer, who can best judge how they compare with your master tape. The lacquers should not be overplayed as they are very fragile and are good for only five or six listenings before noticeable sound deterioration. You will need to save a few plays for the pressing stage, in order to verify the quality of your test pressings. Lacquers should be checked for the following problems:

Neumann VMS–70 disc-mastering lathe. Warner Bros. Recording Studios, North Hollywood, California.

► low overall volume level compared with other records

► variations in volume levels within the songs or from cut to cut

► variations of tempo within each song

► breaking up or distortion in the treble or high registers at peak loudness levels or towards the end of a side

► excessive boominess or airiness in the bass or low registers

► dullness or lack or presence in the mid-range

► skips, buzzes, crackling noises, or dull thuds at the beginnings of notes.

Your engineer and/or producer will probably listen to the reference lacquers on both large and small speakers (like those used in car radios) to be sure that there is adequate treble and bass response.

Once you've approved the reference lacquers (you don't send them back), the disc-masterer will make the master lacquers using settings identical to those used when cutting the reference lacquers. If the engineer has only minor changes to request, he or she probably won't ask for additional reference lacquers.

If the disc-cutting is being done at a separate firm, the final lacquers should be sent to the plating facilities via a quick-freight firm specializing in fast deliveries. Your disc-mastering firm will probably package them for maximum protection. Recording engineers feel that the lacquers should be plated within twenty-four to forty-eight hours of being cut for the finest results. You should coordinate scheduling of disc-mastering and plating so that this can occur.

Plating. Plating, or matrixing, is usually a three-step process that converts the master lacquers into stampers or molds which can exactly duplicate the grooves of the lacquers onto your records during pressing.

The first step, called 'making a master', involves coating the lacquer with a thin film of silver and electroplating it in a tank containing a nickel solution. The nickel plating is then peeled or stripped from the original lacquer. An exact negative impression of the lacquer (grooves projecting upwards) is thus produced in the form of a metal mold, also called a metal part.

What happens in the mastering room is essentially voodoo. It's an art—a matter of ears, sensitivity, good taste, care. There are no real rules to follow because every record is unique. Every tape dictates what the record wants to be—that's why it's so very important to turn in as good a tape as possible. People who think, 'Oh, we can fix it in the mastering room', are crazy. If it's not right on tape, the disc transfer is always going to be a problem.

PHIL BROWN
Warner Bros. Recording Studios

The second step, called 'making a mother', involves electroplating the master to provide a positive impression exactly like the original lacquer to produce a second metal mold. These molds are thicker near the label, so that when the completed records are stacked on top of each other, the grooves won't be damaged.

The third step involves producing negative metal stampers from the 'mothers', which are used to press records.

When record manufacturers quote prices for 'full protection', it indicates that they will follow the three-step process and will make permanent metal molds. These metal molds, or parts, can be stored for up to twenty years. They can also be used to make additional metal molds which can then be shipped anywhere in the world you want to have records pressed, thus avoiding the cost of shipping records overseas.

The original negative master can also be converted directly into the stamper and used to press records, a process called pressing records from a 'converted stamper'. However, the converted master is extremely fragile and, if it gets damaged, new lacquers must be ordered from the disc-masterer and the process of electroplating repeated. For this reason, converted masters are used only for extremely small runs and when no further records will be ordered.

Pressing. The completed stampers mass produce records whose grooves duplicate those on the master lacquer. Each stamper can turn out about 1500 to 2000 records before deteriorating. Labels are pressed onto the records at the time they are formed.

Currently, two quite different methods, and plastics, are used in record pressing. The 'compression method', which uses polyvinyl chloride, is employed universally for LPs as well as for 45s and EPs. In this method, semi-molten vinyl is inserted into a pressure cavity and compressed hydraulically into the stamper. The temperature of the vinyl, as well as the temperature and humidity of the room, affect the overall quality of the pressing. Improper cooling, or 'curing', of finished records can result in warping.

Either 'virgin' vinyl or a combination of virgin vinyl and 'regrind' (melted down vinyl from defective records) or 'flash', (the excess edge of the records which is trimmed off) is used in the compression method. Unless you have dealt previously with your manufacturer and can trust the 'regrind' mixture, insist on virgin vinyl.

Vinyl comes in different grades, each containing a slightly different resin formula. The better the quality, the lower the surface noise. Some pressing plants give you a choice of grades. For example, one California pressing plant offers domestic vinyl (good), Quiex II (better), and Teldec (among the best). If you want premium vinyl, make sure your pressing plant offers it or can get it for you. The difference in price will be as much as 50 to 100% higher than the standard domestic grade.

The other method for pressing records, called the 'injection method', is often used by major labels for pressing 45 rpm singles. This method uses polystyrene, a harder, more brittle plastic than vinyl. In the injection method, hot liquid styrene is poured into the mold and quickly baked and cooled. It's similar to the method used by manufacturers for mass producing plastic toys. Its advantages are that records are turned out twice as fast as with the compression method and that the styrene is cheaper. The records are also ready as soon as they come out of the mold. Its disadvantage is that the records wear out faster and tend to register greater background noise. If you are pressing 45s or EPs and care about quality, avoid manufacturers who use the injection method.

With the injection method, all pressing machinery is fully automated; with the compression method, some may be manually operated. Both types of machinery turn out records at the rate of about two per minute, or 120 per hour.

In addition to operating the machine, the manual operator spot checks records as they come off the presses for defects, such as bubbles or noticeable dropouts in the grooves. Sometimes he or she will also play records at random to check for sound quality and possible deterioration of the stamper. In recent years, pressing plants have had difficulty filling these jobs satisfactorily, still another factor affecting the quality control of record pressings.

With automated machines, there is usually one person checking ten or more machines at a time, or twenty records a minute. Thus it is easier for defects to slip by unnoticed. However, the automated machinery turns out a more consistent product and random errors are less likely to occur.

Test Pressings. Before the final pressing takes place, a few test pressings can be made and shipped to you for approval. These pressings help verify the accuracy of both the plating and pressing processes, and tell you how your finished records will sound.

You should listen to the test pressings with your recording engineer and compare them with your reference lacquer. They should sound the same, or even a little brighter, since vinyl is a harder compound than the lacquer on the master lacquer, resulting in higher frequency output. If the sound is duller, or if the hole is off center, if there are pops, crackles, skips, or other mysterious noises, you should reject the test pressings and order new ones.

Flawed test pressings are not uncommon, and they are usually corrected in subsequent trial runs. However, some manufacturers will use as an excuse the fact that the first records off the machines never sound as good as later ones and will try to talk you out of new test pressings. As an independent who may be unfamiliar with these dealings, you should ask your recording engineer, producer, or disc-masterer to phone in your complaints, since they can be more technically specific and they have the professional credentials to back up their claims.

If the test pressings repeatedly come back flawed, the problem can be traced to either faulty plating or faulty disc-mastering. The reference lacquers can help prove that the disc-mastering process was satisfactory. Without them, the plating manufacturer could (and often will) try to pin it on the disc-mastering, since errors in the plating process will usually require new master lacquers and metal parts—an expense that the manufacturer should bear.

Once you have approved a test pressing, a final run is made. You won't see your records again until they arrive neatly packaged from the pressing plant.

Packaging. When the final pressing is completed, your records are collated with album covers, dust sleeves, and any inserts you may be using. To prevent scratching, warping, or other damage, this is done immediately after the records are pressed and have properly cooled. Each record is then wrapped in cellophane which is shrunk to the exact size of the album cover, a process known as 'shrink-wrapping'. The records are then boxed for shipment.

The way your records are packaged can greatly affect the shape your records will arrive in, and stay in. Ask that your records not be crammed too tightly into the packing boxes. A slightly thicker dust-sleeve than usual and slightly looser shrink-wrapping will help protect your records from warping. European manufacturers often package albums in loose cellophane to

A 'master' and a 'mother'. The master (left) is a negative metal impression of the lacquer produced by the disc-cutting machine. It is then converted into a thicker, positive metal impression—the mother (right). The mother is then converted into a negative metal stamper (pictured on the opposite page), which presses the records.

The metal stampers must be cleaned before mounting on the pressing machinery to assure accurate reproduction of the grooves. KM Records.

Your shipment will be automatically insured by the shippers, but you should inquire about the extent of the coverage. Be very specific. Ask how your records will be protected from excessive heat inside the truck as well as what you should do if you discover warping.

If a shipment weighs less than 100 pounds, you might find it cheaper to ship by United Parcel Service, or even to mail it parcel post (allow at least two weeks). Either way, don't forget to insure your shipment.

An order of 1000 albums will weigh about 600 pounds. Your manufacturer will tell you the exact weight of each shipment.

When your shipment arrives, count the number of boxes carefully, open some of them, and spot check one or two albums from each before you make payment. It's much less effective to complain about the damages once you've had the records a few days. Usually, shipments are sent C.O.D.; you pay when the records arrive.

Defective records can also be the fault of the pressing plant. Spot check carefully for the same defects looked for in the test pressings. Most plants allow you fifteen days after receipt of your records to complain about defective runs.

Storing Records. Don't forget that the records you sell must be in excellent condition. Many independents have lost sizable and badly needed profits from returns of damaged or warped albums, usually because they were not properly stored.

Records should be stored in their original cartons in a dry room where the temperature remains consistently moderate (neither too hot nor too cold). You should not pile the cartons more than 150 records high. If you take some of the records out of their boxes, don't store them flat, but rather standing on end and fairly tightly packed. Store boxes on their sides as well.

When you go out to distribute your albums, don't expose them to direct sunlight or leave them in the trunk of a hot car. The heat will warp or melt the records.

If you do a second pressing, rotate your stock so that you sell the old records before the new ones.

CHOOSING A MANUFACTURER

The major control you have over the manufacturing of your record is in the selection of your manufacturer. It's extremely important to take the time to write to manufacturing plants for information. This way

protect against warping, something which Americans resist, having become accustomed to the glossy, slick appearance of a neatly shrink-wrapped album.

Shipping. Your manufacturer will box your records in lots of twenty-five or fifty and prepare them for shipping. However, you are responsible for making the shipping arrangements. You select the method (mail, truck, rail, UPS), choose the firm, insure the shipment, and then give instructions to the manufacturer, who will notify the firm selected when your records are ready. If you want to have some of your records shipped directly to distributors, your manufacturer can ship them to as many locations as you want, provided you make all the arrangements.

If the weight of an individual shipment is over 100 pounds, the cheapest method is to use a trucking firm. You can locate a company by asking other independent record labels for suggestions or else by looking in the Yellow Pages under the heading 'Trucking'. When you phone, ask for the rate clerk or rate department, give them the location(s) to and from which you are shipping, and tell them the approximate weight of the shipment. Interstate and intrastate trucking rates are set by law and vary according to distance, weight, and the classification of the commodity (bulky loads are charged differently than compact loads of the same weight).

you can become comfortable with the language used, get to know the people involved, and discover what is and is not negotiable. You should write to them long before you start to record your album. Ask for price lists, for samples of their work, for the names of labels using their services, and find out their attitude towards 'custom' work. As an independent, you are classified as a 'custom label', which is a label not distributed by a major company and which often presses less then 5000 records at a time. Names and addresses of manufacturers can be found in *The Billboard International Buyers' Guide* under the headings 'Disc-mastering' and 'Plating, Processing, and Pressing Plants.'

Often, the brochures you receive from the firms will be written in language that assumes you are already conversant with all the processes and variables. Don't hesitate to ask questions if you are confused. Some of the firms have toll-free phone numbers. If they don't, write out your questions and mail them with a letter requesting immediate reply. Keep copies of all your letters.

In most cases, you'll be dealing with a sales or marketing representative or a customer service representative, not the technicians who actually run the machinery or the executives who own the firms. The job of these reps is to answer your questions and to attract your business; later they will also give you price quotations and will field your complaints. If you're wise, you'll hedge from making a definite commitment to any firm until all your questions are answered and you have agreed on detailed prices. Firms will work harder to satisfy you if they feel they're competing for your business. That's the time your negotiating leverage is greatest.

Carefully check the reputations of the firms you consider by asking artists, producers, and engineers who have used their services. At the very least, it will give you some idea of the problems that can arise. When you hear complaints about bad pressings, be sure to take into account how much can go wrong from the record label's end, particularly if reference lacquers or test pressings are not made.

As a general rule, to increase your chances for quality records, use a disc-mastering facility separate from the firm doing your plating and pressing. You'll have a little more control over the work and the disc-masterer can side with you and your recording engi-

Most manufacturers can arrange for shipments directly to distributors. KM Records.

neer should the test pressings or plating be flawed. Choose a disc-mastering lab owned or used by major labels, even though you will pay more for their services. Most of these disc-mastering labs have excellent reputations for superior work. If there's a recording studio in your town that offers disc-mastering but is not used by major labels, be sure to listen to some samples of its work, and check with engineers or producers who have used their services.

Although plating and pressing services can be done at separate firms, most independents prefer to have both processes done by one company. In selecting a firm for plating and pressing your records, you will have to choose between those that specialize in work for independent (or custom) labels and those that service mostly major labels. Both types of firms can deliver high quality work.

The main problems encountered by independents choosing major-label plants center around timing and service. Major labels contract yearly for huge blocks of time from these pressing plants and, in return, receive priority in scheduling their work. In fact, it's not uncommon to refer to these labels as 'owning' this or that piece of machinery. In these plants, work for custom labels happens either as 'filler' or during slack periods. That doesn't mean that the work will be of poorer quality (although some independents have complained that it is), only that it might take much more time than you are led to believe from initial conversations. At these plants, work for major labels or long-time customers will always preempt work for custom labels.

The major advantage in choosing a firm which specializes in work for independent labels is service. These firms will give you more attention and higher priority in scheduling. Quality control during actual pressing may be better.

However, no matter which firm you select, there is no way to guarantee that your records will be perfect. All labels have problems with defective pressings, or flawed test pressings, even from firms with which they have successfully dealt for other records.

When you have selected one or more firms for the manufacturing process, be sure to have final price quotes and any agreements made by phone put into writing. Try to come to some specific agreements about what errors the firms will be responsible for and under what circumstances.

When you place your order with the manufacturer, you will be asked for an advance deposit with payment in full before your order is shipped. This includes work done separately, such as disc-mastering. First-time customers will not be granted credit. Once you have used a firm several times, you can establish an account, sometimes with a reduction in prices.

TIME AND MONEY

If you are pressing records for the first time, you should schedule *at least eight weeks* before receiving your records from the time you send your tape for disc-mastering and your album cover for fabrication, particularly if you are using separate firms for the processes. What takes time is coordinating pressing dates with the completion of album covers and/or special inserts, approval of reference lacquers and test pressings, last-minute changes, and scheduling difficulties within the plants themselves. If problems occur along the way, it can take much longer.

When you choose your pressing plant, inquire about the best months for pressing your record; it's a tactful way of telling them you know your project might have low priority. August through November are usually the busiest months because all labels are preparing for the Christmas buying season. Records pressed in August can be widely distributed in stores by November; records that sell well are usually pressed again in November to meet the heavy December buying demands. However, you should not assume that August through November are the only peak months: each manufacturing firm has its own schedule.

The following should give you an idea of what it will cost to manufacture you records:

▶ When your engineer orders lacquers to be disc-mastered as is, or 'flat', a standard price is usually charged per lacquer. For 12″ LPs, sets of master lacquers for both sides average $200; reference lacquers average $150. For 7″ 45 singles, sets of master lacquers average $80 and reference lacquers $50.

▶ When sound enhancement is requested for disc-mastering, more often an hourly rate is applied. Studio mastering time varies from $80 to $175 an hour, with lower prices offered by manufacturing firms that provide all the processes in-house.

▶ For 12″ LPs, plating, or matrixing, charges average $180 per set of two for three-step, or full-protection, processing. For 7″ EPs or 45s, prices range between $135 and $160 per set. Additional metal molds for LPs average $70 per set, and for 7″ EPs or 45s, about $60 per set.

When my 500 albums came, I opened a few boxes and spot-checked them. The first two records were warped. Then I opened all the boxes and found that the manufacturer had boxed them too tightly—both the bottom and top two or three were damaged. It represented 20% of my order. They more than made up the bad albums in my second order.

LARKIN STENTZ
Wind Sung Sounds

Pressing charges are based on the quantity of records ordered, and there are price breaks as the quantity increases. Here are some average prices:

Quantity	Cost	Unit cost
12″ LPs or EPs		
500	$ 340	$.68
1000	$ 680	$.68
5000	$3050	$.61
7″ EPs or 45s		
500	$ 180	$.36
1000	$ 310	$.31
5000	$1300	$.26

Note that, while the unit cost drops as the quantity increases, the savings are not nearly as dramatic for pressing records as for printing covers. (See Chapter 3, on Printing.) Thus, while it is usually to your advantage to print extra cover slicks, you should only press as many records as you have use for.

► Test pressings are usually figured as an extra charge. For 12″ LPs or EPs, prices average $35 for a set of three, plus postage. For 7″ EPs and 45s, $15, plus postage.

► The collating of records and covers is often figured as part of the pressing charges, but when it is not, average charges are about 2¢ per record. Included in that price is a white dust sleeve.

► Additional items are figured on a per record basis. Some average prices for LP extras are: rice paper dust sleeve—10¢; inserts—2¢; shrink-wrap—4¢; stickers— 6¢. Extras for EPs or 45s might be mailing envelopes—9¢; cardboard pads—8¢; plain white sleeves with no center hole—7¢.

► Packing completed records in boxes is usually done at no extra charge.

Tight Budgets. Let's say you've recorded a whole album's worth of music and, because the sessions were going so well (or so badly), you spent much more money than you intended. Let's also say that, during recording, your graphic designer came up with a beautiful four-color design for your album cover, labels, and a lyric insert. Sometime during the mix, you discovered you had very little money left in the bank, not

We chose to do an EP in accordance with our budget ($2000, which ended up $2500 plus)—not wishing to have such an important step to us result in only a two-song single, but not being able to afford an LP. Also, the record was an experiment to see whether our established audience would come through for record sales, as well as the already proven aspect of ticket sales. Fortunately, we found success.

THE NEW MISS ALICE STONE LADIES SOCIETY ORCHESTRA
Harmony Club Records

enough to press 1000 albums with a four-color cover. What can you do to reduce manufacturing costs?

► Put out a 7″ or 12″ EP instead. Recycle the profits from them into issuing your album.

► Put out cassettes (see Appendix I, 'Cassette-Only Releases'). Recycle the profits from the cassettes into issuing your album.

► You can also go for a 'total package' deal that combines both manufacturing and printing in-house, and cut the frills recommended at the end of the chapter on Printing. Packages include one- or full-color covers and one-color labels for 12″ LPs. Cover backs will be printed in one color only. An average package will include mastering, three-step plating, labels, label proof, pressing (usually on virgin vinyl), dust sleeves, printing, collating, shrink-wrapping, and boxing.

Quantity	Cost	Unit cost
12″ LPs (one-color covers)		
1000	$2000	$2.00
5000	$6000	$1.20
12″ LPs (full-color covers)		
1000	$2500	$2.50
5000	$7100	$1.42

When Quality Is a Priority. Audiophile records provide premium quality to a consumer. You must choose mastering, plating, and pressing plants carefully for their ability to deliver quality control and services. You can also use half-speed disc-mastering for distortion-free, high-frequency sound, and a premium vinyl, such as Teldec. You can expect to pay the following prices for audiophile records. (Note: your pricing policies at the retail and wholesale level should be geared to reflect the premium prices you'll be paying for quality manufacturing.)

HALF-SPEED DISC-MASTERING

Lacquer masters	$175 per side
Reference acetates	$175 (both sides)
Studio charges for half-speed analysis, preparation, EQ	$125 per hour
Premium vinyl	$1.20–1.40 per 1000 (slightly lower for 5000)

Manufacturing Cassettes. For information on cassette duplication and costs see Appendix I, *Manufacturing Cassettes.*

Manufacturing Compact Discs. For information on compact disc manufacturing and costs see Appendix II, *Manufacturing Compact Discs.*

Chapter 6
Recording Procedures

THE VERY SOUL OF RECORDING IS A LOVE OF MUSIC AND a desire to share it. Today's technology makes this possible for every musician. Yet making records differs radically from sharing your music from a stage. You are performing to a far removed audience, without the aids of lights, theatrical effects, and your stage personality. Presenting your music on a record requires different techniques and skills.

In preparing yourself for recording, you will have to be clear on your resources and your goals. You should consider whether your music is ready to be recorded, what instrumentation you intend to use, and how familiar you are with various recording methods and procedures. Have you ever been in a recording studio or watched a recording session in a multi-track studio? Have you ever recorded on someone else's album?

You should also think about what would be your ideal record. What would you do if the sky were the limit? Would you change your arrangements? Would you hire different musicians or a producer? Is there a particular studio, perhaps one not even located in your city, that you would want to use?

Finally, you should determine how much money you have to spend on recording. Recognize first that no amount of money will ever seem enough, whether you have a recording budget of over $100,000 or have to skimp by on less than $1500.

However, there are ways to get almost everything you need, and more of what you wanted than you may think possible. Many independent records have been made under less than ideal recording circumstances. Stories abound of makeshift improvisations and improbable schemes which got the job done. Wonderful records have been made on both large and small budgets —and so have some terrible ones. The bad ones were often a result of musicians lacking, not money, but adequate information upon which to make their choices.

The goal of these next three chapters is to help you record a good first album. The first chapter, Recording Procedures, will help familiarize you with the equipment you'll be dealing with and the procedures common to all methods of recording, from preparing equipment to editing your final master tape. The following chapter, Recording Options, considers the choices that confront you: arrangements, recording methods, recording environments, and personnel. Finally, the third chapter, Recording Time and Money,

provides a general outline of costs, together with tips on saving money and making your sessions proceed efficiently.

When you finish reading all three chapters, you should have enough information to know which questions to ask and how to focus your energies and resources when you start recording.

RECORDING EQUIPMENT

Regardless of their size or sophistication, all recording studios are equipped to record (capture and store) sound, to play back what was recorded, and to improve, alter, or edit sound, during both recording and playback. Six kinds or equipment help provide these capabilities: 1) microphones and pick-ups, 2) tape recorders and tape, 3) noise reduction systems, 4) mixers, 5) signal processing equipment (sometimes also called 'outboard gear'), and 6) speakers, including headphone sets.

This section will discuss briefly these various kinds of equipment. Since modern recording is such a highly technical field, in which the 'state-of-the-art' changes virtually every month, this section will purposely avoid mentioning brands, models, or specifications of particular equipment. It will, however, introduce and explain many of the types of equipment you are likely to encounter when working in the studio.

If you have had some experience with recording, the following will be merely a summary of some of the basic terms and concepts. If you have had little previous recording experience, knowledge of these basics should help you to understand what is happening during the recording process and to ask intelligent questions of the recording personnel. In either case, anyone wishing to pursue further the technical aspects of recording should refer to the books and periodicals listed in the Bibliography.

Finally, in considering equipment, remember *not* to equate the latest state-of-the-art equipment with a good recording. What ultimately produces a good recording is experience with the application of the equipment in the context of the music. The most important question an engineer or producer can ask in selecting or operating equipment is, "What will work best for the music?" In judging a studio, recording situation, or even an individual piece of equipment, let your ears be your guide. Do you like what you hear?

Specifications. All types of recording equipment can be rated in terms of how accurately they reproduce or transmit information about sound in the form of electrical or magnetic signals. The three major specifications are 1) frequency response, 2) distortion, and 3) signal-to-noise ratio.

The 'frequency' of a sound wave refers to the number of cycles of the wave per second. The basic unit is the 'Hertz' (Hz), which is one cycle per second. Variations in frequency are perceived by the ear in terms of the pitch of the sound. The lowest note most humans can hear is around 20 Hz; the highest is around 20,000 Hz, or 20 kiloHertz (20 kHz). The range of frequencies (notes) a piece of equipment can reproduce or respond to is referred to as its 'frequency response'.

Any piece of equipment will be more or less responsive to different frequencies within the extremes of its frequency response range. These differences are measured in 'decibels' (dB), which are units used to compare the relative intensities of audio signals. A one dB difference is considered the smallest that can be detected by a human ear; a three dB difference can be heard by almost everyone. Thus, frequency response is always expressed in terms of a range of sound intensity, such as "30 to 18,000 Hz plus or minus 3 dB." This means that, within the frequency response range of 30 to 18,000 Hz, the intensity of any individual frequency will not vary more than 3 dB from the mean.

The relative intensities of all the frequencies within the frequency response range can be expressed as a 'frequency response curve'. The 'flatter' this curve, the more evenly and accurately the equipment will respond to sounds across the entire frequency range.

The second major specification is 'distortion'. This occurs when the equipment produces audio signals in addition to the input signal which are either multiples of the original signal ('harmonic distortion') or the result of interactions among two or more frequencies ('intermodulation distortion'). Distortion is expressed as a percentage of the original signal, such as ".08 percent total harmonic distortion."

The third specification is 'signal-to-noise ratio'. This expresses, in decibels, the ratio of the maximum audio signal to background noise, caused by the equipment itself. For example, "signal-to-noise ratio: 45dB" means that the maximum audio signal is 45 decibels more intense, or 'louder', than the underlying noise.

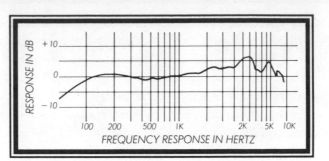

A frequency response curve for a dynamic microphone.

The 'ideal' specifications for each piece of equipment are frequency response over the greatest range, with the flattest curve, least distortion, and greatest signal-to-noise ratio. However, technical specifications are really meaningless unless they are considered in terms of the music to be recorded and how the final recording sounds. Much more important is the person operating the equipment. Skilled engineers can produce excellent results on equipment that does not display superb technical specifications.

Microphones. Microphones convert sound waves into electrical signals, which are then processed through the rest of the equipment. There are three basic types of microphones commonly encountered in recording: 'dynamic', 'ribbon', and 'condenser'. (A fourth, 'crystal', sometimes supplied with inexpensive tape recorders, is inadequate for studio quality recording.) These microphone types differ in the method by which the sound waves are converted into electric signals.

Dynamic and ribbon microphones operate on electromagnetic principles. In a dynamic mike, the sound waves hit a diaphragm which generates vibrations in a coil suspended in a magnetic field. In a ribbon mike, sound waves hit a thin metal ribbon suspended between the poles of a magnet, also setting up vibrations within a magnetic field.

Condenser microphones operate on electrostatic principles. A flexible diaphragm (called a 'plate') is placed parallel to a fixed back plate which has a permanent electrical charge. Thus, the area between both plates stores a fixed electrical charge (called a 'capacitance'.) As sound waves hit the flexible first plate, the capacitance alters, a change which can be measured electrically.

All types of microphones are further classified as either 'directional'—cancelling the sound patterns coming from one or more directions—or 'omni-

Sixteen-track studio at Hun Sound, San Rafael, California

A Speck 800-C mixing console
B MCI JH-10 16-track recorder
C 16-track inputs and outputs
D 2-track, 4-track, cassette inputs and outputs
E Sony TC880-2 2-track recorder
F Sony TC788-4 4-track recorder
G Ashly Audio SC-50 peak limiter compressors (2)
H DBX 165 Over Easy compressor/limiter
I Delta Labs DL-1 digital delay modules (2)

J Ashly Audio SC-66 stereo parametric equalizer
K 364-point patch bay
L Furman PQ-6 stereo parametric equalizer
M White 4003 one-third octave graphic equalizers (2)
N DBX 155 4-channel tape noise reduction systems (2)
O Ashly Audio SC-60 parametric equalizer
P Crown EQ2 adjustable center graphic equalizer
Q Klark-Teknik DN-34 analogue time processor
R Marantz 5030B cassette recorder

directional'—capturing the sounds coming from all directions equally. Directional mikes are further classified as 'cardioid'—capturing the sound directly on axis (in front) and rejecting sounds from back or sides—and 'bi-directional' or 'figure-eight'—capturing sounds from both directly in front and directly in back and rejecting sounds from the sides. Some mikes give a choice of pickup patterns.

All types of microphones have an 'output impedance' rating, which is used to match their signal-providing capability with that of a signal-drawing recipient, such as a mixing console or amplifier, which has an 'input impedance' rating. The unit of measurement is ohms. Low impedance microphones are commonly rated from 50 to 600 ohms; high impedance mikes from 20,000 to 50,000 ohms. So that the signal can be properly accommodated and transferred, the *general* rule is that the input impedance rating of the mixing console (or any other piece of equipment the microphone is plugged into) should be at least ten times greater than the output impedance rating of the microphone.

High impedance microphones have the characteristic of generating a signal that can only travel about 20 to 25 feet through cable before there is a noticeable deterioration in the sound quality. Since low impedance microphones do not display that characteristic, they are the preferred choice in most studio or location recording situations where mike lines may need to extend as far as 200 feet.

These differences regarding type or impedance do not, however, indicate which microphone is best to use for a particular instrument or voice. Microphone choice depends on the instruments and voices being recorded, the kind of music and how it is performed, the other recording equipment being used, the acoustics of the recording environment, and the placement of the microphone itself. (An inch can yield appreciable differences in the sound.) Two musicians playing the same instrument might be miked very differently, or microphones might be changed for an individual musician for the performance of different songs.

To some extent, use has established certain microphones as 'sounding better' in certain situations. For example, some microphones display better 'transient response'—the ability to handle sharp attacks, either sung or played, as when a drummer hits a snare drum suddenly and loudly. Which particular mike will be chosen depends on the judgement of each recording engineer or producer based on experience in working with different microphones in different recording situations. Depending on the circumstances, the least expensive microphone might be chosen for a particular job.

Pick-ups and Direct Boxes. Instead of miking an instrument, a 'pick-up' or a 'direct box' can be used. An acoustic pick-up works like a microphone; it converts vibrations into an electrical signal. The difference is that the pick-up attaches directly to the instrument and is sensitive to the physical vibrations of the

instrument itself. It is most frequently used with acoustic stringed instruments and some wind instruments.

Direct boxes are used with electric instruments. They allow the electric output from the instrument to be routed directly into the other recording equipment instead of placing a microphone in front of an electric instrument's amplifier. Direct boxes can be used with or without an amplifier and speaker. Sometimes, in order to obtain a certain quality of sound, a microphone is used in combination with a pick-up and the signals mixed at the console or during the final mix.

Tape Recorders and Tape. Tape recorders have three main functions: recording sound, playing it back, and erasing. Like microphones, they transform one kind of energy into another.

Magnetic tape recorders convert electrical signals into magnetic ones and imprint those signals as patterns on a recording tape. The tape consists of a plastic backing coated with metallic particles (ferric oxide, chromium dioxide, or other metallic oxides) which react to the electrical signals. The recording head on the tape recorder, functioning like a small electromagnet, aligns these particles into magnetic patterns that reflect the sound being recorded. The reverse happens during playback. The erase function saturates the tape with a very high frequency signal that destroys the previously recorded patterns and leaves the tape

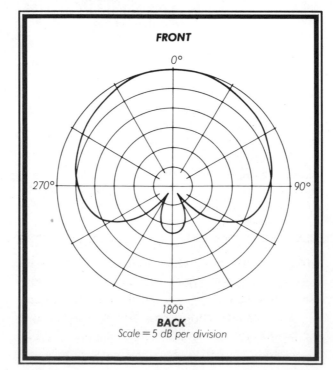

FRONT

0°

270°   90°

180°

BACK
Scale = 5 dB per division

A microphone pick-up pattern. This 'supercardioid' pattern has maximum off-axis rejection at 150°.

particles once again arranged randomly and ready to be rearranged with a new sound pattern.

Magnetic recording tapes differ with regard to the kind of magnetic coating used, its thickness, and, to some extent, the kind of backing. Each type displays different abilities to receive and retain the magnetic signal at any given tape recorder speed, and each requires different magnetic strengths to record the signal properly. These characteristics in turn determine each tape's frequency response, signal-to-noise ratio, and saturation levels.

There are two principal variables which permit a tape recorder to be adjusted to accommodate the properties of a particular type of tape: 'bias' and 'equalization'. The bias control of the tape recorder adjusts the magnetic field strength applied to the tape. All magnetic particles respond non-linearly (or disproportionately) within any magnetic field. By adding the correct amount of a very high frequency signal (100 to 350 kHz), far above the range of hearing, and mixing it with the audio signal, the relative magnetization of the tape particles are changed to react proportionately. Without the proper amount of current, the signal being recorded would be distorted. Different types of tape require different amounts of bias current.

The other tape adjustment, equalization ('EQ'), corrects for the fact that the tape does not respond equally to all frequencies. The EQ setting, expressed in decibels, compensates for this during record and playback, producing a nearly flat response.

Most tape recorders are equipped with bias and equalization controls that optimize performance for each tape. The adjustment of these controls is called 'tape alignment', or 'calibration'. It is accomplished with the help of test tapes which provide test tones at various levels and frequencies for specific tape speeds.

During tape alignment, the recording heads will also be properly positioned with respect to the tape, an adjustment called 'head alignment'. The heads and tape must precisely intersect at right angles. When they don't, tracks will be 'out of phase' (not properly aligned in time to each other). Moreover, the tape must also be centered at the record, playback, and erase heads. Improper positioning will cause loss of audio information.

Tape Speed and Track Format. Tape speed and tape width also affect a tape recorder's overall performance. In any given area of tape, the metallic

particles can hold or retain only so much magnetic information before becoming 'saturated'. Generally, the wider the area of tape exposed to the audio signal, the less likelihood that the signal will be distorted. Running the tape at a higher speed will also maximize the area of tape exposed to the recording signal.

Professional tape recorders usually operate at speeds of 15 or 30 inches per second ('ips') rather than at the slower 7-1/2, 3-3/4 or even 1-7/8 ips found on home recorders. Higher tape speeds also make it easier to splice the tape precisely, since the musical information is spread over a longer portion of the tape. Since the higher speeds use up tape faster, economical long play tape (more footage on the reel) may sometimes be used, particularly for rehearsal purposes. However, the tape backing is physically thinner, thus making the tape susceptible to breaks and stretching.

The accuracy with which a tape recorder maintains its speed also affects the tape recorder's overall performance. Variations in speed produce 'wow' and 'flutter'—audible effects that sound much like their respective names. Generally, operating tape recorders at higher speeds mitigates any inconsistency. Tape recorder specs express speed consistency as a percent of the speed variation over the total length of the tape.

Although constant speed at 30 or 15 ips is used for standard recording and playback, many professional tape recorders also offer variable speed. Varying tape speed alters both tempo and pitch. It is especially convenient when a musician or singer can't perform a song in a particular key, or is off pitch by a hair, or when an instrument is tuned to other than standard concert pitch, as are some non-Western instruments. Variable speed can also produce special sound effects.

Tape recorder heads come in different configurations. Some are made to record (and play back and erase) over the entire width of the tape; some are divided so that they can record two or more separate signals over portions of the tape width (called 'channels' when referring to the mixing board or 'tracks' when referring to a tape recorder). The number of channels that a head can respond to identifies its 'track format'.

For standard quarter-inch tape, the common track formats are:

▶ Full-track mono, which records one signal over the entire width of the tape, in one direction

► Half-track stereo, which records two signals over the width of the tape, in one direction

► Quarter-track stereo, which records four channels (two signals in one direction and two in the opposite direction when the tape has been flipped over)

► Four-track, which records four separate signals over the width of the tape, in one direction. This format is the lower treshhold of 'multi-track' recording.

Multi-Track. 'Multi-tracking', about which more will be said, is the capability of recording four or more synchronized signals on a piece of tape and then mixing them down to a monaural or two-channel stereo master tape. Any channel can be played back, erased, and rerecorded without affecting the others. What gives multi-track tape recorders their incredible versatility is their ability to record the different tracks at different times, termed 'overdubbing', and to synchronize the tracks together, creating the illusion that they were simultaneously recorded.

Some quarter-track tape recorders, notably those sold for home stereo use, do provide the capability of building layers of sound, similar to overdubbing, a feature called 'sound on sound', or more precisely, 'sound with sound'. Each time a new layer of music is added, the old layer is remixed with it and rerecorded. As a result, noise levels and distortion build up quickly. There is also no capability for erasing separate layers of music. Despite these disadvantages, these machines are worthwhile for rehearsal purposes, especially for experimenting with vocal or instrumental harmonies.

Professional multi-track tape recorders use maximum tape widths to maximize their performance. (Semi-professional models, which are discussed later, economize on tape costs by using narrower widths.) Professional recorders use half-inch tape for four-track recording, one-inch tape for eight-track recording, and two-inch tape for sixteen- or twenty-four-track recording. Multi-tracking in thirty-two-, forty-eight-, and sixty-four-track formats is also available, but this involves interlocking two or more tape recorders, since two-inch tape is presently the widest that can be accommodated by the recorder. Each tape format must also provide room for non-magnetized bands between each tape track to prevent signals from spilling onto other tracks, referred to as 'cross talk', or 'fringing'.

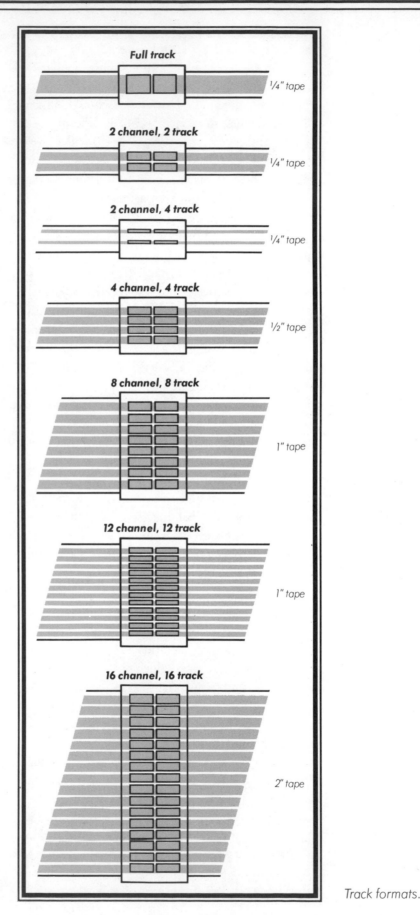

Track formats.

Sony PCM-3324 Digital Audio Multi-Channel Recorder.

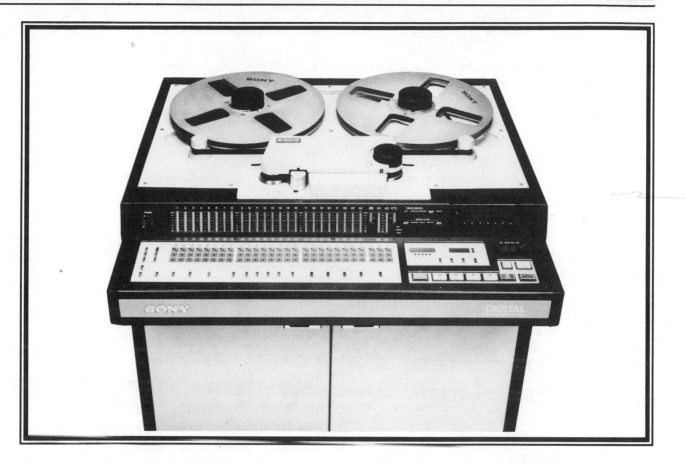

Studios providing multi-tracking will frequently be equipped with a multi-track recorder, a half-track recorder for mixdown, and one or two quarter-track tape decks and cassette machines for making copies.

Digital Recorders. The digital tape recorder converts electrical audio signals to binary code which is stored on tape and decoded upon playback. Digital recording eliminates most of the problems inherent in magnetic tape recording. These recordings have superb clarity, good transient response, wide dynamic range, and virtually no audible distortion or degradation at either extremely low or high volumes. Multi-track digital recording is available at premium prices. Sony's new rotary head digital recorders (R-Dat) will result in less expensive direct to two-track digital recording or two-track digital recording simultaneously mixed from a multi-track digital or analog mixing board. For more information on R-Dat see Appendix II, *New Technologies.*

Noise Reduction Systems. Magnetic tape and tape systems inherently produce noise, which is most commonly experienced as high frequency hiss on playback. It is more apparent when music is recorded at low volume levels. Unfortunately, if the music is recorded at high volume levels, which effectively masks the hiss, distortion can occur from tape saturation. In an ideal situation, where fast tape speeds are used together with high quality tape, machinery that is both mechanically precise and thoroughly clean and aligned, and an engineer who can adjust volume levels, or 'ride gain' so as to make the soft passages a bit louder, extraordinarily quiet tapes can be made.

In addition, within the past decade noise reduction equipment has become a standard feature of recorders and recording studios. Some systems, such as Dolby and DBX, manipulate the dynamic range of the signal before it reaches the record head by compressing the dynamic range of the signal ('encoding'). When, during playback, the signal is restored to its original dynamic range ('decoding') using the opposite principle of expansion, the high frequency hiss inherent in the tape falls into the background.

The DBX system (used most often in semi-pro recording equipment) compresses the total frequency band of the signal. The Dolby A system (used in most professional recording studios) divides the frequency band and independently works within each band to compress its dynamic range. The Dolby B system (used in cassette recorders) compresses the dynamic range of the signal at high frequencies only. Other systems, such as the Burwen System, use equalization to accomplish the same net result. Sometimes these noise reduction systems are built into the tape recorder; more often they are separate pieces of accessory equipment.

Noise reduction systems do affect the total sound of the recording. For this reason, many professional studio engineers prefer to record at 30 ips without using noise reduction at all.

Whatever noise reduction system is used for recording must also be used for playback; otherwise the encoded signal will not be restored to its original state. Moreover, different brands of noise reduction systems are incompatible; the same brand must be used throughout the entire taping and disc-mastering process. Basic tracks recorded in one studio equipped with DBX can't be mixed in a studio equipped with Dolby. Moreover, not all disc-mastering labs are equipped to handle all noise reduction systems. It is therefore wise to check with the labs before recording a master tape.

Mixing Console. The piece of equipment that always accompanies the multi-track recorder is the 'mixing console', or 'mixing board'. This piece of equipment, which visually dominates the studio, amplifies the signal very precisely to the level at which it can be processed and recorded. At that point, two or more signals can be combined onto one tape channel (pre-mixing); volume, tone, or spatial positioning can be adjusted; and the signal can be routed via switching or patching to any number of places, such as a specific tape channel, the musicians' headphones, or the right or left monitor speakers. Once the music has been recorded on two or more channels, the mixer can also be used to combine them further onto one channel (mono mix), two channels (stereo mix), or even four channels (quad mix).

Although the average console contains over a hundred knobs and dials concentrated in a small space, many of them simply repeat a series of functions for each channel of mixing provided. The following are basic control functions for each channel found on most consoles:

► The 'mic/line switch' selects between a low level signal from a microphone and a high level input called a 'line level signal', such as from the playback output of a tape recorder.

► 'Attenuation' cuts down the amount of signal entering the console should it be too high, thus preventing overloading the microphone pre-amp.

► 'Faders', or 'sliders', control volume for each channel. 'Master faders' control volume for several or all of the channels.

► 'Equalization controls' permit precise adjustments of tone in selective frequency ranges.

► 'Cue sends' route the signals to particular tape channels, to the headphones, or to the monitor speakers.

► 'Talkback switches' permit the engineer to communicate with the musicians in the recording room.

► 'Pan pots' permit spatial positioning of the signal between the right or left channels of a two-track recorder, headphones, or speakers.

► 'Solo switch' permits listening to any channel of the mixer alone without affecting the recording.

► 'VU meters' or 'LEDs' provide visual monitoring of the signal.

In some consoles various signal processing effects (such as echo or reverb) may be built into the mixer itself and made accessible by separate controls. More common is an auxiliary piece of equipment, called a 'patch bay', which provides access to the inputs and outputs of every piece of equipment in the studio. In addition, the console may have several access points in each input and output channel.

Dozens of brands of consoles are on the market; consoles are also custom designed. Each can be judged by the sheer number of inputs and outputs and controls available to accommodate everything from microphones to outboard gear, as well as by their technical specifications, mechanical precision, and ease of operation and maintenance. In the more complex consoles, where multiple pieces of equipment are accommodated, ease of switching and access to circuitry become features to be judged.

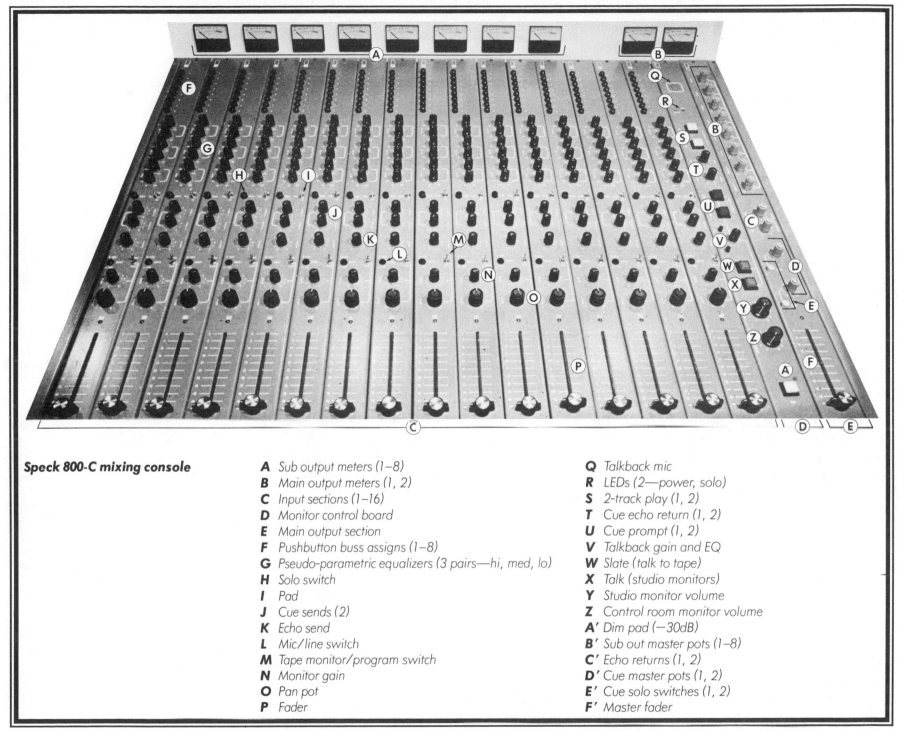

Speck 800-C mixing console

A	Sub output meters (1–8)
B	Main output meters (1, 2)
C	Input sections (1–16)
D	Monitor control board
E	Main output section
F	Pushbutton buss assigns (1–8)
G	Pseudo-parametric equalizers (3 pairs—hi, med, lo)
H	Solo switch
I	Pad
J	Cue sends (2)
K	Echo send
L	Mic/line switch
M	Tape monitor/program switch
N	Monitor gain
O	Pan pot
P	Fader

Q	Talkback mic
R	LEDs (2—power, solo)
S	2-track play (1, 2)
T	Cue echo return (1, 2)
U	Cue prompt (1, 2)
V	Talkback gain and EQ
W	Slate (talk to tape)
X	Talk (studio monitors)
Y	Studio monitor volume
Z	Control room monitor volume
A'	Dim pad (−30dB)
B'	Sub out master pots (1–8)
C'	Echo returns (1, 2)
D'	Cue master pots (1, 2)
E'	Cue solo switches (1, 2)
F'	Master fader

Rather than considering a mixing console, or board, from the standpoint of functions and switches, think of it as a series of circuits waiting to be told what to do and where to send the audio signals. How they are used depends very much on the music being recorded and the recording philosophy of the engineer, producer, and musicians working on the session. In all cases, the choices among the many options offered by multi-track consoles and recorder, are ultimately resolved in terms of which will allow the best recording and the most flexibility during the mix.

Signal Processing Equipment. Auxiliary pieces of equipment permit further processing or editing of the signal. Some, like compressors, limiters, and expanders, compensate for the deficiencies of the tape recorder in capturing the dynamic range of music efficiently. Others, like reverb, phasing, and variable speed oscillators purposely alter the sound. As previously mentioned, some of these pieces of equipment are used as accessories to the mixing board and are routed through it to the appropriate channels being recorded or played back. Others are accessories to the tape recorder or the musical instruments.

Although new, more sophisticated pieces of equipment are constantly being developed, some of the most common signal processing devices are the following:

▶ 'Equalizers' break the audio spectrum into separately controllable frequency ranges. Equalizers are, in effect, super tone controls which can be used in addition to the equalization controls provided by the mixing console. They give the engineer control over the harmonic balance of the instruments ('timbre') and can be used to make instruments sound different, to increase the separation between instruments by rolling off leakage frequencies, and to make the music from all tape tracks blend better. Professional recording studios use several different kinds of equalizers.

▶ 'Graphic equalizers' provide control over many frequencies simultaneously; the relative positions of the knobs provide a visual ('graphic') display of the overall frequency response curve.

▶ 'Parametric equalizers' enable the engineer to zero in on a particular tone that he or she wants to accent or attenuate, thus offering more specialized control than a graphic equalizer.

▶ 'Filters' cut out offending frequencies at the extreme ends of the frequency spectrum, such as rumble, air conditioning noise, and hiss, without disturbing the music.

▶ 'Compressors' reduce the dynamic range by automatically lowering the level of the loudest sounds. A compressor guarantees a signal that can be recorded louder than the background noise and yet will never distort. The trade-off is diminished dynamics.

▶ 'Limiters' are similar to compressors, except they are designed to cut off sudden peaks, such as when a singer comes in abruptly on a loud note.

▶ 'Expanders' increase the dynamic range on playback. They compensate for the work done by the compressor. Expanders are also called 'music gates' because they provide the capability of shutting off a channel at a preselected low threshold, eliminating noises and leakage.

▶ 'Reverb' and 'echo' create discrete, repeating sound (echo), or a combination of echoes so close together that they sound continuous (reverb). There are a number of different devices for producing echo and reverb.

▶ 'Digital delays' electronically delay the signal in time by adjustable amounts. Digital delay can produce a much shorter echo called 'slap echo' or 'doubling', which delays the signal so little that a vocal part may sound like one person singing exactly the same part with him- or herself.

▶ 'Phase shifters' delay the signal and recombine it with itself, producing a signal that is out of phase with itself. The resulting effect has a wooshing sound like a jet plane.

Every year sees the addition of dozens of pieces of signal-processing equipment. The choice of when, where, and how to use them should be left to the discretion of the engineer and/or producer of the session.

Speakers. None of the equipment described so far produce any sound; they merely process electrical impulses. It is only when these electrical impulses are transformed back into physical vibrations of air that any music can be heard. That is the function of the speakers.

Studio monitor speakers are chosen for their ability to provide a flat response over the widest possible frequency range. However, that response is affected by the acoustics of the room. The same set of speakers can sound entirely different when placed in different environments. Studios therefore employ a sophisticated method of standardizing speaker response to the room, called 'tuning', or 'equalizing'. This attempts to eliminate the problems caused when music is recorded in one control room and either mixed in a different room in the same studio or in a different studio entirely.

The major problem with this sophistication in speaker selection and tuning is that the people who buy the finished records or who listen to them on the radio seldom hear the mix as it was engineered in the studio. Not only will they be listening on different and often inferior speakers, but their rooms will also not be equalized to provide flat response. For this reason, many studios are equipped with one or more additional sets of speakers, including a set of small speakers simulating those found in car radios or small hi-fi sets. The engineer attempts to reach a mix which sounds good on all types of speakers.

In addition, the studio will have headphone sets so that musicians can listen to the sounds they are recording or, in the case of multi-tracking, accompany their music to the previously recorded tracks. Once again, the choice of headphone sets is critical, since the musicians' performance will be greatly influenced by what they hear while singing or playing.

Semi-professional Equipment. Several manufacturers now offer equipment that can outfit an adequate four- to eight-track home studio for less than $12,000. This includes multi-track and two-track tape recorders, mixing console, microphones, mike stands, cables, amps, and speakers—and perhaps one or two extras, like noise reduction, limiters, and a reverb unit.

The innovation which makes possible this economy equipment is a change in track format. 'Semi-pro' tape recorders use narrower tape widths than their professional counterparts. Instead of two-inch tape for sixteen-track recorders, the semi-pro models use one-inch tape; for eight-track tape recorders, half-inch tape instead of one-inch tape; for four-track models, quarter-

Good sound and ease of use make multi-track cassette recorders great composing and rehearsal tools.

inch tape instead of half-inch tape. The semi-pro models provide tape speeds of 7-1/2 and 15 ips, but not 30.

Most semi-pro recorders provide bias and equalization controls to be set to the tape that will be used. However, use of these controls is almost impossible without good test equipment to measure the signal and frequency; thus these controls are often preset by the store from which they are purchased to accommodate a specified tape. A maintenance program must also be planned for when the recorders go out of alignment or need their bias reset for some other tape brand.

The second design innovation has been to package the tape recorder with a complementary mixer that provides key functions for all tape channels, but is not as elaborate as the more expensive professional consoles. For example, the consoles generally provide bass and treble tone control, but not the ability to isolate particular frequency ranges. They provide a headphone mix for the musicians, but not different mixes for each musician; nor do they provide as many inputs and outputs.

Since these innovations, almost every tape and console manufacturer is competing for the semi-pro market. Each console and recorder has slightly different design features to catch musicians' attention and dollars. What should be kept in mind is that the difference in track format does result in somewhat noisier tapes, and that these semi-professional models are neither as rugged nor as durable as professional equipment. Using and maintaining them properly requires time and attention. However, they are built with the beginner in mind, and ease of use is an important feature in all the semi-pro recorders and consoles. They are excellent rehearsal and arranging tools, and good tapes and records have been made on them.

THE RECORDING PROCESS

Recording sessions, whether they take place in a studio or at home, usually follow a set of procedures designed to maximize quality and to help the musicians perform effectively. These procedures include 1) preparing the equipment, 2) set-up, 3) testing, 4) recording and playback, 5) mixing, and 6) preparing the tape for disc-mastering. The actual performance of the music takes up a relatively small amount of the total time; in fact, many musicians describe the recording experience as one in which they learned to *listen* to their music.

Preparing the Equipment. Before any sound is recorded, all equipment must be checked so it doesn't cause problems during recording sessions. Whether the session takes place in a recording studio using hundreds of thousands of dollars worth of equipment or in a living room with a two-track recorder and one microphone, the equipment must be tested before every session and every mix to be sure it is in excellent working condition.

Preparing the equipment includes cleaning and demagnetizing tape heads, making sure the heads are in alignment, and, if necessary, adjusting bias. Anything that might have broken down during the last session must be repaired. Properly functioning headphone sets are especially important; their malfunction at a crucial moment during recording may break the flow of a session or interrupt a brilliant performance.

In a recording studio, preparation is usually done when musicians are not present, often between sessions, as part of the studio's regular maintenance program. If you are recording on location or at home, preparation should be done before the other musicians arrive. Schedule at least two hours for this work.

Before going to a session, professional musicians thoroughly check their instruments and equipment for problems that could interfere with sound quality, such as worn-out strings, rattles in a drum set, chord connectors that cut out, or a loose ground in an amplifier

Set-up for piano and vocal at Different Fur Recording Studios, San Francisco, California. Engineer: Steve Mantoani.

When recording, my sense of the performance comes mainly from what I hear in the headphones. That's why the right mix is important.

IDRIS ACKAMOOR
Idris Ackamoor Quintet

that produces a low buzz. These problems frequently elude the audience at a live performance, but are never missed by the tape recorder. Instruments should be tuned in advance, although fine tuning is always done in the studio.

Set-up. To a great extent, the quality of the final recording is determined by the set-up, which is primarily carried out by an engineer, following directions from a producer or group's leader. In the absence of a producer, the engineer will assume the entire responsibility.

Depending on how many tracks the tape recorder will accommodate, as well as the number of instruments and voices to be recorded, the engineer will assign tracks to specific instruments. The engineer will also decide how best to capture the sounds made by each instrument—whether to use microphones and/or pick-ups, or to record an electric instrument 'direct'. (There are probably as many ways to set up for recording drums as there are recording engineers.)

Set-up also involves isolating the instruments as much as possible in the studio; ideally, only the sound of one instrument will be heard through its assigned microphone. The goal is to minimize leakage of the sound of other instruments onto other tracks during recording as well as to minimize the effect of room acoustics,

which could cause sound to reverberate off walls and back into the microphone. If one part later needs to be done over (a guitar lead that is out of tune, for example), it won't show up as a 'ghost' on other tracks.

During set-up, musicians should tell the engineer how they need to be positioned around one another. A bass player may need to see the guitar player's hands; a drummer may prefer working close to the bass player. Maximum sound separation can always be achieved by putting all musicians in special 'isolation booths' or by recording each instrument individually—but usually at some discomfort to the musicians. Mediating between sound quality and performance ease is one of the trade-offs encountered in recording.

An engineer can use several techniques to maximize separation while still meeting the musicians' need to communicate with one another. Instruments can be isolated from each other with separating materials. In a home, an engineer might use speaker boxes or a sofa; in a studio, low 'flats', or 'baffles', which are partitions made of wood or other sound absorbent material. A blanket can be draped over the open lid of an acoustic piano to keep other sounds from entering the piano's microphone. Sometimes isolation booths will be assigned to vocalists or to relatively quiet instruments such as the acoustic guitar, or noisy ones, such as drums.

In an on-location or home situation, extraneous noises, such as slamming doors, ringing telephones, sirens, and street noises, have to be eliminated. Sometimes blankets are draped over windows, or recording is done late at night when everything quiets down.

Testing. After set-up, the equipment and instruments are tested, a process also referred to as 'getting a sound'. First, the musicians tune their instruments precisely to the standard 'A' (440 Hz) pitch. To some extent, they must be dependent on the engineer's ears for accuracy, since the level at which instruments are recorded tends to influence pitch.

Each instrument is then adjusted, with the engineer listening for whether the instrument has the desired sound quality. Each musician will be asked to play his or her instrument apart from the others at extremely low volume, to make sure that the controls are adjusted to capture soft tones, and at extremely high volume, to make sure that distortion does not occur. Distortion can be a problem when an instrumentalist or vocalist shows great and unpredictable dynamic range. If too much distortion is anticipated, the engineer might add a limiter. The engineer will also listen closely for buzzes, clicks, pops, rattles, and hiss, and will do what is possible to eliminate them.

Musicians with little recording experience frequently complain that their sound isn't right. They need to understand that the sound of each instrument is being considered in the context of the final mix—not individually. Learning how to record 'for the mix', technically and aesthetically, takes a great deal of recording experience.

The musicians will each be assigned a headphone set to help them clearly hear the other instruments being recorded (as well as tracks previously recorded) and to receive instructions from the engineer or producer in the control room. Depending on the sophistication of the equipment, the engineer will adjust the sound in the musicians' headphones. Once again, unless musicians communicate their preferences, the engineer can only guess whether the individual headphone mixes are appropriate.

Once each instrument has been tested, a proper balance will be found when they are all played together. The level at which an engineer records the instruments is as critical as how each instrument is actually played. Not only do instruments sound different at various levels, but musicians also play their instruments differently depending on the level they hear in their headphones. Set-up and testing can take one to four hours, depending on the number of instruments and voices involved.

Record and Playback. Only when the instruments sound correct and the musicians feel comfortable in the studio can recording begin. During sessions, the engineer will record a song, or part of a song, and then play it back so that everyone can listen to it from both an aesthetic and a technical point of view. Sometimes a 'take' might be brilliantly played, but the recording is marred by a mysterious buzz coming from an amplifier. The buzz has to be eliminated before taping resumes. Conversely, a take might be perfectly recorded but flawed by inconsistent tempo or notes incorrectly played or sung.

Some preliminary editing might occur during sessions as the engineer, producer, and musicians choose between various parts of takes and splice them together.

This is a time-consuming operation that frequently breaks up the flow of performing.

Each mike and track assignment is noted in a session log kept by the engineer or producer. During sessions, the engineer or producer will keep track of each take with the help of a tape counter or stop watch. Occasionally the producer will write out each part of a score to facilitate keeping track of every detail, such as a solo that needs three bars redone and spliced in.

Sessions usually alternate between recording a song and playing it back. It often seems that there is more listening and analysis happening than actual playing, particularly in sessions in which multi-track equipment is used. Musicians who come in 'hot to perform' are often frustrated by the long hours of set-up and testing and by the start-and-stop procedures of the actual sessions.

Mixing. Mixing involves blending the signals recorded from all channels into two signals, one for each stereo channel (or, in the case of mono, one signal; in the case of quad, four signals). The mix is made directly onto quarter-inch tape on a half-track tape recorder, usually at 15 or 30 ips, resulting in a master tape that is used for disc-mastering.

In two-track recording, the mix is accomplished at the same time the instruments and voices are recorded;

Most of the fifty-plus hours in the studio were spent by Kay, Marilyn, and me getting the best sound we could from the best takes we could make. The work was thrilling, nervewracking, boring, and always intense.

ALIX DOBKIN
Women's Wax Works

in multi-track recording, the mix usually occurs afterwards, in mixing sessions. The advantage of mixing the tracks afterwards is that special attention can be paid to tone, volume, and overall balance, and changes can be made without affecting the performance itself. Moreover, special effects, such as delay or echo, can be added or deleted and different parts of the same tune can be spliced together to make one good take.

With a multi-track mix, each track will first be listened to separately. The engineer and/or producer listen carefully for ghosts, leakage from other tracks that were subsequently rejected, or for extraneous noises which can be edited out. This initial listening to each track also makes it easier to remember individual lines in the music and to note certain phrases which might be emphasized in the final mix. Then the engineer will begin to blend several tracks together, often repeating the order in which they were recorded: basic tracks first, then overdubbed lead instruments, then vocals and harmonies.

The engineer and producer have two concerns during mixing. Technical considerations involve the quality of the overall sound and the tone and level of each instrument as well as disc-mastering requirements. Aesthetic considerations include when and how much

to emphasize certain rhythms, melodies, or lead solos, their relationships to one another, and whether or how to alter the sounds of individual instruments or voices. It's much like cooking—too much or too little of even a minor ingredient can mar the result.

No two engineers or producers will mix a song exactly alike. In fact, a song can sound like two entirely different pieces of music depending on the way it's mixed. The engineer relies on the producer to provide guidelines as to what is to be emphasized. It's the engineer's job to translate such general directives as, "it needs more presence," or "the rhythm instruments aren't strong enough," into audible changes. What makes mixing a specialty is knowing how to choose among the many options available, not just for the abstract properties of the sound, but also for its appropriateness to the musicians who created it and the audience they want to reach.

The more tracks used in the recording sessions, and the more complex the vocal and instrumental arrangements, the more complicated the job of mixing will be, whether it happens during recording or afterwards. It can take from six to twelve hours for one song to be mixed, as the engineer and producer make literally hundreds of decisions—where to bring up the guitar a bit more and bring down the piano, when to omit a third harmony, when to add just a little more reverb to the lead vocal. Just executing a fade properly can be painstakingly slow.

Once all the decisions are made, a mix usually has to be made from beginning to end without interruptions and with all cues remembered. (Some songs can be mixed in sections and spliced.) During the final mix, the engineer's fingers are in continual motion on the console. Sometimes both engineer and producer 'play' the console so that all the cues can be executed, particularly if the arrangements are complex. Engineers and producers have to concentrate and almost always prefer to mix by themselves, without the presence of musicians in the studio. For this reason, rough mixes are often made so that band members can hear and discuss them before the final mix.

Stereo mixes are usually made for albums, and for singles to be sold commercially or played on FM radio. Monaural mixes are commonly made for singles slated for AM radio airplay or for films and commercials. While most FM stations broadcast in stereo, few AM

Take notes on what you do and how you obtain certain sounds— first, so that you can concentrate exclusively on the music, and second, because you will find that taking notes prevents you from getting into the situation of wondering what track you recorded something on. Also, you'll find that when you are busy working on a session, your memory isn't putting much effort into remembering all of what went down.

CRAIG ANDERTON
Author, *Home Recording for Musicians*

stations have that capability. Singles slated for DJs will therefore often provide a mono mix on one side and stereo mix on the other.

Although mono mixes can be accomplished in the disc-mastering phase by mixing the stereo signals together, producers almost always prefer to make their own mono mixes. They can edit the songs, cut them down to under three minutes, and emphasize frequencies that come across better over AM radio. Mono mixes are apt to sound awful on studio monitors, but terrific over the air waves.

Preparing for Disc-mastering. After the music has been mixed, the next step is selecting the tunes and putting them in order for the record. The amount of music that can be accommodated in either the 12″ or 7″ size depends on: 1) the playback speed intended for the records (either 33-1/3 rpm or 45 rpm), 2) the dynamic range of the music, 3) the amount of low frequency information the music contains (how much bass), and 4) the level the master lacquer will be mastered at. In general, the faster the speed, the greater the dynamic range, and the more bass present, the hotter the mastering level and the fewer the minutes that

can be accommodated on the record without sound deterioration. Thus, most pop and disco music records average 19 minutes per side for a 12″ LP, 12 minutes for a 7″ EP and 3 minutes for a 7″ 45. On the other hand, some classical music and spoken word records can accommodate twice that much.

Decisions regarding selection and sequence are those of the musicians and producer, not the engineer. Sequence should be considered in terms of tempo and key changes as well as thematic or musical continuity. Sales and promotional considerations should also play a part. DJs, concert promoters, and store owners will often listen only to the first thirty seconds of the first and last songs on each side of your record.

Once these decisions have been made, the engineer edits and precisely times each song. Then the songs are spliced into the desired sequence, leaving three to six seconds of 'plastic leader', or 'biased blank tape', between songs. Each side of an album is put on a separate reel of tape.

The engineer will provide alignment tones at the head of each reel so that the disc-mastering machines can be aligned identically with the machines on which

Mixing session. The execution of the final mix is best left to the engineer and producer.

Here's how we did the mix: first, Grey and Malcolm would premix all the tracks, working carefully on each one until they were satisfied with the echo, the equalization, etcetera. Then our engineers would come in and comment on their work. When each individual track was perfected, all four would do the final mix until it sounded right to all their ears. Sometimes there were as many as eight hands on the board controlling each of the eight tracks.

JACK WRIGHT
Engineer, June Appal Recordings

the tape was recorded. These tones will permit adjustment of playback level and equalization.

At this point, some engineers copy the two-track master as an insurance against loss; that tape is then referred to as a 'safety master'. Since a transfer is involved, some sound quality is lost, however imperceptible. (If the safety is ever used for disc-mastering, the engineer should indicate how to compensate for that loss.)

A 'matrix number' is assigned to the master tape for each side, to be used for identification throughout the manufacturing process. The same matrix number is also placed on the artwork for the record labels so that labels and sides can be matched. The matrix number should end with either '-1' or '-A' for the first side of the album and '-2' or '-B' for the second. The matrix number is an arbitrary one; sometimes it is the same as the album number that will be used for cataloging; if not, it should be entirely different so that there will be no confusion between the two.

The matrix number, names of songs, sequence, and timing are written on each tape box, along with any special requirements the engineer may request of the disc-masterer, such as the addition of sound enhancement or information about noise reduction equipment used. Finally, the tape will be carefully packaged for shipping to the disc-masterer. (See 'Disc-mastering' in the chapter on Manufacturing.)

Information on mastering for cassettes and compact discs will be found in Appendix I, *Manufacturing Cassettes* and Appendix II, *Manufacturing Compact Discs.*

Chapter 7
Recording Options

EVERY ASPECT OF MAKING YOUR RECORD INVOLVES DE-cisions—how best to promote your record, what sales possibilities to pursue, which graphic material you want to represent your music. In the actual recording of your album, there are four key choices to be made which will determine how your record will sound: 1)how your music is arranged for recording, 2) what recording method you use, 3) where you conduct your recording sessions, and 4) which personnel assist you in both the technical and musical aspects of the sessions.

This chapter will describe the options available to you in each of these areas and suggest some of the practical considerations that should help you make your decisions. As you make your choices, you should realize that your primary goal is to create *music,* not just to make a record. The fact that you are recording your music might require that you create it somewhat differently than the way you normally perform.

As you read this chapter, evaluate your experience and skills, and those of the other musicians involved in the project. It's difficult, but extremely important, to judge honestly whether you are capable of making decisions that are both objective and appropriate to your music. You must also assess whether you can and want to provide the leadership necessary to execute those decisions, both during the planning stages and after the sessions have begun. Preparing musicians for recording and directing sessions requires considerable skills—many of them learned through experience. Decide how much you want to learn on your own and how much to rely on the experience of others.

Finally, in addition to how your record will sound, you will have to consider how much it will cost. Before you read this chapter, prepare yourself for the fact that your budget might well limit some of your musical aspirations. The time and money involved in recording will be covered in the next chapter.

ARRANGEMENTS

Your first decision is how to arrange your music for recording. There are three basic possibilities: 1) record your music as you perform it, 2) add some supplementary instrumental or vocal parts to your regular arrangements, or 3) rearrange your music entirely, recasting it as a completely new creation.

Many independents choose to keep their performing arrangements because they are counting on initial sales to come from people who regularly attend concerts and club dates. Their audiences expect to hear the music they have become familiar with and are often disappointed if the artist makes a 'studio' record full of lavish arrangements that cannot be repeated on stage. Keeping the arrangements you use for performances is certainly the easiest and most economical choice. You may even be able to avoid the need for overdubbing and thus choose a less expensive method of recording.

You may find, however, that the arrangements you use for performing do not work equally well for recording. They may sound too cluttered, or they may have overlong tags or instrumental bridges. In the critical atmosphere of a multi-track studio, where each instrument can be isolated and analyzed, you might simply hear how to arrange your music better.

When your original arrangements begin to be altered, or when new instrumental or vocal parts are added as 'sweetening', the recording process becomes more expensive and time consuming. You will have to learn new musical parts and perhaps even hire extra musicians. You will probably be committed to recording your music on multi-track equipment and to using overdubbing procedures. You will almost certainly spend more time getting a good 'take'. Adding parts will also complicate the execution of a good mix.

You should not consider completely rearranging your music unless you have had some prior experience at both arranging for recording and recording itself. It is not easy to 'hear' how a new part or an added instrument will work in the final mix. It also takes considerable skill to play a new musical line with the precision required by the overdubbing procedures. All too often, bands recording for the first time recognize these problems *after* recording sessions have begun. They attempt to test and practice new arrangements in the studio. As the recording environment becomes an arena for experimentation, nerves shatter and costs skyrocket.

If recording weren't so expensive, a multi-track studio would be the perfect place to improvise arrangements. The resources provided can inspire creativity and develop perfection. One can hardly blame a musician for wanting to turn a recording session into a practice session. It takes discipline to realize that money must be saved for promotion and sales.

This is not meant to scare you, just to help you plan for what will be involved. One of the luxuries of recording is the possibility of adding parts that you cannot include in your regular performances. If you have clear musical ideas and the musicians to perform them, by all means consider arrangements for supplemental parts. Keep in mind, however, that as a performing group you have achieved a certain musical unity. Your music as it is performed might leave little room for additional instruments or voices without resulting in an overly busy, cluttered, or muddled sound. You will probably have to simplify your present arrangements to accommodate the new parts.

Regardless of how extensively you plan on arranging your music, you should consider seeking some professional assistance well before you begin recording. (See the section on 'Recording Personnel' later in this chapter.) If you are going to use new arrangements, test them in an inexpensive four-track studio to make sure that they work musically and that they can be competently played. The choices you will make about recording method, environment, and personnel depend on your music being arranged, rehearsed, and ready to record.

RECORDING METHODS

Two broad philosophies reign with regard to the 'sound' of recorded music. According to one philosophy, the most beautiful and natural sound results when the signal is recorded with both minimal equipment and as little alteration as possible. The most direct route from original signal to master tape is achieved by using high quality microphones and a high quality two-track tape recorder. No coloration is added or subtracted, on the theory that the more processing a signal receives, the greater the possibilities for sound degradation.

The second philosophy acknowledges that multi-track recording provides unlimited possibilities for editing sound and minimizing distortion and noise. The signal can be enhanced in a variety of ways, such as emphasizing or diminishing certain frequency ranges, adding special effects, such as reverb, echo, and phasing, and combining or separating different musical elements. The resulting noise build-up can be minimized with noise reduction equipment. The goal is to produce a captivating sound, but one which does not necessarily duplicate the original 'live' sound. Thus, recording can become a creative endeavor in which the technology itself plays a part in producing the art.

Few musicians are totally committed to either philosophy; both approaches can produce recordings which are technically excellent and musically brilliant. What follows are descriptions of the principal recording methods, which represent various degrees of these two philosophies. As with all the subjects discussed in this chapter, the selection of recording method is interrelated with the other choices you will be making regarding arrangements, recording environments, and personnel.

Direct to Two-track. The simplest way to record music is direct to two-track, using one tape recorder and no more than two microphones, even if more than two instruments are being recorded simultaneously. The instruments and voices are recorded and simultaneously mixed directly onto a stereo half-track tape. (Some very high quality tapes have also been recorded direct to two-track using a three-head high quality cassette recorder, although they cannot be used directly for disc-mastering.)

In the direct to two-track method, the engineer determines the best position for the microphones while the musicians try to balance their sound by controlling their performing dynamics. This method allows for some flexibility in editing; if the music is consistently played, multiple takes can be recorded and the best parts of each spliced together.

Direct to two-track has four advantages over other methods of recording. First, it produces high quality, natural-sounding tapes. Second, it allows for

I hunt people down. It's a mania of mine. Some people call it producing. I call it making records. I let people sing whatever they sing. I try to record live as much as I can. I find that it takes people a half hour to warm up and get a good feeling going, then they're good for two hours in the middle, and then they get tired. To me music is live. If you have good music you don't need all that bullshit background.

CHRIS STRACHWITZ
Owner, Arhoolie Records

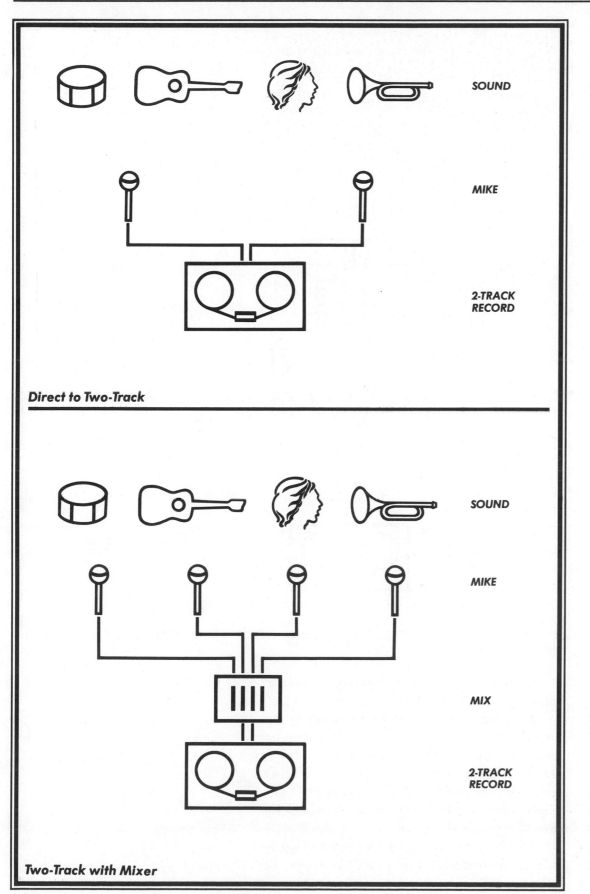

SOUND

MIKE

2-TRACK
RECORD

Direct to Two-Track

SOUND

MIKE

MIX

2-TRACK
RECORD

Two-Track with Mixer

the greatest mobility and ease of set-up. Some two-track tape recorders can even be battery operated. Third, it permits great ease of performing. Musicians don't have to be carefully set apart from each other, headphone monitoring is unnecessary, and the simplicity of the equipment and the method seems to minimize tension. Finally, direct to two-track is usually the least expensive method of recording.

Music best recorded with this method includes traditional folk, blues, jazz, classical, symphonic and choral music, and solo performances. Generally speaking, since it's up to the musicians to control their playing dynamics, this method works best for instrumental acoustic music and not as well for mixtures of acoustic and electrical instruments, or instruments and voices. When used to capture live concert performances, the recordings reflect the spontaneity and inspiration that an enthusiastic audience often generates.

The key to judging whether this method is right for you is how your music sounds when performed. Are you able to clearly hear all the instruments and/or voices? Does the blend sound pleasing to you? If it does, the chances are that it will to the tape recorder as well. With the right engineer, good equipment, and music performed well, excellent recordings can result.

Two-track with a Mixer. In this method of recording, each instrument and voice is miked separately and the signals routed through a mixing board. As the music is performed, it is simultaneously mixed directly onto a half-track tape.

Not only musicians must be able to hear each other, but the engineer must also be able to distinguish what is recorded from the sounds as played in the room. In a studio or home situation, this usually requires that everyone wear headphone sets, and that the engineer work in a separate room. In a concert situation, the on-stage monitor system gives musicians the chance to hear themselves while the engineer monitors the signal through headphone sets and close watch of the VU meters.

The need for a simultaneous mix means that the musicians and the engineer share the responsibility for controlling the dynamics of the music, although more control is vested with the engineer. Ideally, each microphone should be placed so as to minimize leakage into it from other instruments or voices. Sometimes this is accomplished by placing the musicians at greater distances from each other than they are accustomed to when performing or rehearsing. Baffles or other separating materials can also be used. (If a concert performance is being recorded, the engineer may also hang additional microphones at a distance from the performers to add depth to the sound.) The goal is control over the mix so that solos can be turned up, key sub-rhythms emphasized, and lead voices brought to the foreground. Special effects might also be added to selected instruments or voices. As in direct to two-track, the results can be edited by recording multiple takes of each song and splicing together the best parts of each.

This method is a compromise one. It has neither the simplicity of direct to two-track nor the advantages of multi-track recording for controlling the sound and dynamics. It is best used when acoustic and electric instruments or voices can't be successfully recorded direct to two-track or when multi-track recording is not financially feasible. It is also essential that the engineer be thoroughly familiar with the music, and that a spirit of trust and cooperation exist between the engineer and musicians. Under these conditions, great tapes can be made.

Multi-track/Ensemble. The set-up for this method is much the same as for two-track with a mixer. The musicians perform together at the same time, but each instrument and voice is recorded onto a separate track of a multi-track tape recorder. The mix is postponed until the music has been recorded. At that time, decisions about tone, balance, and spatial positioning of the signal can be made.

This method permits the engineer to concentrate during recording on capturing each instrument as clearly and accurately as possible. It also permits different versions of the final mix to be tested until the right balance is achieved. It offers much more editing flexibility than two-track recording.

By performing the music ensemble, the musicians can preserve much of the spirit and spontaneity of an actual performance, while keeping the time spent in recording sessions to a minimum. This method is therefore a very good compromise for groups who cannot afford to log many hours of studio time, yet who still want maximum control over the dynamics of their final recording. As with the previous methods, multiple takes can be spliced together. It is also possible to

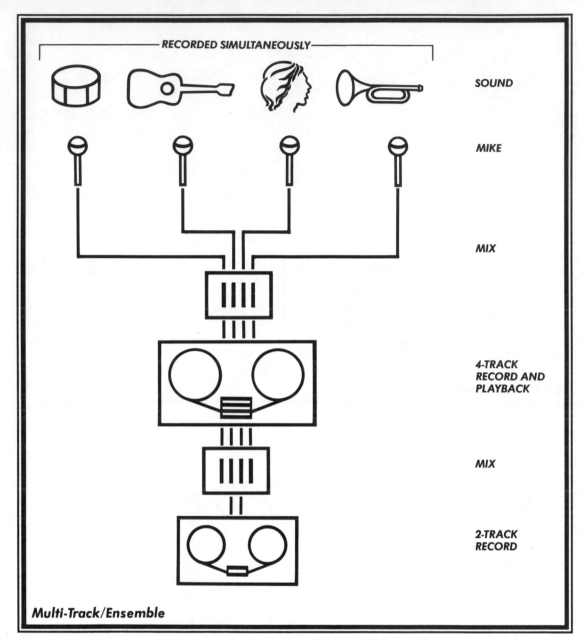

RECORDED SIMULTANEOUSLY

SOUND

MIKE

MIX

4-TRACK RECORD AND PLAYBACK

MIX

2-TRACK RECORD

Multi-Track/Ensemble

rerecord a single track, or to leave some tracks open for adding supplemental instrumentals or vocals.

Multi-track/Overdubbing. Breaking up the music into sections or layers and recording them on different tracks at different times is called 'overdubbing'. Mixing is postponed until all the tracks are completed. This method allows musicians the most flexibility in both arranging their music and editing the results. They can build a few layers of music, erase tracks they don't like, and substitute others. They can fix a sore spot in the music by 'punching in' corrected ones. They can improvise different lead solos on three separate tracks and select the best one. They can adjust tone and stereo placement in the mix, or add or subtract special effects. Or, as some major label artists have done, they can record rhythm tracks in San Francisco, vocals and lead solos in Nashville, and instrumental arrangements in London with musicians from the London Philharmonic.

When the music involves a complex arrangement for many different instruments and voices, a basic foundation is recorded first—a process known as 'laying down basic tracks'. Most often these basic tracks will be drums, bass, and rhythm guitar or keyboards—whatever instruments carry the rhythmic or melodic foundation of the music. Once the basic tracks have been satisfactorily recorded, other voices and instruments are added in overdub sessions. Overdub sessions are usually organized to add lead or solo instruments to the basic tracks first and then all other harmonizing or secondary instruments, a process referred to as 'sweetening'. Lead vocals and harmonies are recorded last, although a trial, or 'work', vocal is often recorded with the basic tracks to orient musicians unfamiliar with the song. Lead vocals or lead instruments are recorded individually, while strings and brass are usually recorded in sections.

In a typical overdubbing situation, the engineer sets up the musician(s) in the studio and plays the previously recorded music through the headphone set while the musician adds his or her part, accompanying the music heard through the headphones.

The main concern of the engineer and producer is a precision performance from the musicians with exact pitch and tempo, especially during recording of basic tracks, since all overdubbed instruments will accompany them. Sometimes a musician will be asked to repeat a part dozens of times, until it is satisfactory to both the producer and the engineer. If the tempo is not exact, a 'click' track may be added through the headphone set to help the musician keep time.

Overdubbing can be expensive, not only because of the need for complex machinery and an engineer properly trained in operating it, but because of the inordinate amount of time that is required, especially when compared to other methods. Hundreds of hours can be spent before satisfactory results are achieved.

Overdubbing is also extremely demanding. Performing ease is difficult to achieve in an atmosphere where precision playing is a priority and the start-and-stop procedures of sessions are often uncomfortable. Much more time is spent listening than playing. Musicians are liable to become so analytical that every note is played self-consciously, or so critical that nothing sounds right. Since virtually anything is possible, indecision and disagreements can take over the session. For these reasons, musicians recording for the first time should carefully consider whether they want to take on multi-track overdubbing.

Best results are realized when procedures are thoroughly grasped, the music is rehearsed and arranged,

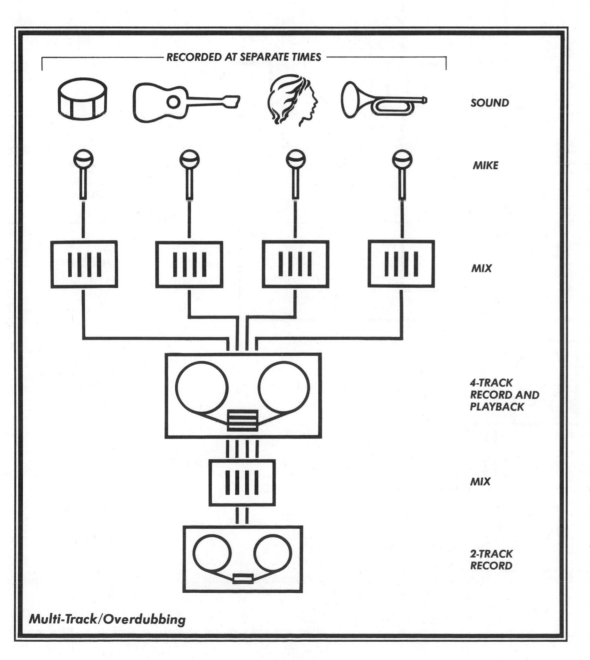

RECORDED AT SEPARATE TIMES

SOUND

MIKE

MIX

4-TRACK RECORD AND PLAYBACK

MIX

2-TRACK RECORD

Multi-Track/Overdubbing

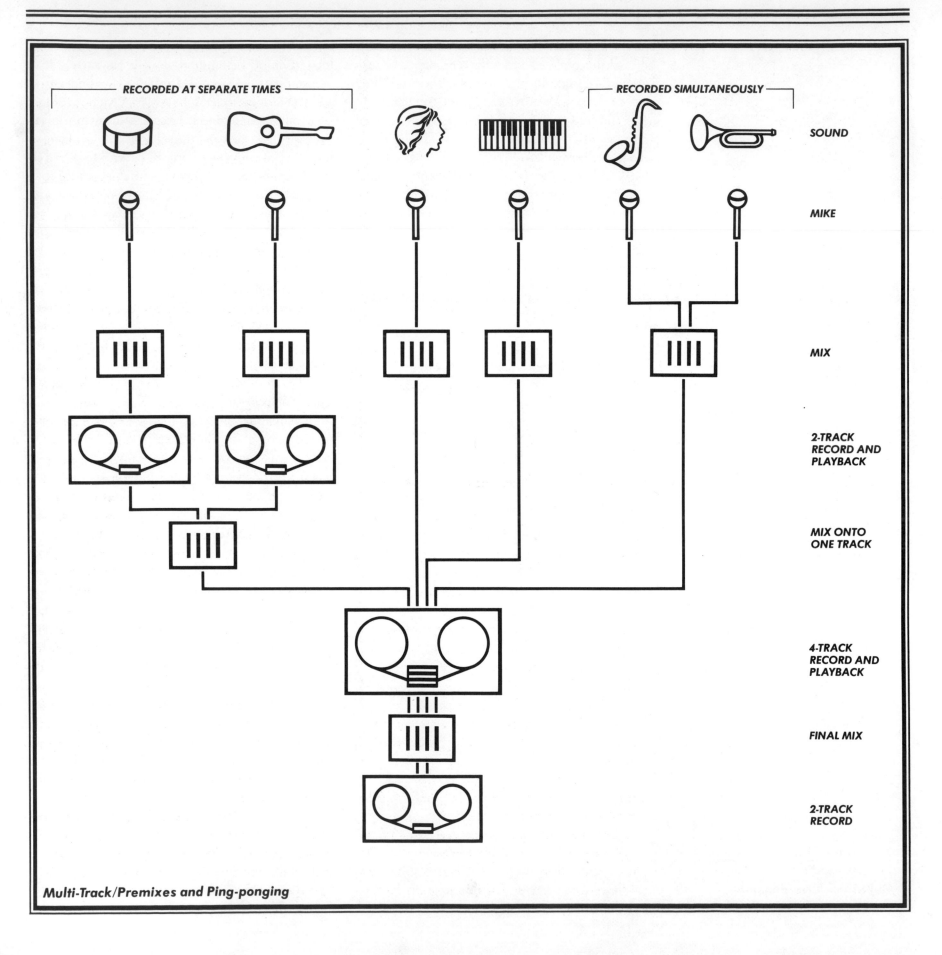

RECORDED AT SEPARATE TIMES

RECORDED SIMULTANEOUSLY

SOUND

MIKE

MIX

2-TRACK
RECORD AND
PLAYBACK

MIX ONTO
ONE TRACK

4-TRACK
RECORD AND
PLAYBACK

FINAL MIX

2-TRACK
RECORD

Multi-Track/Premixes and Ping-ponging

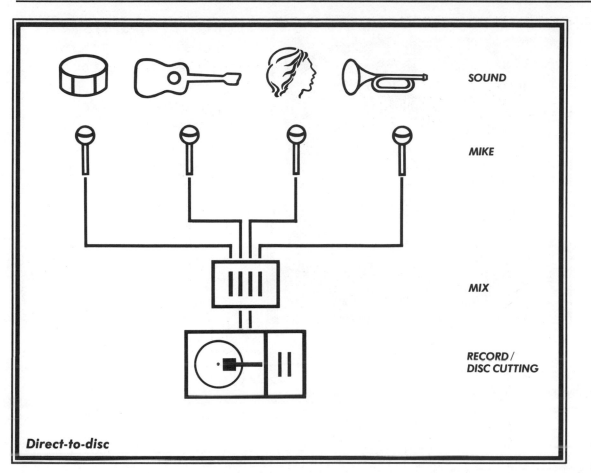

Direct-to-disc

ever, is that noise levels build up quickly on the ping-ponged tracks, with resultant sound degradation.

Sometimes both methods will be used; for example, a live concert that has been initially recorded direct to two-track can be transferred onto four- or eight-track tape and the other tracks used for overdubbing additional instruments.

The goal of both methods is the same: economizing the number of tracks that need to be used and thus cutting recording costs. Although the concept sounds easy, the execution is relatively difficult. Care must be taken both in organizing which instruments are to be grouped as well as recording at proper levels to insure quiet tracks.

Direct-to-disc. In direct-to-disc recording, the music is cut directly onto a master lacquer with the same type of lathe used for disc-mastering. The instruments are usually miked separately and routed through a mixer. The music is always simultaneously mixed directly onto the lacquer. The time limit for each side is 17 to 18 minutes for a twelve-inch record at 33 rpm.

This method requires perfection from both the performer and the engineer, since the music must be performed from start to finish for the entire side of the lacquer without pause. Every time a mistake is made, due to either equipment failure or musical error, the lacquer must be scrapped and the process begun again. Direct-to-disc recording often unnerves even the most seasoned musicians and engineers, who find themselves under tremendous pressure to perform correctly and brilliantly. Days can go by without one satisfactory lacquer being cut. This method is definitely not recommended for musicians inexperienced in recording or unaccustomed to performing their music perfectly under pressure.

The advantage of direct-to-disc is the chance for an excellent quality recording. This method produces recordings with the least sound degradation because the route from sound to record is direct. Furthermore, a much greater dynamic range is possible than with magnetic tape recording.

The major disadvantage of direct-to-disc, barring expense, is that only about 12,500 records can be pressed from each lacquer. For that reason, some direct-to-disc facilities use four or more lathes to maximize the number of records that can be manufactured from one performance, as well as to have extra lacquers

and, in most cases, the entire project is led by a producer. Mastery of multi-track recording is almost always extremely rewarding for musicians. The ability to control the sound opens up exciting new dimensions. It's no wonder that most musicians, at some point in their careers, want to try it.

Multi-track/Premixes and Ping-ponging. When finances do not permit the luxury of one track per instrument, fewer tracks can be used to obtain similar effects. In one method, instruments are grouped together and simultaneously mixed and recorded on one track. Additional tracks are thus reserved for either overdubbing or for simultaneously recording other instruments or voices. Tracks 'pre-mixed' cannot be altered in the final mix. Basic tracks, lead and harmonizing vocals, and string or brass overdubs can all be successfully recorded with this method.

In a second method, instruments are assigned individual tracks and the tracks are then 'submixed'. The resulting mix is then placed, or 'ping-ponged', onto one or two tracks, thus freeing up the others for further use. The big disadvantage of this method, how-on hand should something go wrong in the plating process. Most direct-to-disc records are cut by independent companies and marketed primarily through audiophile stores at prices in excess of $12 per album. Because of the high retail price necessary to cover the recording and manufacturing costs, this method is presently not appropriate for a record that is aimed at a general audience.

RECORDING ENVIRONMENTS

Any of the recording methods described in the previous section (except direct-to-disc) can be used in the recording environment of one's choice: recording studio, club or concert auditorium, rehearsal studio, or home. In choosing an environment, the important considerations are room acoustics and comfort. (Since price is also a determining factor, the following chapter offers suggestions for estimating recording time based on the method and environment chosen as well as general information on booking time and negotiating rates with recording studios and location recording services.)

Recordings sound different depending on the acoustics of the room in which they are made. Sound waves leave their source in an arc. Some of the waves will reach the ears of a person, or the diaphragm of a microphone; some will be absorbed by soft surfaces, such as drapes or rugs. Still other sound waves will be reflected off the surfaces of the room and then to the listener, a phenomenon known as 'reverberation'.

Each environment has its own reverberation pattern. This reverberation can enhance the sound quality of a recording, as with classical music recorded in concert halls; it can result in muddy, distorted recordings, as with electric music recorded in a large, empty gymnasium; or it can be entirely eliminated during studio sessions and added artificially as a desired effect in the mix. Because all spaces differ acoustically, listen to a tape made in environments you are thinking of using and decide whether you like the sound quality in that room. Personal preference is the most reliable guide.

Finding an environment in which you feel you and your musicians can perform effectively is also vitally important. The pressure to perform well often escalates into anxiety. Here are some factors to consider that will help you judge how you're likely to feel in a particular environment:

One of the hardest trips for me was altering my guitar playing in the studio. Live, we perform as an acoustic trio. In the studio, I had drums, a lead guitar, and a bass player. I had to be cleaner, less busy, and let the musicians fill the spaces. I had to learn to play for the tape.

STEVE SESKIN
Bald Ego Records

► Can the room accommodate your musicians and their equipment, as well as any recording gear, comfortably?

► Are the aesthetics of the space conducive to performing? Color and lighting have been found to be extremely important to temperament and mood.

► Are temperature and humidity regulated? Playing in a cold or hot room, or one that is drafty or excessively humid, can make you uncomfortable as well as affect the sound quality of your instrument.

► Do you need an environment free of external distractions or interruptions? Some musicians prefer an audience to inspire them, whether that audience is a few friends in a living room or thousands of enthusiastic concert fans. Still others are more comfortable in the sealed off atmosphere of a recording studio, set up to maximize concentration.

► How accessible is good food and a place to relax or take a break? This consideration is important enough for some studios to provide catered food services as well as saunas and Jacuzzis for shattered nerves.

► At what time of day or night do you perform best? Can the environment support your preferences? Is the time available to you open-ended or, as in some studio or concert situations, limited to a specific set of hours?

After weighing all of the above considerations, the important question is: how do you feel? What is the overall vibe? An environment may check out well in all areas and still leave you feeling ill at ease. Eliminate it from your list. It's your record and your money. The following pages outline some of the pros and cons of different recording environments.

Recording Studios. For many musicians, the recording studio provides the ideal work environment: a wide selection of microphones and/or pick-ups, choice of track format and recording method, adequate recording rooms, personnel dedicated to providing good service, and a quiet, undistracting atmosphere geared for concentration. On the other hand, some musicians feel very uncomfortable performing their music in a recording studio. The atmosphere is too cold and impersonal—a problem accentuated by the plate glass that separates the control and performing rooms and by the need to communicate through headphone sets. They feel that their music will be better served recorded in other environments.

The best way to get acquainted with studios in your area is to visit them. If this is your first record, or you have a limited budget, first check out modestly equipped and priced studios with reputations for good engineering and maintenance. They can turn out tapes sounding as professional as those made in state-of-the-art facilities. Generally, you should be looking for a studio that 1) has a reputation for producing good tapes, 2) works with musicians at your level of recording experience, 3) has experience with recording instrumentation similar to yours, 4) provides the recording

Recording session at Different Fur Recording Studios. Idris Akamoor Quintet.

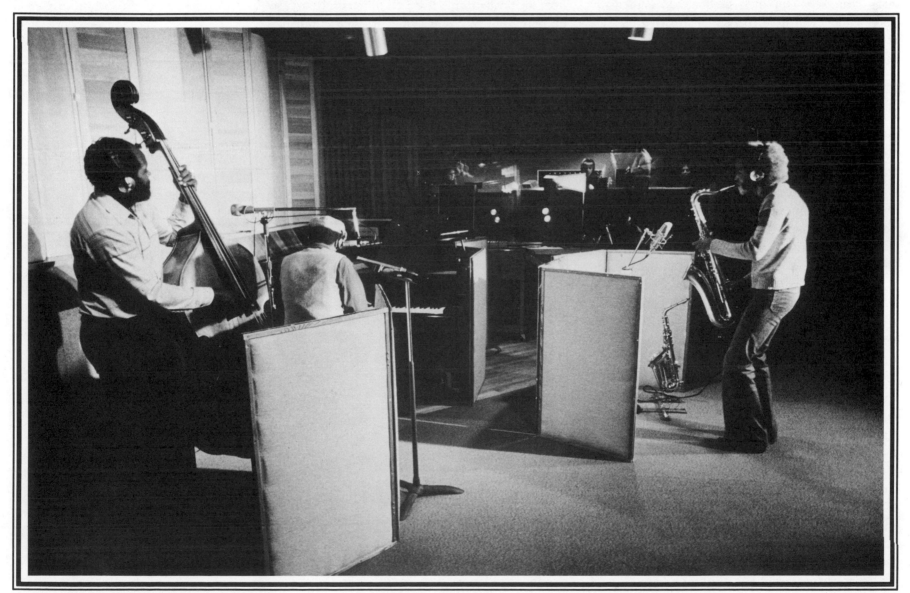

equipment necessary for your project, 5) has the space to accommodate your musicians and their instruments, 6) has time available when you need it, 7) wants your business, 8) fits your budget, and 9) feels right for you.

Call first and tell them you are planning to cut a record and are shopping for a studio. This gives the studio the opportunity to 'sell' you. When you do make an appointment, ask if there is a time when you can meet their engineers and listen to a tape on one of their monitor systems. It's best to bring your own tape, since you can use it for comparison in other studios. You should also ask to check out the 'cue' (headphone) system—particularly in the funkier or cheaper studios. A studio might have a great board and monitors, but a poor cue system. It is extremely important that musicians hear clearly in their headphones. Particularly good studios will have cue systems that enable each musician to have his or her own mix. Allow about an hour for each studio you plan to visit.

Later, when you have decided that a studio is the right place to record and have narrowed your choices, you can involve these studios in your recording plans, ask their advice on such matters as estimating time, and negotiate service and price. (See the next chapter on Recording Time and Money.)

Location Recording—Concerts. The key question with concert recording is how much sound quality are you and your musicians willing to sacrifice in order to capture the feeling and inspiration of a live performance? You will have to make a trade-off, no matter how optimal the conditions.

First, you must find a location with good acoustics. The best person to help you evaluate the acoustics of any concert location is an engineer experienced in this type of recording. He or she should be familiar with most clubs or concert halls in your area and can advise you as to their suitability. The engineer will look for environments that are not overly resonant (having too much reverb), a common problem in halls with many exposed hard surfaces of wood or concrete. Halls with deadening materials such as drapes, curtains, cushioned seats, or pillows help absorb resonance, as do full audiences. The engineer will also look for a 'dead' stage—one that is solid and doesn't produce vibrations when musicians stomp their feet or when the drummer hits the drum set. He or she will also check for outside noises, temperature and humidity, and drafts.

Even when the acoustics of the location are optimal, the engineer will have to contend with both the main PA system and the monitors on stage to help the performers hear themselves. The sound coming out of the monitors will affect not only the clarity and overall recording blend, but the level at which the sound of any instrument can actually be recorded. Sounds from instruments leaking into microphones used for other instruments further complicate the situation. Any feedback from the main PA can ruin an otherwise flawless take.

Set-up and testing time is also at a premium in concert performances. Seldom will there be time for a long sound check prior to the performance. Furthermore, set-up and testing the PA for the audience and the monitors for the performers will take precedence over set-up testing for recording. Under these circumstances, the engineer will have to adjust the sound for the first two or three songs and may never get ideal results.

Finally, cooperation between PA and recording personnel is extremely important. Equipment is often shared, particularly microphones, and everyone needs to take care not to clutter the stage with gear and cables.

At this point you might be asking why, considering all these difficulties, recording a live concert is even attempted. First, location concert recording can be less

Location recording inside Filmways/ Heider Recording mobile unit with API 24-track console, Hollywood, California. Note the television monitor used to check the musicians visually.

Alex de Grassi's Southern Exposure *album was recorded live to two-track digital using a Sony PCM 1600. Steve Miller was the engineer.*

expensive than multi-track recording in a studio. Second, a truly great recording can be achieved if all the conditions are exactly right—a good room, cooperative personnel, musicians attentive to staying on mike and maintaining pitch and tuning, and, of course, an inspired performance.

Location Recording—Home. The main reason home environments are chosen as a place to record is because musicians feel more relaxed performing their music and, often, because their family or friends surround them with support and warmth. The spirit of home sessions is often friendly and loose and the recordings reflect that ease.

Once again, engineers are the best people to use for checking out the room acoustics. Meanwhile, you can check for extraneous noises. Will telephones ring, traffic screech, or doors slam? Are children likely to be wandering in and out?

Home Studios. The advantage of a home studio is apparent: it places recording tools in your hands and makes it possible for you to learn techniques at your own speed and leisure in a comfortable environment. If you have an idea for a song at 3:00A.M., you can put it down on tape, add a few harmonizing lines, and go back to bed. You can take the time to work out complicated arrangements with your band, record and play them back, and analyze them to your heart's content. You can work on training your ears. You can mix and remix tapes. And you don't have to count the dollars whizzing by. Moreover, the sound quality that you can

get in home studios can be quite good, as proven by many home-made records.

The disadvantage of a home studio is that it takes time and money just to build. With the money and energy you would spend on setting up your home studio, you could record your first album and learn a great deal about recording in the process. It all comes down to being clear about your goals and recognizing your priorities.

If you want to know more about what it takes to put together a home studio, and how to learn to use the equipment effectively, consult an excellent book called *Home Recording for Musicians* by Craig Anderton, which is listed in the Bibliography. It includes instructions on the selection, use, and care of equipment, and techniques for recording and mixing two-to sixteen-track tapes. It also contains a primer on sound wave characteristics and how they are affected by various pieces of recording equipment, which is clearly and straightforwardly written and illustrated.

RECORDING PERSONNEL

Recording is a partnership among many different people, each of whom makes an important contribution. In addition to a group of musicians who balance each other's skills, the recording team includes an engineer, a producer or arranger, and perhaps studio musicians. These people influence the sound and character of your music and they must be carefully chosen and directed for your record to appeal to its intended audience. Even though you are an artist, you will be depending on them to help shape your artistry. Putting together a good recording team is as much of a challenge as finding compatible band members.

One of the choices you will have to make is how many of these jobs you want to take on yourself. Don't let your budget (and your ego) deprive you of the valuable knowledge and objectivity that others can offer. If this is your first recording experience, look for people who can provide the skills that you and other members of your band lack. They will be able to shortcut the time needed to solve problems that arise.

Putting together teams that work well is one of the skills you will acquire during your career. You can start with just your band and end up with a loose conglomerate of managers, agents, producers, record companies, song publishers, and promoters. Mutual respect, trust, and acknowledgement will help make the members of your team feel that their efforts are worthwhile and will lead to a personal commitment and involvement worth much more than just dollars.

The Engineer. Your recording project needs an engineer for four main tasks: 1) to evaluate the recording environment and make the musicians comfortable in it, 2) to select, set up, and operate the recording equipment, 3) to execute the final mix, and 4) to prepare a tape for disc-mastering. One engineer may be hired for each or all of these functions.

To an untrained observer, the engineer is just a technician, an operator of complex machinery. But to many musicians and producers, the engineer is a magician. He or she can create the illusion of fantastic, original, and (when multi-track equipment is used) simultaneously recorded sound. From the moment the engineer chooses the first microphone up until the completion of the final mix, sound quality is the prime consideration. As they are often extreme perfectionists, engineers will spend hours, if necessary, working to get the sound just right. The engineer's skill to a large extent determines the sound quality of the final record.

If you are recording with two mikes direct to two-track, the engineering will be the least complicated. Once the equipment is chosen and set up in the recording environment and the proper sound obtained, the engineer's primary job will be to see that everything functions properly.

It's not necessary to find a studio engineer if you are recording direct to two-track. Many freelance engineers are experienced in operating basic recording equipment, and are likely to be more available for recording on location. Other musicians and even local studios can put you in touch with qualified freelancers who will suit your needs and your budget.

In the more complex two-track method, where several mikes and a mixer are involved, the engineer will be executing the mix while the recording is in session. You will be relying heavily on his or her judgement and should definitely seek an engineer who has had experience with simultaneous mixing.

A recording studio is not the only place to find an engineer with this skill. Companies which specialize in producing sound for concerts often offer recording as an additional service. Some radio and television stations also make available for hire the engineers and remote

trucks they use for live broadcasting. In some cases, the engineers from these operations may be more familiar with this method of recording than their counterparts in studios. Their jobs demand results from the very first take. Thus, they may be more adept at 'live' mixing. Whomever you use, ask to hear a tape or record that demonstrates the engineer's ability with location recording. Be sure that the tape was mixed simultaneously and is not a multi-track tape that was mixed later.

If you are going to be recording with multi-track equipment, you definitely need an experienced engineer. Most engineers skilled in multi-track techniques are on the payrolls of recording studios. Often you will be choosing a studio as much for its engineer as for its equipment or atmosphere. Occasionally, you will find freelance engineers who can use the facilities of recording studios in your community. Some of them may also be able to assist you with production.

The engineer's recording experience can be extremely helpful to musicians who are new to studio procedures. In the absence of a producer, an engineer can help organize and direct sessions efficiently, make clear what options are available, and foster a professional attitude among the musicians. Often, musicians get their first inkling of what really good sound quality means from their engineer.

It is important that your engineer be sympathetic to working with you at your level of experience and in your musical style. Some engineers are not comfortable working with amateurs; some prefer recording jazz or

It is really not enough to listen to records a lot and to feel that you have a special understanding of what makes a hit. If you don't speak either the musical language or the technical language of the recording studio fluently, you aren't going to get your ideas across in the very limited time available in recording sessions. That doesn't mean you have to give up your goal of becoming a producer, but it does mean you are going to have to educate yourself, first either as a musician, or as an engineer, preferably both.

PAT GLEESON
Producer and Musician

rock to classical or country music. Try to find an engineer who is reasonably sensitive to your music and the personalities of your musicians.

Generally, unless specifically instructed to do so, an engineer will not try to correct musical errors or make aesthetic judgments about the non-technical aspects of the recording. When working with producers and professional musicians, engineers are trained to take direction and impeccably follow it, regardless of whether they disagree. Bad music, poorly played, can and should be captured authentically by the engineer. It should be recognized, however, that the distinction between sound quality and good music is not always clear-cut. Music that is arranged for too many instruments playing simultaneously in one frequency range can result in muddled sound, no matter how well the engineer tries to adjust for it.

Arrangers. An arranger can be hired for various purposes: 1) to adapt your regular performance arrangements for recording, 2) to simplify your regular arrangements to make room for additional instrumental or vocal parts, 3) to score those additional parts, or 4) to score arrangements for the entire session. Depending on the complexity of your music and your own experience with recording, you should seriously consider hiring an arranger, if only for a brief consultation.

Many arrangers specialize in a particular kind of music or instrumentation, such as synthesizers, brass or string sections, or vocal harmonies. Most have distinctive arranging styles, which should be an important consideration in your choice. Recording studio managers and engineers, producers, or other musicians who have used arrangers on their records can give you the names of experienced arrangers that might be appropriate for your style of music and the instrumentation you need. College music departments or music conservatories are also good places to look for arrangers.

When you hire an arranger, play your music for him or her and explain in general terms what you'd like to hear. Do you want melodic or abstract lead lines? Do you have preferences for unusual instrumentation? What mood do you want the song to convey? This input will be valuable in steering the arranger in the proper direction.

Studio Musicians. If you are going to use additional musicians on your record, they should be skilled in adapting their playing to your style of music. They should be able to learn the arrangement quickly and either follow your arranger's score or improvise their part. They should be familiar with studio procedures. Most important, they must be proficient with their instruments.

You can create problems for yourself by having someone play on your album just because he or she is a friend. If they have the skills, your friends can be a welcome addition to your album; if they don't, they will cost you time and money, and it will be much more difficult to ask them to step out of the session if it is just not working.

Professional studio musicians are numerous in the major recording centers. They can be located through studios, producers, arrangers, the local musicians' union, or a local symphony orchestra. Unless you are seeking musicians who are nationally famous, you will probably find that most musicians will want to play with you if they like your music. Professional musicians can not only save you money in the long run, but can be helpful in teaching you studio techniques.

Regardless of which musicians you use, make sure that you have at least one rehearsal *before* you step into the studio.

The Producer. The producer of a record is the person who can facilitate and direct the making of all the choices discussed in this chapter. He or she can help gear your arrangements for the recording method, as well as toward your intended audience and promotional plan. The producer can help choose a recording method and environment appropriate to your music and your experience. He or she can help direct sessions so that they proceed smoothly and creatively. The producer usually takes responsibility for making decisions regarding the final mix. Finally, the producer can help you complete your record efficiently, producing a good sound within a given amount of time and money.

To do this, the producer must be experienced in working with different arrangements, methods, environments, and, most important, in working with recording personnel and musicians. The best producers know how to bring out your talents and teach you how to choose among the infinite possibilities that recording makes available.

A producer is also your objective conscience—the one person who can step back from your music and honestly tell you what does and doesn't work. It's extremely difficult to be impartial when your own music is at stake. Objectivity is essential in helping you decide which songs to record, which arrangements work and which should be redone, when you and your musicians are properly rehearsed and ready to begin recording, which takes are satisfactory, what editing needs to be done, and when the mix is complete. Objectivity is also needed for mediating group conflicts or smoothing out tensions. This detachment helps avoid mistakes that will hurt when your albums reach the marketplace.

When simpler methods of recording are used, such as direct to two-track, or when the music has already been arranged by the group or a professional arranger, the leader of the group can often act as a producer. However, in multi-track recording where overdubbing is planned, a professional producer from outside the group is more essential to provide leadership. Multi-track sessions produced 'communally' often flounder as analysis turns into endless discussions, wasting both time and money.

Musicians who have worked with good producers swear by them. They'll tell you how much they learned about recording, about their music, and about themselves. They'll tell you that the producer helped them make a record that excites the listener as much as their live performances—perhaps more!

When looking for a producer, shop the way you would if you were adding a member to your band. Look first for the skills that balance those you lack, and then consider compatibility. Someone with an agreeable personality and a love for your music may not have the experience necessary to provide the many and diverse skills you and your group may need. Finally, no matter how experienced or personable a producer may be, the final test is to listen to records he or she has produced.

Unfortunately, in the case of most independents, producers, particularly the experienced ones who have the most to offer, usually find you and not the other way around. Supply and demand rules; there are few really good producers and many groups needing their services.

Many of the best producers are on payrolls of major labels; others contract their services on a freelance basis exclusively to major label recording groups. Many of the best freelance producers scout for talented groups for whom they'll produce a record and then sell it to a major label for distribution, getting both an advance for their services, a rebate for production expenses (both of which the group will end up paying for in the long run), and usually a percentage on every record sold. This type of recording contract, quite common in recent years, is called an 'independent production deal'. You may be able to hire some of these independent

The first record I produced was an album by Be Be K'Roche— an already existing band with a clear concept of the songs they wanted to record and their arrangements. My job was clearly defined—it was like being the coach of a football team. Also, it wasn't my own music. I took on a lot more emotional responsibility when it became my own project, and it took a lot out of me. I wouldn't want to be my own producer on the next album. I think it's good to turn that power over to someone else.

LINDA TILLERY
Olivia Records

A good producer is an illusionist, a musician's magician—if you can get magic in the studio, then you're a successful producer. The real duty of a producer is to the music. You have to love the music and the people who are making it. You have to have confidence in them and you can't cop an attitude. You have to really open your heart to them.

MICKEY HART
Drummer with the Grateful Dead and producer of the Diga Rhythm Band

producers on a freelance basis, but their fees are liable to be exorbitant.

If you desire production help but can't afford or find a professional producer, what should you do? First, because of their experience in working with diverse groups and instrumentation, engineers can often double as producers, or be hired to provide one or more production skills. They can be extremely good at organizing and directing sessions. Their greatest weakness will usually be in helping arrange the music. If

that skill is needed, hire an experienced arranger, who may also be able to provide direction during rehearsals or sessions, even if new arrangements are not required.

Sometimes musicians with a great deal of recording experience also make good producers, particularly if they themselves have worked with good producers.

You might also be able to persuade an experienced producer in your community to give you a few hours of time on a consultant basis to help you with particularly thorny problems. Play the producer your rehearsal or demo tapes. His or her advice about your arrangements, studios, and engineers can save you countless hours and wasted money. Sometimes a producer can also be hired on an hourly basis to direct rehearsals, conduct complex overdubbing sessions, or to direct the mix.

If other resources are not available, one of the members of your group can take on the responsibilities of a producer. If you do this, make sure you select someone whose objectivity you trust. You should also consider prior recording experience and the ability to direct the other musicians in your group. If you are going to be your own producer, you might find helpful the tips listed in the next chapter under the heading 'Making Sessions Work'.

Finally, whomever you choose as your producer, follow his or her direction. Trust in the choice you've made, and concentrate your energy into giving your best performance.

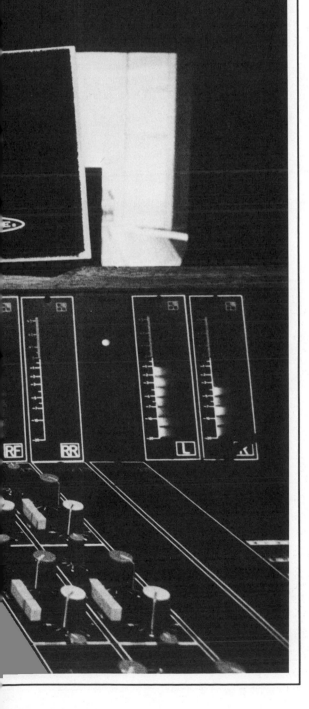

Chapter 8
Recording Time and Money

THROUGHOUT YOUR PROJECT, YOU WILL BE DEALING with your dreams and your finances. It's not that they have to conflict, but rather that your finances will determine how you shape your dreams. You must set limits on the time and money to be spent on recording and stick to these limits, so that, when your record comes out, you will have money left for promotion and distribution.

For many musicians it seems that no amount of money is enough. Recording—especially with multi-track equipment—is highly addictive, given all the possibilities it presents for creating and arranging music. From the very first session, you will hear your music differently and see how you can make it better. Without a clear sense of your limits, you might never finish your first album.

ESTIMATING TIME

The cost of recording depends on the method you choose and the time it takes. As a rule, the more complex the method, the longer you will spend recording, unless you are recording a concert. When you estimate the time you will need, take into account 1) the recording experience of the musicians, 2) the organization of the sessions, 3) whether you have a producer, 4) whether the music and recording method have been rehearsed, and 5) how much deviation from the planned arrangements might occur during the sessions. Finally, no matter how carefully you estimate your time, add fifty percent for the unexpected. Recording *always* takes longer than you think it will.

What follows are guidelines to help you estimate the time you will need, based on actual experiences of groups making albums for the first time. The guidelines include time for set-up and testing, listening to playback, retakes, and final sequencing of the songs. For purposes of standardization, when the word 'song' is used in these guidelines, it means a musical piece (vocal or instrumental) lasting three to four minutes.

▶ For direct to two-track, estimate 90 minutes per song. No one session should last more than 6 hours.

▶ For two-track with mixer, estimate 3 hours per song. The number of instruments and voices being miked, and the number of inputs they are routed through on the mixer, increase the time needed for both set-up and recording.

▶ If you plan to use multi-track/ensemble to record a single performance within the studio with no over-dubbing, estimate 5 hours per song. The extra time will be spent mixing. If you plan to use one or two tracks for overdubbing and an additional vocal or instrument, add an extra hour per song.

▶ If you are planning on multi-track with extensive overdubbing and are a relatively inexperienced band, estimate no less than 15 hours per song. The breakdown goes like this: 4 hours for basic tracks, 5 hours for lead instrumental and vocal overdubs, 2 hours for vocal harmonies and other instrumental overdubs, and 4 hours for mixing.

Why does overdubbing consume so much time? Mainly because each track is worked on with great care. The goal is technical and aesthetic perfection, and that means perfection on each track individually, as well as in the final mix.

Basic tracks and vocals take the most time because of the need for precision in tempo and tone. Singers with little recording experience sometimes have a problem staying perfectly on pitch. Instrumental overdubs usually take the least time, especially when experienced studio musicians are used.

▶ If you plan to economize by using ping-ponging or premixing, you should still figure on 15 hours per song. You'll save money, not on the time consumed, but on the lower rates for a two-, four-, or eight-track studio.

Finally, you will save set-up time by grouping songs which use similar instrumentation and recording them at one session. If you will be using additional musicians on several cuts, try to record those songs all at one session.

RECORDING RATES

If you live in a large metropolitan area, you will be able to find everything from cut-rate basement studios to beautifully furnished and equipped, state-of-the-art complexes, as well as location recording services. When you start shopping, first check the Yellow Pages of your phone directory; call several studios and request their rate cards. This way you can eliminate studios clearly beyond your means. In addition, a knowledge of the rate spreads in your town may help you bargain with a studio you especially like.

Recording Studios. Hourly rates for four- to thirty-two-track studios vary considerably, particularly in cities that are recording centers and have many studios. Even in these inflationary times, some rates have actually gone down, not up—perhaps because of competition. In Los Angeles and San Francisco, rates for two-, four-, and eight-track vary from $15 to $90 an hour; rates for sixteen-track, $40 to $175 an hour; rates for studios offering twenty-four or more tracks start at $125 an hour. The highest rates are usually charged by the better-known recording studios used by major-label recording artists.

These basic rates usually include some free time for set-up and breakdown, as well as the provision of microphones and certain instruments, such as pianos or organs. (Synthesizers are almost always extra.) When comparing studio rates, determine what is included.

Basic rates do not often include extras, such as automated mixdown, noise reduction, or special effects. Mixing sessions often cost less per hour than recording sessions. When shopping for studios, find out what services are available and at what rates.

Sometimes studios charge less in the morning hours, which are unpopular with musicians. In addition, hourly rates are often cheaper when you contract for a block of time. Ask studios whether they have block rates and how much time you have to book to get the special rates. You might be able to negotiate a further discount if you offer to pay cash in advance.

Remember that you don't have to use the same studio for all stages of your work. You might use one studio for recording basic tracks and another for overdubbing. Mixing might be done in a studio whose engineer is especially skilled or in one with automatic mixdown.

When negotiating rates, be sure to let the studio owner know you are an independent artist making and selling your own record. Studios that deal mostly with major-label clients charge them top dollar because they know that the label can pay; you might find a sympathetic studio manager who is willing to work out more favorable rates for you.

You should also give the manager some general information about your recording plans—the number of songs you plan to record, their instrumentation, and the method of recording you are considering. Bring your worksheets listing the instrumentation for each song. Many studio managers will help you evaluate the feasibility of your plans and offer suggestions for organizing sessions and estimating the time required.

Don't try to hype or impress the studio managers; straightforwardness is the best approach. Remember that you are going to hire the studio and not *vice versa.*

Location Recording. Location recording services usually charge by the half-day or day rather than by the hour. If the equipment and personnel have to travel far out of town, you might also be charged for mileage. For two-track, rates vary from $40 to $20 a day; for two-track with a mixer, which requires more equipment and sometimes an extra person, $150 to $500 a day. You might be able to negotiate lower rates by booking consecutive days.

Location recording that requires a remote unit with sixteen- to thirty-two-track equipment will cost around $2,000 a day. You will also have to book studio time for mixing, which could take fifty to one hundred additional hours. If you are recording a concert, not only is the price high, but the risk is great, since you stand to lose your money if the performance or recording is unsatisfactory. It's not a risk many independents choose to take, unless they are experienced in recording and are reasonably sure the circumstances will be optimal. Few groups hire remote services for recording in their homes.

If you're shopping for two-track location recording services, it's a good idea to check out sound reinforcement companies, since the only extra piece of equipment they need to perform these services is a good two-track tape recorder. Some night clubs also provide two-track recording equipment as an extra benefit to bands. Even if you can't get your group booked in such a club, you might be able to rent the club's facilities for morning or off-day use at a fraction of what the recording time would cost you elsewhere.

Sound reinforcement companies are also good places to rent individual pieces of recording equipment. Here are some day rates from one major West Coast PA company: $12.50 per microphone, including stand and cable; $100 for a sixteen-channel mixing console; $50 for a two-track tape recorder; $100 for a four-track tape recorder.

Although a recording studio is the standard place to look for remote multi-track services, sound reinforcement companies, radio stations, or TV stations

We did things backwards. Instead of performing first, we went right into the studio, bartering time in a first-class sixteen-tracker for painting and carpentry. It allowed us to log over 1000 hours in a two-year-period. One of the most important things I personally learned, since I was chief songwriter for the group, was that you better go in and cut that baby as fast as you can, because you lose energy and feeling with every consecutive take. You've got to get the energy while it's hot if you're after the perfect elusive take.

JIM McGUIRE
Companion
Sleepy Eye Records

sometimes offer them at lower rates. You will need to make arrangements with a recording studio for mixing, however—one that will accept a tape you make elsewhere.

Tape Costs. The choice of track format and the number of songs to be recorded will dictate the width and length of tape you will need. Since multi-track recording requires mixing down to a two-track machine, you will need at least one reel of standard quarter-inch tape in addition to the multi-track tape. You will also need tape for cassette and reel-to-reel copies for listening between sessions ('work tapes') and for your personal use until the album is manufactured.

Tape for professional studio recorders comes in two standard lengths—2,500 feet and 3,600 feet. To fit the extra length onto the same size reel, however, requires the longer tape to be thinner and thus more fragile. Studios use the thinner tape mainly for tape copies or trial mixes.

Studio recorders run at either 15 or 30 inches per second. For 2,500 feet, you will get thirty minutes recording time at 15 ips, fifteen minutes at 30 ips. For 3,600 feet, you will get forty-five minutes at 15 ips, twenty-two-and-a-half minutes at 30 ips.

You can calculate how much tape you'll need after deciding on the songs, their length, track format, and tape speed. Then *triple* your figure to allow for all the false starts, retakes, and other waste that's bound to happen during sessions.

Most studios will insist that you buy your multi-track and mastering tape from them if they are to 'guarantee' the quality of the final project. Ask for prices, and be aware that they will be higher than wholesale. Like everything else, costs keep rising. At the time of publication, studio prices for good quality tape (including reels) averaged as follows:

Tape width	2,500 feet	3,600 feet
1/4-inch	$ 17	$ 23
1/2-inch	$ 45	$ 60
2-inch	$200	$225

Recording studios that deal with major labels are likely to charge even higher prices since they are accustomed to the big companies' footing the bill. Tell studios you are an independent; you may be able to negotiate lower tape prices. Recording studios that specialize in a particular track format—for example, eight-track—may charge lower prices for tape as a means of attracting business and keeping their studios fully booked. Some studios also will allow you to bring in your own quarter-inch tape and cassettes for personal copies.

Payment. Payment for all recording is usually C.O.D., with advance deposits required as a protection against last-minute cancellation of a session. In most cases, you won't be allowed to take your master tape until your bill is completely paid. It's the only leverage studios have.

When booking time, clarify all costs and payment policies with the business manager. With studio recording, where rates are usually figured on an hourly basis, you should settle certain questions before sessions begin: Who takes responsibility in case of equipment failure? If you are paying musicians hourly rates, will the studio pay for their time while they wait for equipment to be repaired? In location recording, technical problems sometimes come up that escape notice until after a session is over. Will the recording company redo the taping at no charge? Resolve issues like these before you sign a contract.

Once you agree on rates and time, spell it all out in writing. It needn't be anything more formal than a letter to the recording company stating the agreements as you understand them.

Home Studios. One way to save costs over the long run is to construct your own home recording studio. For direct to two-track recording, your basic equipment needs are a two-track tape recorder and two microphones, which shouldn't cost more than a total of $1,800. For the more complex two-track method, another $2,000 will buy an adequate mixing board and some additional microphones. The mixing board and the microphones can also be used as part of your PA system when performing. Two-track tape recorders are easy to operate; you don't have to be a technical wizard. If you shop carefully for used equipment, you can reduce the outlay by about half.

You can also purchase equipment for an eight-track studio for less than $10,000—cheaper than a sports car or van. Building a studio room, or sound-proofing an existing one, will add both time and money to your project.

In considering a home recording studio, you should first decide on your priorities. How do you want to spend your money? Are you willing to invest two to six months of hard work? Your money and time can either be spent building a home studio or making and selling your own record—the two can seldom happen simultaneously. A multi-track home studio is a business in itself, with the demands for planning and budgeting that go along with any business.

HIRING PERSONNEL

Your other major recording expenses will be for the services of people who assist you with the recording sessions. Some of these costs, such as the engineer's fee, may be included in the cost of the studio you select. Other services, such as those of an arranger, studio musicians, or producer, will be contracted for separately. The financial arrangements you make with these people can vary widely, depending on the extent of their services and the nature of your project.

The Engineer. Most engineers are paid by the studio, rather than by the performing group, unless they are hired on a freelance basis. It is still customary, however, to tip the engineer anywhere from $25 to $100 at the end of a project for a job well done.

If you hire an engineer to operate equipment you provide, it is normal to pay a flat day rate. That rate can vary from $50 to $200 depending on the engineer's experience and reputation.

Arrangers. If you are asking studio musicians to improvise a part for your song, you seldom have to pay them anything other than their agreed-upon recording fees. If you hire an arranger to compose music to be played by other musicians, you will pay a fee computed on the length of the arrangement and the number and kinds of instruments involved. Most experienced arrangers belong to the American Federation of Musicians (AF of M), which sets minimum arrangers' fees ('scale'). Some arrangers, understanding that independents might not be able to afford scale, might agree to work for less, either to gain experience or to do you a favor. The only way you can find out if they're willing to do so is to set your overall budget, allow a percentage for arranging, and present that information to an arranger. Be sure to credit the arranger on your album cover.

Studio Musicians. It can be expensive to use extra musicians on your record if they're members of AF of M or the American Federation of Television and Radio Artists (AFTRA). (See 'Labor Unions' in the chapter on business.) The basic session rate established by the AF of M is $178.15 per musician. The AFTRA rate is $110 an hour for a soloist or for two vocalists. A three-piece jazz or classical trio recording for three hours could cost more than $500; a five-piece rock band, more than $900. Budgets for popular albums recorded for major labels often allow as much as half the total for union fees to musicians.

Many independents can't afford to pay union scale. If union musicians play on your album for less than scale, and are discovered by the unions, they risk suspension or fine.

Whether or not you hire union musicians, you will have to decide how to pay the musicians who record for you. A common method is to agree on an hourly rate, and, to be fair and to avoid hard feelings, pay all the musicians at the same rate. To do this, you need to fix an overall album budget well before making these arrangements, carefully figuring out how many musicians you need for each session.

An alternative to an hourly rate is to pay each musician a flat fee, whether they record for five hours or fifty. This is ideal if you have a tight budget, because it allows you to predict accurately the cost of musicians. Until you have more experience recording, it will be difficult to predict when one song might take twenty extra hours of recording time.

On occasion, you might use extra musicians who are friends of yours and offer to record for free. This is fine if the agreements are clear on both sides. If you are paying some musicians but not others, just make sure they all know that fact in advance and feel comfortable about it.

Incidentally, it's unusual to pay session musicians a percentage of the profits, no matter how famous they might be, and you should be skeptical of anyone who demands it. If a record makes it big, however, it's common to give bonuses to the session musicians.

In addition to whatever money you pay your musicians, you should be sure to credit them on the album cover, specifying which instruments were played on what songs. Sessions musicians would also be happy to receive a couple of free albums when the record is completed.

The Producer. Some producers charge an hourly fee, some a flat fee for the entire album. Some also ask for a percentage of the money from record sales. The amounts may depend on the producer's opinion of your record's sales potential. Some producers, for example, may ask a low flat fee for a talented but destitute group but make a secondary agreement that when the record sells over a certain quantity or is picked up by a major label for distribution, they will get a percentage of sales. A flat fee of $1,000 to $1,500 for an independent record would not be unreasonable to pay an experienced producer; expect to pay more for a producer with a reputation for hits. One to three percent of the wholesale record price is the range of average producer royalties. Hourly rates will seldom be less than $35 an hour.

If you have asked your engineer to handle production as well as engineering, you should pay a fee directly to the engineer in addition to the hourly studio fee. This can be either an hourly rate or a flat fee and should be scaled to the tasks involved and the time the engineer spends as producer.

If an engineer is asked to assume *only* production duties and has little experience producing, you might try negotiating a flat fee of $500 to $750, roughly half of what you'd pay an experienced producer.

Band Members. Members of groups producing independent records usually waive any recording fees and wait for payment from record sales. They share the risks, and they may or may not invest equal amounts of time and money. Whatever investments are made, you should put all financial agreements into writing, including various contingencies that might arise.

If your band is made up of close friends, is it really necessary to put agreements in writing? Yes. It's not to prevent rip-offs but rather to prevent honest misunderstandings that can occur months or years later, when memories have dimmed.

The group should discuss questions like these: How will you feel when monthly expenses for running the business eat away at the profits? What happens if one of the members of the group quits after a few months? What should you do with offers from a major label? How are royalties to be divided? The situations will differ, but it is important to talk things out at the beginning when the air is clear. Read the sections on financing and partnership agreements in the Appendix and spell out arrangements that seem appropriate to your group.

MAKING SESSIONS WORK

On tight budgets, ingenuity and efficiency must substitute for state-of-the-art equipment, 'hit-maker' personnel, and the luxury of hundreds of hours in the studio. What follows are some suggestions to help you make the best album you can on a limited budget.

► Visit some actual recording sessions so that you can observe and get a sense of the lengths of time different

Producer David Kahn got his 'chops' doing demos and records for 415 Records. One of his greatest skills was rehearsing our bands prior to recording so that costs were kept to under $10,000 an album. His good work led to his current job as staff producer at CBS Records. Now we can't afford him anymore.

STEVEN SEID
415 Records

procedures take. It's surprising how many people contract for recording time without ever having sat in on a session. Make your request either to the studio manager or to the manager or leader of the group. If you are allowed to watch, be as unobtrusive as possible. Don't ask questions until after the session.

► Attend courses or seminars on recording offered in your community. Look for courses given by large music stores to encourage the sale of four- or eight-track home studio equipment as well as courses offered in music schools, at community colleges or universities, or by private organizations. The courses are often relatively inexpensive. You will gain familiarity with equipment, studio terminology and procedures, and the science of recorded sound. Most such classes demonstrate common miking techniques, and some will give you 'hands-on' experience operating the equipment.

► If you don't live near a large city and have no access to such courses, look through issues of such magazines as *Modern Recording* and *High Fidelity,* which regularly run articles on audio technology and recording techniques. Several good books are also available and are listed in the Bibliography.

► Plan on recording fewer songs with multi-track methods. If you've planned to do your whole album in a multi-track studio, look again at your songs and consider using a less expensive recording method for some of them. As you have seen, prices go up in proportion to the amount of equipment and knowledge needed to operate it. Consider which songs might work well with direct to two-track or two-track with mixer.

► Plan on using professionals for producing, arranging, and engineering. It's a temptation to use amateurs who offer to help for cut-rate prices, but it usually doesn't save you money. One good engineer or arranger can save you endless hours and can perform a multitude of services.

► Make demos of your arrangements so that you know what you're doing before you step into the studio. If you will be recording direct to two-track, a reel-to-reel or cassette recorder should be adequate for the demo. If you are planning multi-track recording, do a quick demo in an inexpensive four-track studio. By trying out different mixes emphasizing different instruments, you'll be able to check the effectiveness of each part in the arrangement.

► Play your demos for as many professional musicians, producers, and arrangers as will listen, and ask their advice about your arrangements. Consider hiring an experienced arranger or producer as a consultant.

► Rehearse your songs and studio procedures in a low-cost studio before you begin actual sessions. You might ask the engineer in the small studio to drill you in studio techniques.

► Have your musicians get accustomed to accompanying the music through headphones and to stopping and starting at various places in each song. The most common editing technique is to record a song or its parts several times and then to splice together the best parts of each. Musicians should be thoroughly comfortable with such instructions as "Let's rerun the first couple of phrases in the second verse" or "Let's take it from the bridge." Instructions should be arbitrary, rather than based on actual errors, to help musicians follow instructions without attaching emotional energy to them. This will be crucial during sessions.

► If multi-track will be used, rehearse the music in sections (rhythm, lead instrumentals, and vocals) to test precision in pitch and tempo. Check separately the intonation and phrasing of the vocalist and the lead instrumentalists. These are often problems, particularly when parts played through headphones are accompanied. The musicians will be less nervous during sessions if they can perform it right in rehearsal.

► Rehearse alternate arrangements so there will be no changes of mind in the studio. Practice 'punching in' corrections or alternate arrangements. This is one of the most common multi-track editing techniques and it takes some getting used to.

► Book enough continuous studio time to accomplish what you need, but not so much that your musicians will begin to lose their effectiveness. Usually no less than three and no more than six hours per session should be booked by inexperienced groups. The high degree of concentration that's required involves intense energy and isn't easy to maintain over long periods of time.

► Organize sessions so that you will be working with the same instruments throughout each session.

One of the things I realized was that you could do a song too much. In recording the vocals over so many times, some of them got stilted. At the same time, it got me past the point of being afraid of not singing in tune. Now I can work on just getting across better, singing with the emotion that's in the songs. I no longer take it for granted that if I sing my songs in tune people will love them.

BECKY RYAN
Blossom Records

You might record all the basic tracks using bass, guitar, and drums for several songs in one session, and the basic tracks requiring brass, keyboards, and drums in another. Check with your engineer before sessions, however, to make sure you aren't trying to cram too much into one session.

► Stagger recording sessions so as to leave time in between for listening to rough mixes or for further rehearsals.

► Buy your own tapes to record rough mixes for use after the session. There's no reason to pay extra for them at the studio.

► Arrive at sessions on time. This may seem like an obvious suggestion, but engineers and producers will tell you that late arrivals are common among musicians. This wastes money. Even if the engineer sets you up quickly, you can use the waiting time to tune your instrument and get your fingers or throat warmed up.

► Arrive with your instruments and amplifiers in excellent working condition. Guitars and basses should have their strings checked and necks aligned; drums should be checked for rattles; amps should be checked for buzzes or loose grounds. Drummers should bring extra sticks; string players should always have an extra

set of strings. It's absurd to interrupt a session to chase down new strings.

► Don't bring lovers or friends to studio sessions. There is little for them to do and they are apt to resent the silence that must be maintained. Moreover, their presence can increase tensions, especially if the musicians are having difficulty during a session.

► Relinquish control to the people you have chosen to direct the sessions and follow their leadership, whether or not you agree. If you have ideas for changes, hold them until after the session or bring them up at rehearsal.

► Let the producer and engineer do the mix on their own. Directing a successful mix is not a skill that most musicians have. Usually they lack the technical language required to communicate with the engineer. More important, most musicians are accustomed to hearing their music through monitor speakers rather than from the perspective of an audience. (This accounts for the fact that musicians frequently complain that their instrument or vocal part isn't loud enough in the mix.) Moreover, even the mix the audience hears is quite different from the mix that goes on the record. Let the professionals handle it.

► A corollary to this is simply to stay away from mixing sessions. The fewer people who are present during mixdown, the more the engineer and producer can concentrate. Usually they will make rough mixes so that the band can voice suggestions and air disagreements. During final mixdown, however, when the failure to bring up one guitar lead properly can ruin the whole mix, it's best to stay away.

► Finally, be prepared to say, "It's done." Naturally, you want your record to be perfect, but you've got to recognize the point at which more time spent won't significantly improve the recording. If you are recording for the first time, don't worry about making your ultimate statement as a musician. Think of your record as the first of many that you will be making during your career.

Chapter 9
Song Rights

ORIGINAL SONGS CAN BE A MUSICIAN'S GREATEST ASsets. They can produce more income over a longer period of time than either performing or recording. They can earn 'performance royalties' from being played on radio, television, or in clubs or concert halls. They can be recorded by other artists and earn 'mechanical royalties' on each record sold. They can be issued as sheet music and earn further income from their sale. Large fortunes have been reaped from songs which became popular and have been recorded time and again by numerous artists and in several countries.

This chapter will discuss the various aspects of musical property. We have loosely called these 'song rights', although the information applies as well to musical compositions without words. The first part of the chapter explains how to establish your rights to your original compositions and your record. The next section outlines the ways in which income can be earned from them. Finally, the last section discusses what is involved if you record songs written by other musicians.

SONG PROTECTION

Before you put your record out for sale, you need to establish your rights so that you can earn royalties from your songs and protect yourself. To do this, you form a publishing company, register both your songs and your record with the Federal Copyright Office, and join one of two performance rights organizations, the American Society of Composers, Authors, and Publishers (ASCAP) or Broadcast Music, Inc. (BMI). Because you will need to print the information on your album cover and labels, you will need to begin this work well in advance of preparing final cover copy.

Copyrighting Your Songs. The Copyright Law, which went into effect on January 1, 1978, grants all songwriters specific rights regarding the use of their songs, whether or not they choose to register them with the Federal Copyright Office. These rights include 1) the right to publish the song, 2) the right to record and distribute copies of it, 3) the right to perform the song in public, 4) the right to make what are known as 'derivative works', such as different arrangements of the song, and 5) the right to 'display' the musical work, such as printing a lyric sheet or a picture disc. With regard to songs created or published after January 1, 1978, these rights automatically belong to the songwriter for his or her lifetime plus fifty years.

The most important step in securing these rights is to place the proper copyright notice on your album cover and record label. You do not have to register your songs with the copyright office to put the copyright notice on your works. The notice must include 1) the symbol '©', the word 'Copyright', or the abbreviation 'Copr.', 2) the year of first publication, and 3) the name of the owner of the copyright; for example, "©1979 by J. Smith." If the copyright owner is a publishing company, the notice could read, "Copyright 1979 by J. Smith Publishing Company."

Without this notice, you stand a chance of forfeiting your rights and losing any royalties that might be earned from the use of your songs by other artists. If you do omit the notice, you can correct your error under certain circumstances, but you could still lose all or part of your royalties.

Copyright Registration. To effectively insure protection of these rights, you will need to register your songs with the Copyright Office in Washington, D.C. Registering your songs will help establish proof of authorship as well as the identity of each song, something the courts will need if there is ever a dispute.

To register your songs, write to the Register of Copyrights, and request Form PA, Application for Copyright Registration for a Work of the Performing Arts. Request a Form PA for each song you wish to register. These forms are free. At the same time, ask for a copy of the Copyright Law as well as copies of any regulations or informational publications that apply to copyright of musical works. You might also be able to obtain the forms and information by phoning the federal information number in major metropolitan cities.

The forms are not complicated and are accompanied by detailed instructions. The form has space to indicate collaborations by several people on a composition, as well as to state the specific contribution of each person. The copyright is secured in the name of the 'copyright claimant'. If the songs have not been assigned to a publishing company, the copyright claimant is you (and any collaborators). If you have assigned your songs to a publishing company (your own or someone else's), the copyright claimant is the publishing company. (In such cases, you would also file a notice of transfer with the Copyright Office.)

You also need to deposit something which identifies your song, either a tape or a leadsheet (the song's notes, words, and rhythm written on paper). In the opinion of many attorneys, it is best to file both a leadsheet and a tape of your music. If your composition depends on multiple rhythms and melodies (like choral pieces or symphonies), you should 'score' the music, indicating all the separate elements involved.

Leadsheets or scores should be done by professionals. Charges are usually figured on an hourly basis, ranging from as low as $7.50 to as high as $40 an hour. A leadsheet for a song that is three to five minutes long and includes only chord changes, rhythms, and melodies should take no more than an hour to do, particularly if you've taken the trouble to write out the words clearly and indicate the chord changes. A professional copyist can make leadsheets by listening to a tape or record. If you don't know anyone in your area who does leadsheets, call your local musicians' union, the head of the music department in a nearby college or high school, or a member of the local symphony orchestra.

For each song you want to register, send Form PA, your deposit, and $10 to the Register of Copyrights. You can register your songs as a collection by using one name for all of them together, with each song indicated as a 'chapter'. However, if you are putting out a record, you should register you songs separately, so that you can easily license individual songs to others and collect royalties.

Although you can choose not to register your songs with the Copyright Office, the Copyright Law does require you to deposit two copies of a published record with them within three months of the time you first offer it for sale. This is absolutely mandatory. Usually this is done at the same time as registering the copyright for the record. (See 'Copyrighting Your Record', later in this chapter.)

The address of the Copyright Office is listed in the Directory at the end of this book.

Alternatives to Copyright Registration.
Some songwriters try to establish proof of authorship by sending a copy of their song to themselves by registered mail and not opening the letter. They feel that the postmark on the letter is evidence that the song was original as of that date. This method, commonly referred to as a 'poor man's copyright' or as 'common law copyright', is considered risky by most attorneys.

An alternative method for establishing proof of authorship and song identity, as yet untested in the

courts is to register your songs with a bonded song registration service, such as Songwriters Resources and Services (SRS) in Los Angeles. You send them a copy of your song on tape, cassette, disc, or lyric sheet. When your song is received, SRS will put a seal on it, give it a registration number, file it in a vault, and send you a receipt with your registration number. Since SRS's services are completely bonded, you need not suspect any tampering with your songs. At this time, SRS is the only nationally bonded organization offering such a service.

Since its founding in 1974, SRS has proved to be useful to songwriters who have composed a great deal of material that they are showing to publishers, producers, or artists, but who don't want to pay for copyright registration until they are sure their songs are actually going to be recorded. As soon as songwriters know that their songs will be recorded, they register them with the Copyright Office to receive 'official' protection.

According to Los Angeles music publishing attorney Alfred W. Schlesinger, the courts would very likely find the registration service satisfactory for proving authorship because "it involves a third party who can attest to the fact of who registered the song, the date of the registration, and the fact that it was given a registration number in sequence and the contents

Since I am not a commercial songwriter, I do not limit myself to sure shots, even if I knew how to write them. I write about anything that interests me, that moves me and that seems to move into a song. Like most songwriters, I think songs, just as poets think poems, fiction writers think in stories. One of the things I think about are the nuclear installations being constructed all over the country. I have written a song called 'Power Plant Reggae'. You may not believe this, but I get more satisfaction out of the fact that this song is in the front lines in a battle I care about than if it were on the charts.

MALVINA REYNOLDS (1900–1978)
Cassandra Records

Copyright Form PA is used to register an original song. It lists basic information about the composer and lyricist as well as the publishing company to which the song has been assigned. The forms can be obtained free from the Copyright Office.

sealed as of the date of receipt. In brief, this would be evidence that, even though [the contents] were unsealed prior to trial, there would be a witness to the facts concerning the registration and its unsealing" (Alfred W. Schlesinger, *Legal and Practical Aspects of the Music Business,* Songwriters Resources and Services, 1977). For further information regarding SRS, you can write to them at the address listed in the Directory.

Copyrighting Your Record. Legally, the record you sell is considered an entity in itself, apart from the songs contained on it, and you must copyright the record separately to protect against its illegal duplication. The Copyright Law grants recording companies much the same rights to their creations as songwriters. The companies are officially referred to as 'authors' and their work as their 'sound recordings'. According to the Copyright Office registration form, "When a record company issues a new release, the release will typically involve two distinct 'works': the 'musical work' that has been recorded, and the 'sound recording' as a separate work in itself. The material objects that the record company sends out are 'phonorecords', physical reproductions of both the musical work and the sound recording."

You secure your rights as a record company issuing records by printing the correct copyright notice on the label affixed to your record and on the album cover. Include the following: 1) the symbol 'Ⓟ,' 2) the year of first publication of a sound recording, and 3) the name of the owner of the copyright; for example, "Ⓟ 1979 J. Smith Records." You can print the copyright notice without registering your record with the Copyright Office.

To protect your rights as a record label, however, you should register your record with the Register of Copyrights in Washington, D.C. Request Form SR, Application for Copyright Registration for a Sound Recording, as well as Circular R56, which provides additional information. The forms and circulars are free. You might also be able to obtain them by telephoning the federal information number in major cities.

The copyright will be secured in the name of the 'copyright claimant', or 'author', in your case the name of your record label. Form SR can also be used to copyright songs, if the name of the copyright claimant for both the song and the recording are the same. (In such case, the correct notice would be "ⒸⓅ 1979 J. Smith Music".) Usually, however, the copyright claimant for the record is the name of your record company while the copyright claimant for the songs is you or your publishing company. Even if you have recorded songs written by other people, you still can, and should, copyright your record as an entity in itself.

To register the copyright on your record, you will need to deposit a copy of your work. If the work is

---

FORM PA

UNITED STATES COPYRIGHT OFFICE

REGISTRATION NUMBER

PA   PAU

EFFECTIVE DATE OF REGISTRATION

Month   Day   Year

DO NOT WRITE ABOVE THIS LINE. IF YOU NEED MORE SPACE, USE CONTINUATION SHEET (FORM PA/CON)

① Title

TITLE OF THIS WORK:

NATURE OF THIS WORK: (See instructions)

PREVIOUS OR ALTERNATIVE TITLES:

② Author(s)

IMPORTANT: Under the law, the "author" of a "work made for hire" is generally the employer, not the employee (see instructions). If any part of this work was "made for hire" check "Yes" in the space provided, give the employer (or other person for whom the work was prepared) as "Author" of that part, and leave the space for dates blank.

1

NAME OF AUTHOR:

Was this author's contribution to the work a "work made for hire"? Yes___ No___

DATES OF BIRTH AND DEATH:
Born___ (Year) Died___ (Year)

AUTHOR'S NATIONALITY OR DOMICILE:
Citizen of ___ (Name of Country) or Domiciled in ___ (Name of Country)

WAS THIS AUTHOR'S CONTRIBUTION TO THE WORK:
Anonymous? Yes___ No___
Pseudonymous? Yes___ No___

AUTHOR OF: (Briefly describe nature of this author's contribution)

If the answer to either of these questions is "Yes," see detailed instructions attached.

2

NAME OF AUTHOR:

Was this author's contribution to the work a "work made for hire"? Yes___ No___

DATES OF BIRTH AND DEATH:
Born___ (Year) Died___ (Year)

AUTHOR'S NATIONALITY OR DOMICILE:
Citizen of ___ (Name of Country) or Domiciled in ___ (Name of Country)

WAS THIS AUTHOR'S CONTRIBUTION TO THE WORK:
Anonymous? Yes___ No___
Pseudonymous? Yes___ No___

AUTHOR OF: (Briefly describe nature of this author's contribution)

If the answer to either of these questions is "Yes," see detailed instructions attached.

3

NAME OF AUTHOR:

Was this author's contribution to the work a "work made for hire"? Yes___ No___

DATES OF BIRTH AND DEATH:
Born___ (Year) Died___ (Year)

AUTHOR'S NATIONALITY OR DOMICILE:
Citizen of ___ (Name of Country) or Domiciled in ___ (Name of Country)

WAS THIS AUTHOR'S CONTRIBUTION TO THE WORK:
Anonymous? Yes___ No___
Pseudonymous? Yes___ No___

AUTHOR OF: (Briefly describe nature of this author's contribution)

If the answer to either of these questions is "Yes," see detailed instructions attached.

③ Creation and Publication

YEAR IN WHICH CREATION OF THIS WORK WAS COMPLETED:
Year___
(This information must be given in all cases.)

DATE AND NATION OF FIRST PUBLICATION:
Date___ (Month) (Day) (Year)
Nation___ (Name of Country)
(Complete this block ONLY if this work has been published.)

④ Claimant(s)

NAME(S) AND ADDRESS(ES) OF COPYRIGHT CLAIMANT(S):

TRANSFER: (If the copyright claimant(s) named here in space 4 are different from the author(s) named in space 2, give a brief statement of how the claimant(s) obtained ownership of the copyright.)

- Complete all applicable spaces (numbers 5-9) on the reverse side of this page.
- Follow detailed instructions attached.
- Sign the form at line 8.

DO NOT WRITE HERE
Page 1 of ___ pages

unpublished, you need to deposit only one complete phonorecord. If the work is for sale to the public, you must deposit two complete phonorecords, including your album cover and any special inserts.

Mail your deposit, the form, and $10 to the Register of Copyrights.

SONG EXPLOITATION

In the music industry, the term 'exploitation' commonly refers to the process of making money from songs. Your original songs are commercially valuable. In order to take fair advantage of them, you need to be well-informed about how songwriters earn money from their creations.

Forming Your Own Publishing Company. The 'publisher' of a song is simply the person or business entity responsible for making it available for public sale, whether in the form of sheet music, a record, or tape. Therefore, when you offer your record for sale to the public, you are 'publishing' your songs, whether or not they are available as sheet music and whether or not you have formed an actual publishing company.

Once a song is published in the form of a record, the song may be used in various ways, and the 'users' must pay the composer. The record can be played (or the song performed) on radio, television, or in concert halls or clubs, thus entitling the composer to 'performance royalties' for the song. If the song is recorded by other people, the composer should receive a fee for each record sold, called 'mechanical royalties'.

Most independents form their own publishing companies under whose name copyrights are filed and royalties collected. You can do these tasks yourself; there's no reason to assign your songs to someone else's publishing company and pay them a portion of your earnings. If your songs are later recorded by other artists, or if larger publishing companies want to further exploit them, the paperwork and contractual obligations warrant expertise from both experienced attorneys and publishers. These matters are outlined later in the chapter.

To form your own publishing company, you must first devise a name you like which has never been used by another publishing company. This name will be used to conduct all official business. To find out whether a name is original, write or call ASCAP or BMI and ask them to research it for you. It's wise to

give them three to five names at a time. You'll be surprised at how many names you think are unique that have already been used by someone else. When you find a name that is original, ask both BMI and ASCAP to reserve that name for you until you join one or the other. Both ASCAP and BMI will reserve a name for up to six months before requiring you to join. (The addresses for ASCAP and BMI are listed in the Directory.)

Once you have chosen a name, use it every time you copyright a song, make a record, or put out sheet music. Display it on your album cover and label, lyric sheet inserts, or sheet music, thereby informing others that you've officially established your rights as a composer and publisher and complied with the copyright law. This information also makes it easy for others interested in your songs to contact you.

If you want to open a separate bank account for your publishing company, you will need to obtain a fictitious name certificate. (See the chapter on Business.) Many independents, however, simply keep track of the monies earned and spent by their publishing companies in their bookkeeping ledgers for their recording project.

Performance Rights. Since one of the rights granted to songwriters by the Federal Copyright Act is the right to perform the songs publicly, you need to give a 'user', such as a radio or television station, the right to do so. Both ASCAP and BMI are non-profit societies which grant your performance rights for you and collect a fee for their subsequent use. By joining either organi-

The record label should list the composer and ASCAP or BMI affiliation for each song, and must include a copyright notice.

FORM SR

UNITED STATES COPYRIGHT OFFICE

REGISTRATION NUMBER

SR   SRU

EFFECTIVE DATE OF REGISTRATION

Month   Day   Year

DO NOT WRITE ABOVE THIS LINE. IF YOU NEED MORE SPACE, USE CONTINUATION SHEET (FORM SR/CON)

① Title

TITLE OF THIS WORK:

Catalog number of sound recording, if any:

PREVIOUS OR ALTERNATIVE TITLES:

NATURE OF MATERIAL RECORDED:
(Check Which)

☐ Musical   ☐ Musical-Dramatic
☐ Dramatic   ☐ Literary
☐ Other:

② Author(s)

IMPORTANT: Under the law, the "author" of a "work made for hire" is generally the employer, not the employee (see instructions). If any part of this work was "made for hire" check "Yes" in the space provided, give the employer (or other person for whom the work was prepared) as "Author" of that part, and leave the space for dates blank.

1

NAME OF AUTHOR:

Was this author's contribution to the work a "work made for hire"? Yes..... No.....

AUTHOR'S NATIONALITY OR DOMICILE:
Citizen of .... (Name of Country) or { Domiciled in .... (Name of Country)

AUTHOR OF: (Briefly describe nature of this author's contribution)

DATES OF BIRTH AND DEATH:
Born .... (Year) Died .... (Year)

WAS THIS AUTHOR'S CONTRIBUTION TO THE WORK:
Anonymous? Yes...... No.....
Pseudonymous? Yes...... No.....
If the answer to either of these questions is "Yes," see detailed instructions attached.

2

NAME OF AUTHOR:

Was this author's contribution to the work a "work made for hire"? Yes..... No.....

AUTHOR'S NATIONALITY OR DOMICILE:
Citizen of .... (Name of Country) or { Domiciled in .... (Name of Country)

AUTHOR OF: (Briefly describe nature of this author's contribution)

DATES OF BIRTH AND DEATH:
Born .... (Year) Died .... (Year)

WAS THIS AUTHOR'S CONTRIBUTION TO THE WORK:
Anonymous? Yes...... No.....
Pseudonymous? Yes...... No.....
If the answer to either of these questions is "Yes," see detailed instructions attached.

3

NAME OF AUTHOR:

Was this author's contribution to the work a "work made for hire"? Yes..... No.....

AUTHOR'S NATIONALITY OR DOMICILE:
Citizen of .... (Name of Country) or { Domiciled in .... (Name of Country)

AUTHOR OF: (Briefly describe nature of this author's contribution)

DATES OF BIRTH AND DEATH:
Born .... (Year) Died .... (Year)

WAS THIS AUTHOR'S CONTRIBUTION TO THE WORK:
Anonymous? Yes...... No.....
Pseudonymous? Yes...... No.....
If the answer to either of these questions is "Yes," see detailed instructions attached.

③ Creation and Publication

YEAR IN WHICH CREATION OF THIS WORK WAS COMPLETED:
Year ....
(This information must be given in all cases.)

DATE AND NATION OF FIRST PUBLICATION:
Date .... (Month) (Day) (Year)
Nation .... (Name of Country)
(Complete this block ONLY if this work has been published.)

④ Claimant(s)

NAME(S) AND ADDRESS(ES) OF COPYRIGHT CLAIMANT(S):

TRANSFER: (If the copyright claimant(s) named here in space 4 are different from the author(s) named in space 2, give a brief statement of how the claimant(s) obtained ownership of the copyright.)

• Complete all applicable spaces (numbers 5-9) on the reverse side of this page
• Follow detailed instructions attached
• Sign the form at line 8

DO NOT WRITE HERE
Page 1 of .... pages

Copyright Form SR is used to register a phonorecord.

work television stations far more than network radio stations, not only because they reach wider audiences, but because they have greater advertising revenues.

The licensing fees collected are then distributed among member authors and publishing companies according to how frequently their songs were performed in any given year in a given medium. Both ASCAP and BMI have different and complicated methods of monitoring ('tracking') television and radio programming to determine what is being performed and how often.

The writers and publishers with 'hits' on the radio get the greatest share of the fees collected. If the songs on your record attract airplay in your hometown, or even on several major AM or FM stations in your state, you won't receive much in performance royalties. Your song needs to be a minor hit before royalties amount to anything substantial. Occasionally, a record that sells well and even becomes one of the top one hundred selling albums does not receive much airplay. In such a case, no significant performance royalties are earned, since earnings are based solely on songs being played on the air and not on sales of albums.

There is no practical way to collect performance royalties without joining ASCAP or BMI. (You cannot join both in the same year or for the same songs, and you cannot join until you know you are publishing your songs.) Both the authors of the songs and the publishing company which administers their copyright must become members.

It costs nothing to join BMI as an author and $25 as a publisher (a one-time cost); ASCAP charges $10 for authors and $50 for publishers. To join, write and request free information and forms for yourself as both an author and a publisher. The addresses are listed in the Directory.

Although you can become a member of ASCAP or BMI after your record is out, most people choose to do so before, so that they can include their affiliation on the album cover and label. If all the songs are your own or belong to the same publishing company, you can print on the cover "All selections from J. Smith Publishing Company, BMI." On the record label, list the affiliation after each song. If some or all of the songs are composed by someone else and belong to another publishing company, you need to print that information on the cover and the record label. (See the section on 'Using Other People's Songs' later in this chapter.)

zation, you are technically assigning your performance rights to them. In return, they keep track of who is performing your song, charge all users a 'licensing fee', and pay you your share of performance royalties.

Licensing fees are charged yearly and vary according to how many people are reached by a particular medium, as well as how much profit that medium realizes in a year. For example, ASCAP and BMI charge net-

NOTICE OF INTENTION TO OBTAIN A COMPULSORY LICENSE
FOR MAKING AND DISTRIBUTING PHONORECORDS

To:_____, copyright owner of the

musical work entitled:_____

music by:_____, lyrics by:_____

Pursuant to the compulsory license provisions of the United States
Copyright Act and the interim regulations issued by the Copyright
Office, we hereby apply for a license to make and distribute phonorecords of the above nondramatic musical work, and provide the
following information.

1. Full legal name of the person or entity intending to obtain the
compulsory license:_____

2. Ficticious or assumed names used for the purpose of making and
distributing phonorecords:_____

3. Street address:_____
_____

4. Business organization:__corporation, __partnership, __proprietorship

5. Names of individuals who own a beneficial interest of 25% or more
in the entity:_____
_____

6. If a corporation, names of the corporation's officers and directors:
_____
_____

7. Type(s) of phonorecord configuration(s) intended to be made under
the compulsory license:__single disk, __long playing disk, __cassette,
__cartridge, __reel-to-reel.

8. Catalog number(s):_____

9. Label name(s):_____

10. Principal recording artist(s):_____
_____

11. Anticipated date of initial release:_____

We agree to pay royalties at the statutory rate provided for by the
Copyright Act; however, we request that we be allowed to render statements and pay royalties quarterly rather than monthly.

Date:_____   By:_____
                                (signature)

                             _____
                                (typed name)

A sample notice of intention to obtain a compulsory license. This notice is an application for a mechanical license to record a song written and recorded by someone else (see 'Using Other People's Songs'). It should be sent to the publisher of the song.

On the issue of home taping, I would like to point out the following. Windham Hill is a community of artists who depend upon the income from the sale of their records and concert appearances for their livelihood. I ask only that everyone weigh the possible economic impact on Windham Hill and the artists represented by the label in the taping of our records. . . . In all respects we count on you people to support our efforts, and for your help we are all sincerely grateful.

WILLIAM ACKERMAN
*Chief Executive Officer,
Windham Hill Records*

Mechanical Licenses. Once you publish a song by distributing copies of phonorecords (that is, you make it available to the public on records or tape), other artists have the right to record that song as long as they file a 'mechanical license' with the publisher. This license states simply that the artist will pay your publishing company mechanical royalties (whatever fee that you negotiate) for the right to record your song and will also make regular accountings of all records sold and returned.

The Copyright Law sets a ceiling rate (called a 'statutory rate') for the use of songs by others on a record at 5 cents per song or .95 cents per minute, whichever amount is larger, per record sold. For example, if an artist records six of your songs, each of which is three minutes long, the amount of mechanical royalties owed is 30 cents per record sold. If the artist records two songs, each nine minutes long, the amount of mechanical royalties owed would be 17.1 cents per record sold.

A rate lower than the ceiling rate can be negotiated by the artist or the record label, if the songwriter and the publishing company agree. The mechanical royalties that are collected by your publishing company are equally divided between the publishing company and the songwriter.

When another artist records your song with the intent of selling it to the public, that artist's record label should request a mechanical license from your publishing company. (A sample request is shown on page 116.) One of the reasons for including the address of your publishing company on your album is to make it easy for other artists to contact you.

If you have never published a song you wrote, you can refuse another artist or group the right to record it for the first time, since that is one of the rights granted songwriters by the Copyright Law. In some cases, however, it is advantageous for you to give up that right, particularly if a famous artist wants to record your song. In that case, you need to make sure that you go through all the steps outlined in this chapter for protecting and exploiting your songs. Before making any final agreements, consult an attorney.

If you find that another artist or group has recorded your songs without filing mechanical licenses, you can sue them, and at that time you should definitely consult an attorney.

If one of your songs becomes really popular, dealing with many requests for mechanical licenses and keeping track of the number of records sold could become complicated and time consuming. For this reason, many name artists (actually, their publishing companies) become affiliated with an organization known as the Harry Fox Agency, whose headquarters are in New York City. The publishing company authorizes the Harry Fox Agency to issue licenses to would-be recorders of its songs and to collect the mechanical royalties. The agency deducts a percentage fee for its services. Artists requesting mechanical licenses also go through the agency to handle their reporting and payment obligations under the Copyright Act. (The address of the Harry Fox Agency is listed in the Directory.)

Selling Your Songs. It can be extremely lucrative to persuade established producers or artists to record your songs. It is also very difficult, even when your songs have been published. Not only do many groups and artists write their own material, but the competition among established publishers for the attention of artists and producers makes it difficult for songwriters with independent publishing companies to get a foot in the door.

However, it can be relatively easy to convince talented but undiscovered artists to learn and perform

your songs, with the hope that, if and when they are discovered, their recordings will earn additional money for you and your publishing company.

At some point, you might want to assign one or more of your songs (or your entire publishing company, which may contain the songs of other writers) to a larger publishing company that can further exploit your songs and increase your income. Selling your songs to other artists is not the only means of earning money from songs. Sheet music can be issued, your record released and promoted in foreign countries, or your talent as a songwriter can be sold to movie and television companies or advertising agencies.

Before you sign contracts with any publishing company, you must be convinced that they will produce tangible results in one or all of these areas. Publishers should work as hard to exploit your songs as should a good booking agent to sell your performances to a club or concert promoter.

Although it is very difficult for a publishing company to guarantee to sell your songs, you can require that, if they fail to do so within a reasonable amount of time, they give you the songs back. You can also test them by assigning only a few of your songs until they prove to you that they are doing a satisfactory job. If your songs or talents are sold, your publisher should collect the royalties due and pay you your share regularly.

Agreements between you and a publisher are called 'Songwriter/Publisher Agreements', and they go beyond the scope of this book. You should never try to take care of this yourself. It requires an attorney experienced in these matters to negotiate a contract that will protect your rights.

Songsharks. You may have noticed ads in music publications from companies offering to help songwriters publish their songs and even to promote them. They will usually promise to take your tape demos and press records from them, or publish sheet music, and send the results to producers and radio stations, as well as place them for sale. Variations include offering to put your words to music, or *vice versa,* or to have someone else record your completed song in a 'professional recording studio with professional musicians'. For this service, you are expected to pay a set fee, usually between $500 and $2000, and to sign away some of your rights as a songwriter and publisher. Sometimes these companies will offer to guarantee some portion of your money back

SICK OF YOU · SLEEPY

if they don't deliver the services that they promised within a specified amount of time.

These deals are referred to as 'songsharking' within the music industry because they are just about worthless to the songwriter.

Three things are wrong with these deals. First, no legitimate record or publishing company asks you to pay for the services of recording and pressing albums—at least not up front. All payments are advanced and then repaid out of actual monies earned from the sale of the record or from performance royalties. Second, the promise merely to mail albums to radio stations or producers or to put them out for sale is of little value to you if the records are merely dumped into the nearest wastebasket. Third, any rights you sign away as a songwriter or publisher should be accompanied by a very strong songwriter/publisher contract specifying how the publisher intends to exploit your song and when you will be paid when results are realized.

Any deal of this kind should be checked by a lawyer, who can also investigate the legitimacy and reputation of the publisher. The reason these companies are not legally fraudulent is that they do deliver what they promised. It doesn't matter that this doesn't benefit you—or that it costs you a bundle of money.

USING OTHER PEOPLE'S SONGS

Most of this chapter has dealt with how you should protect your original compositions. Of course, some or all of the songs on your record may have been written by someone else. In such a case, you will have to make sure that you do not infringe upon their rights.

Once a song has been recorded and distributed, you have a right to record that song and to make your own arrangement of it, provided that you obtain a mechanical license from the writer's publishing company. The license states that you will pay the statutory rate (or the fee negotiated) for the use of the song, based on records actually sold, and that you will make regular accountings of all records sold and returned.

If you do not know the address of the publisher of a song you want to use, you can write to the record company or the performance society listed on the album cover or record label.

For songs that have not been previously recorded (or published), you will need the permission of the songwriter to record that song for the first time. That right can be granted through a contract which specifies the details of your agreement. This agreement should always be written by an attorney knowledgeable in song publishing.

Chapter 10
Business

ALTHOUGH YOUR ALBUM IS A CREATIVE ENDEAVOR, AS soon as you plan to sell it, you become a small business, with all the legal and professional obligations of other small businesses. This chapter details the forms and legalities that help establish your credentials in the industry, protect your financial interests, and satisfy government regulations. Information on financing your project and the legal forms under which you can operate your business are discussed in the Appendix.

ESTABLISHING YOUR BUSINESS

The most important unwritten rule of business is to separate your personal and business life completely, particularly with regard to finances. Aside from the necessity of doing so for tax purposes, you'll find that paperwork spreads like wildfire unless you organize and control it from the very beginning.

Giving your business a name different than your own helps establish its separate identity. Having a place where you can conduct most of your business and collect your paperwork helps prevent your business from taking over your personal life. This place might be a corner of a room that contains a desk, typewriter, stationery, business phone, business checkbook, ledgers, and a filing cabinet for documents, contracts, memos, and receipts. Later on you might want a separate office.

Lawyer and Bookkeeper. Two professionals essential to setting up your business are a lawyer and a bookkeeper. Both should be hired on a part-time basis in the planning stages of making your record.

The job of your lawyer is to help you set up the form of your business (sole proprietorship, partnership, corporation; see the Appendix) so that you can raise and spend money legally, to help you write and negotiate contracts, to advise you on major business decisions, and, hopefully, to steer you away from trouble. Try to find a lawyer who specializes in entertainment law. He or she will be familiar with standard contracts (recording, publishing, and management) and the acceptable variations. Music industry lawyers frequently know people working in record companies, agencies, and management companies, and they will sometimes put you in contact with people who can further your career. Fees can vary from $35 to $150 an hour. Musicians in your community should be able to refer you to lawyers who specialize in music business law.

The job of a bookkeeper is to help you keep track of money by setting up ledgers which correspond to the form of business decided on by you and your lawyer. Once set up, maintaining the ledgers is fairly routine. Your bookkeeper can show you how to properly list income and expenses, file receipts, and 'read' your ledgers so that you can determine how best to spend money. He or she can also take care of all federal and state tax returns.

Services of bookkeepers vary from $7.50 to $25 an hour. You don't need a bookkeeper skilled in music business finances; the service of any reliable person used by any small business will do just fine. If you don't know people who can recommend a bookkeeper, look in the Yellow Pages under the heading 'Bookkeeping Services'.

Accountants, or Certified Public Accountants, are a more specialized type of bookkeeper, knowledgeable in such things as investments, tax shelters, and pensions. They can be called upon when your business starts making more money than you can properly manage with the help of a lawyer and a bookkeeper, generally when your business turns a profit. CPAs ask fees comparable to those charged by lawyers.

Bank Account. Most helpful in keeping your business finances separate is to open a business bank account. Your business bank account gives you an easy way to keep track of both income and money spent on legitimate business expenses. You should also keep written receipts for your checks as well as invoices for income, and carefully file them. You might use a credit card earmarked only for business expenses, and pay the monthly bill with a business check, filing the statement sent you every month as a written receipt.

When it is inconvenient to use a business check, be sure to collect receipts for everything paid with cash; at least once a month add up the receipts and pay yourself back out of your business account. File these receipts along with all other receipts for business expenses.

Ledgers. At the end of the year, you'll need to know the total amount of income and expenses and how it breaks down by category. You'll need to know how much you spent on printing, postage, and transportation, as well as how much of your income came from the sale of records in stores, at concerts, and from mail order.

A set of ledgers, or 'books', lists all the checks you write, as well as all the deposits made, chronologically and by category. These books are necessary for filling out tax forms and they give you accurate and easily accessible information about the state of your business. You can read your ledgers to find out how much of your income came from performances and how much from sale of records, how many records your distributors sold, how much you spent on postage or office supplies in a given period of time, or how much you spent on graphics or manufacturing. That information will tell you which parts of your project were most profitable and where expenses were excessive.

Setting up your books with your bookkeeper shouldn't take longer than several hours, especially if you come equipped with some knowledge about future expenditures and expected income. Once your books have been set up, you can keep them up to date yourself. However, if you can afford it, let your bookkeeper do this and the other financial paperwork, such as filing sales tax returns.

Business Telephone. Having a business phone is more expensive than a personal one—the telephone company limits the amount of outside calls included in your monthly rate and has a higher rate for businesses than for homes. However, separating your business calls from your personal ones is tedious work, and you'll find it worthwhile to invest in a business phone.

When you get your business phone, be sure to list your label's name in the Yellow Pages of the phone directory under the heading 'Records: Phonograph, Wholesale and Manufacturers'. List your label not only in your county Yellow Pages, but in the directory of the largest metropolitan area nearest you. The Yellow Pages' fee depends on the prominence of your listing and whether you also take out a display ad. The charge is added to your phone bill every month.

Postal Services. You will be a frequent visitor to the post office. You'll be mailing out records, press packages, business letters, and promotional material. You needn't pay premium first class rates for anything except personally signed letters.

The most convenient way to do promotional mailings is in batches of more than 200 pieces at a bulk mailing rate. For $80 the first year and $40 for subsequent years, the post office will give you a bulk mail permit and an official number. You can use them to send as many bulk mailings a year as you like for 45¢ a pound. There are a few rules: all pieces in the mailing

have to be identical in size, weight, and content, and the batches have to be presorted and bound by zip code. Two hundred one-page letters in envelopes seldom weigh more than 10 pounds.

You can also send promotional mailings, flyers, and duplicated press releases for a special third-class rate assigned to printed matter. The cost is 11¢ per piece when the piece weighs less than 3¾ ounces, or 45¢ a pound.

Records and tapes go by a special fourth-class rate of 63¢ for the first pound and 23¢ for each additional pound. Each package must be stamped 'Records: Special Fourth Class Rate.'

Some people find it convenient to rent a post office box to receive all their business mail, especially when they are using a room in their home as an office. Rates for a P.O. box vary.

Stationery. Stationery and business cards printed with your business name, address, and phone number are good to familiarize others with your name and to do business formally. Your graphic designer can adapt the lettering and logo design used on your album cover to produce camera-ready artwork for business cards, letterheads, and envelopes. It shouldn't add too much to your graphic costs to have your designer prepare these at the same time as your album cover and other promotional materials.

You can buy paper stock for your stationery and envelopes inexpensively from a paper wholesaler in

Olivia Records provides the opportunity for women to have artistic control over every aspect of their recording project—from planning the budget; to choosing producers, engineers, and musicians; to approving final packaging and marketing direction.

bulk quantities. A quick-print service can then be used for duplication of your letterhead. White is always a practical paper color; if you choose a colored paper, make sure that you can be supplied with a matching correcting material for typing errors. You'll find that 1000 sheets of stationery go quickly. If you can afford it, buy twice that amount initially.

Record mailers can be purchased through pressing plants, often at cheaper prices than at a paper store. You should also print mailing labels with your return address for use on record mailers or larger packages you send out.

GOVERNMENT REGULATIONS

Anyone who operates a business, including independent record labels, must comply with a number of city, county, state, and federal regulations. These regulations are designed to protect both the business and the public as well as to insure that taxes are paid. Regulations, procedures, and fees vary from one geographical area to another. The paragraphs that follow provide general information about what types of regulations exist and how you can comply with them.

Fictitious Name Certificate. If you are not doing business as a corporation, most states require that you file a fictitious name certificate. A fictitious name certificate establishes the name of your business in your county and prevents other businesses in the area from using the same name. It will not, however, prevent someone in another county from using your name.

In choosing the name of your business, take care not to use a name similar to one being used by another business with an established reputation since you could be sued for 'trading' on that company's reputation. Usually you give a name to your record label. You might also file for fictitious name certificates for your publishing company and your music group.

To obtain a fictitious name certificate, fill out a form available at the county clerk's office located in your county's administration building. It's usually a simple form that states the name under which you will be doing business. There is a small filing fee and a requirement that a newspaper of general circulation in your county publish the information for four consecutive weeks. Use whatever newspaper has the cheapest rates; generally it will be a law journal that serves the county court system.

You cannot copyright a name, whether it's for your label, group, or publishing company. Only by establishing a name through continual use does it become officially 'yours'. You establish your business name by using it as often as you can—on your bank checks, letterhead, business card, invoices, album cover, label, and advertising—or for anything else you do to sell and promote your records.

There is a procedure whereby you can register your record label name as a trademark, but until your business becomes well-known and has been operating for a number of years, there is no reason to go through the paperwork and pay the filing fees required for registration. For further information on trademarks, contact the local office of the Federal Department of Commerce.

Seller's Permit. Unless you are living in a state with no sales tax, you will need to obtain a seller's permit, sometimes referred to as a 'resale license'. This permit allows you to sell your records, whether directly to the public or through distributors. The seller's permit insures that the state sales tax will be collected, either by you or your distributors, for every record sold to the public, and will then be remitted to the state.

You will usually be charged a filing fee for this permit and asked to post a bond, or security deposit, as a guarantee that you (or your distributor) will collect the sales tax and remit it to the state. The board will usually base the amount of your deposit on the volume of records you say you will sell directly to the public.

Putting out my own record led to a deal with Kaleidoscope Records. We work as an integral team: they respect me for what I know because I once took all the steps for making and selling records by myself, and I respect them because of what they free me up to do. I still manage myself and book my own concerts.

KATE WOLF

Since you will need to demonstrate how you arrived at your estimate, you must state the number of records you will be manufacturing and then determine how many of them you intend to sell.

When you acquire the seller's permit, you will receive the forms to prepare sales tax returns. Each month, quarter, or year (depending on your volume of sales) you will send in the forms and any sales taxes collected during that period.

In most states, your seller's permit allows you to purchase goods at wholesale without paying sales tax —*if* those goods are going to be resold. That would include your record manufacturing and album cover fabrication costs, but not furniture, tools, or equipment.

Local Business License. Most major cities now require that your business file for a local business permit, or license, which gives you official permission to do business locally. Some also require that you have a business address that is not residential. Usually you obtain your license from city hall and pay a permit fee based on the nature of your business.

Federal ID Number. If your business hires regular employees, paid weekly or monthly, you will need a Federal ID number, which automatically informs the IRS that you will file quarterly and year-end payroll tax returns. When you do have regularly paid employees, the paperwork increases and you will have to count on paying for benefits, such as workman's compensation and social security. When you are ready for that step, a good reference book is *Small Time Operator,* by Bernard Kamoroff (see the Bibliography).

Federal and State Tax Returns. Whatever business entity you set up, be it a sole proprietorship, partnership, or corporation, you will need to file federal and state tax returns—both business and personal. The IRS must be able to distinguish between the two. This is simplified if you do business under a fictitious name and keep your personal income and expenses separate from your business income and expenses.

You must remember to keep a receipt for absolutely every penny you spend on legitimate business expenses. If you don't know what legitimate business expenses are, check with your accountant, or the IRS can send you free brochures on the subject. In case you are audited by the IRS, receipts are obligatory in order to prove every tax-deductible expense that you claim on your income tax.

Until your business makes a profit, or until your own personal income reaches an amount established by the IRS, you won't have to pay taxes, although you will have to file the returns. When your income exceeds expenses, you will pay taxes on the profit. Some people spend as much as they can on their business, in order to build their business *and* to avoid paying extra to the IRS. At some point, however, your business should make money faster than you can spend it.

JOINING THE INDUSTRY

There are several ways to enhance your business's chance of success. The paragraphs that follow detail some standard business practices that apply to the recording industry. These practices are simple and relatively inexpensive. They will help people locate you and help you locate them.

Publications. Two comprehensive national and international directories of music industry resources are published annually. *The Billboard International Buyers' Guide* lists names, addresses, and phone numbers valuable to people making and selling records, such as record companies, distributors, pressing plants, and discmasterers.

The *Talent and Booking Source Directory* lists names, addresses, and phone numbers important to people in the music business, such as recording artists, personal managers, booking agents, and colleges (complete with the names of the director of student activities, entertainment chairman, and pop concert chairman or pro-

If I want to keep offering good records, I have to make money on the ones I already have. I have to be a businessman. I have to learn how to work with people, how to work with distributors, how to collect money, how to be a hardnose— how to be businesslike and reality oriented.

MIKE RICHEY
Owner, Ridge Runner Records

start your recording project, you should definitely acquire them. *The Billboard International Buyers' Guide* costs $35 (postage included) and *The Talent and Booking Source Directory* costs $60 (plus $4.50 postage). Both are available by mail order only, from the addresses listed in the Directory at the end of this book. You might also be able to find them in the business reference section of your public or university library.

Information listings in both directories are free. They are as comprehensive and up-to-date as possible. It is, however, the responsibility of each business to inform the directories of new listings or changes. The deadlines for information are usually six months preceding publication. To be sure that your record label or publishing company is listed, write and request the forms and send the information in as soon as it is available. Remember to include all the services that your business offers.

NAIRD. The National Association of Independent Record Distributors (NAIRD) was founded in 1972 for the purpose of exchanging information on marketing, promotion, manufacturing, and advertising records. NAIRD members make and distribute independent records, most of them selling records in quantities under 50,000. Both the manufacturers and the distributors who are members of NAIRD are committed to providing buyers with alternatives to the music available from the major labels.

Most of the association's business is done at its annual trade convention, usually held in the Spring, for members only. Members display their records and catalogs and attend seminars and workshops on topics such as "Starting a New Distributorship," "Mass Merchandising" and "Advertising and Promotion." NAIRD also sponsors its own "Indies" Awards for the best independent records released during the year. The convention provides an opportunity for independent labels to meet distributors, introduce them to their records and map out promotional and sales campaigns.

Distributors or record labels may join NAIRD for $125; with an annual fee thereafter of $95. This fee entitles members to attend the annual convention and take advantage of co-op advertising in *Billboard Magazine* and a press release mailing program. Convention fees (separate from membership fees) cover display tables, all workshops and seminars and include quite a

The Billboard International Buyers' Guide *and the* Talent & Booking Source Directory *are standard reference sources for services in all aspects of the recording business. They should be part of your library before you start researching and planning your record project.*

gram director). Both directories also provide extensive supplementary listings of sound and lighting companies, recording studios, clubs hiring musicians and singers, public relations firms, and manufacturers of instruments and recording and P.A. equipment. *Talent and Booking* additionally supplies touring information, such as seating capacities and stage and lighting facilities of major concert auditoriums in the United States.

These two directories are the unofficial Yellow Pages of the music industry. When you are ready to few brunches and dinners. For information on NAIRD or their annual convention, write to the address listed in the Directory.

NARM. The big business counterpart to NAIRD is the National Association of Recording Merchandisers, Inc. (NARM). NARM is composed of the biggest record manufacturers and record distributors in the United States. Its annual convention is a music business spectacular. At the 1978 convention, the keynote speaker was Clive Davis, President of Arista Records, and evening banquets featured such artists as Donna Summer, Dolly Parton, Lionel Hampton, and Anthony Newley. Seminars dealt with issues pertinent to big business: "Maximizing the Use of Radio Today," "Bar Coding: Its Impact and Opportunities," "Everything You Always Wanted to Know about Tax Shelters But Were Afraid to Ask." When your record label finds that subjects like this are relevant, join NARM. Its address is listed in the Directory.

NARAS. The National Academy of Recording Arts and Sciences (NARAS) is an organization designed to promote artistic, creative, and technical excellence in the recording industry. Much of the business in this organization centers around the annual Grammy Awards. Grammies are awarded nationally and locally to members of NARAS' seven chapters located in Atlanta, Chicago, Los Angeles, Nashville, Memphis, New York, and San Francisco. The national awards presentation is televised nationally. Member chapters also hold monthly meetings, both for informational and social purposes.

Voting membership is open only to people involved in the creative aspects of recording: musicians, singers, engineers, producers, arrangers, conductors, songwriters, art directors, photographers, artists, and designers. These people nominate and vote for the Grammy winners. Record labels and publishing companies do not belong to NARAS and neither do record promoters, DJs, store owners, or record label executives (unless they qualify under the above-mentioned categories).

Qualifications for voting membership are as follows:

Vocalists, Singers; Leaders, Conductors, Producers; Engineers; Instrumentalists, Musicians; Arrangers; Speakers: Must have recorded and commercially released at least six sides of an album or one-half of a 45.

Songwriters, Composers: Must have six recorded and commercially released selections, or the equivalent of one complete side of a commercially released long-playing record.

Art Directors, Photographers, Artists, Designers: Must have commercially released six album covers.

Annotators and Literary Editors: Must have written liner notes for six commercially released albums.

Associate memberships are available to persons who don't yet qualify for voting membership, but who are actively involved in the recording industry.

Nominations for Grammies are conducted solely by NARAS members. If you feel that the awards don't fairly represent independent labels, join and make your voice heard. The address for information about joining NARAS is listed in the Directory.

Voting members of NARAS also receive the *NARAS Awards Guide,* published every two months by Record Source International (RSI) as a service to NARAS. It lists newly released albums that voting members can purchase at greatly reduced prices so that members can become familiar with the year's releases by awards time.

Listings in the *NARAS Awards Guide* are free and are not limited to records by members. They are sent in by record companies. If you want to offer your album(s) for sale to NARAS members, send a list of your new releases to the RSI address in the Directory. Your list should include the album title, artist's name, label name, and album number. After each listing, indicate whether the release is a single, an LP, or a two-record LP. It can take as long as three months before an order is placed with your label.

NARAS members pay $3.68 each per LP. The record company, however, is paid only $1.50 per LP. Before sending in your listing, consider that you will be selling your record for that low price to as many NARAS members as order it.

Labor Unions. Two major labor unions serve the recording and performing musician and singer: the American Federation of Musicians (AF of M) and the American Federation of Television and Radio Artists (AFTRA). In general, instrumentalists belong to the AF of M and vocalists to AFTRA. These unions set wages and working standards for their members by entering into agreements with employers using their services, such as record labels, concert promoters,

If it hadn't been for NAIRD, it would have delayed my progress by maybe a year or two. If somebody has a record that looks good, he could get from two-thirds to all of the distributors at their convention. If he could do that, he already has something resembling national distribution. It's a good start.

BRUCE KAPLAN
Owner, Flying Fish Records

by members is not respected. Neither union acts as an employment agency.

To join either union, musicians and vocalists have to demonstrate their proficiency, agree to abide by all rules and regulations, and pay dues regularly. Most major American cities have a local branch of both AF of M and AFTRA. With a few exceptions, AFTRA initiation fees are $300 and annual dues are $36 a year. Initiation fees for the AF of M vary greatly from city to city, running as high as $300 or more in major recording centers and as low as $60 in cities seventy-five miles or more from those centers.

Not all musicians and singers belong to these unions. In some cases, they do not join because they are just beginning their careers and want to be free to take jobs in non-union situations, or because it is hard to find union jobs, particularly in communities with high populations of musicians and singers. Some people hesitate to join because they think the unions don't provide enough value or service for the money required to sustain membership.

As long as neither the employee (musician or singer) nor the employer (record label or club) are party to union agreements, the unions cannot step in and regulate wages or working conditions. Many small or independent labels are not signatory to union wage and working agreements because they do not operate on a large enough financial scale. However, a small label will usually sign union agreements if it makes a distribution agreement with a larger label which is a signatory to union agreements. If you want to sign union agreements, write or call the local branches of AF of M or AFTRA and ask for the appropriate forms and regulations. (The addresses are listed in the Directory.)

orchestras, and television producers. All major labels (and some minor ones) are signatories to either the Phonograph Record Labor Agreement, which is regulated by the AF of M, or the National Code of Fair Practices for Phonograph Recordings, which is regulated by AFTRA. These agreements bind labels who are signatories to paying union-set wages to member musicians and vocalists. The wages are figured according to the number of hours and time of day worked, the number of instruments played, and the type of sessions.

Both unions prohibit members from performing or recording with employers who have not signed such agreements, as well as recording with other musicians who are not union members. The goal of these unions is to help members earn a fair living and to provide them with recourse in the event that a contract signed

Chapter 11
Planning

By now, you are probably wondering how one person can carry out all the tasks suggested in this book. It can be done, as thousands of independents have demonstrated, but many of them accomplished their goals only after much frustration, delay, and unexpected expense. There's no guarantee that every aspect of your project will proceed perfectly, but you'll save considerable time and money if you map out a plan of action before you plunge in. The purpose of this final chapter is to help you estimate the time and money your record will require and coordinate all the necessary steps in producing it.

A good plan will help you maintain a sense of valor and adventure throughout your project, and insure that there will be enough money and energy to promote and sell your record. When cartons of records are delivered, you'll feel excited and ready to launch into your sales and promotion plan, rather than tired and impoverished and wishing that someone had convinced you to plan things better.

Good plans are also catalysts; they draw people with skills and show how those skills can be meaningfully used. Throughout your project, you will be calling on many people—friends, family, investors, musicians, engineers, studio owners, producers, arrangers, graphic designers, printers, and manufacturers —to help carry out your ideas. Good plans will show them that your ideas are grounded in reality, not fantasy.

TIME

What's a reasonable amount of time on which to plan from the point you decide to make a record until you have them shipped to you, ready to sell? If you've never made a record before, figure about a year. At first, you will think that a year sounds like much too long, especially since the idea of having a record of your music is very exciting and you naturally want to have it in hand instantly. That's why it's important that you think carefully about all that has to be done before you step into the studio, and about the follow-up work needed to produce a well-made product and prepare for sales and promotion.

Most people who make and sell their own records for the first time expect things to happen much too quickly. Some pros can record an album in a week; some major labels can launch an album successfully in a month. But that kind of speed comes only with a great deal of experience. Trying to make your project happen too fast will lead you and others to have false expectations or to foul up entirely some part of your project.

What follows is a suggested time plan designed to have records in hand one year from when you start your project. That year is divided into six two-month segments for research, financing, preparation, recording and graphics, editing, and presales. When you start to analyze everything to be done in each of those periods, you'll soon realize that that year will be a busy one.

Your first temptation will probably be to cut short the research and start talking to your rich friends about investing their money in your record. Don't be tempted. If you really hope to get others to lend you money, you will have to demonstrate that you are serious enough about your project to have planned it financially. Even if you have money of your own, force yourself to investigate the audience and media outlets for your record, and prepare a preliminary budget for your entire project before you spend a dime. The time you spend doing research will pay off. Plan on two months to assemble all the information needed to make your budget and another two months to line up your financing.

The following two months should be spent setting up your business and lining up commitments from the various people and services that will play a part in the production of your album. By the end of this period, your selection of songs to be recorded and their arrangements should be fairly set and well-rehearsed.

Plan on two months to record and mix your album, and make sure that the graphics for your cover are being prepared as well. You should then plan on *another* two months to produce the final mechanicals for your cover once you have edited your master tape. Again, your first inclination will probably be to try and get this done more quickly. Consider first, however, that your final selection of songs and their sequence will most likely not be made until after the recording and mixing sessions. You will waste much of your graphic designer's time (and your money) if you keep making changes in the back cover copy. Furthermore, you are likely to get so wrapped up in your recording sessions that you won't have the energy to write the cover copy and plan for all the graphics for your cover. Remember, your album cover makes a first impression. Give it the time it deserves.

It will probably take another two months from the time you ship off your master tape and camera-ready mechanicals until you receive your finished albums. For many independents, this time is spent just waiting and feeling frustrated. Actually, this should be another busy time. Aside from approving your reference lacquers, test pressings, and cover proofs, you should be spending this time preparing your sales and promotion plans so they can go into high gear once your records arrive. If by chance you do get your records a couple of weeks early, don't jump the gun getting your record 'out there' until you've got all your promotional materials, mailing lists, and sales arrangements ready. This will be another frustrating temptation, but just make up your mind beforehand that you're going to do it right and try to make the most of the sales and promotion potential of your record.

Finally, you should plan on at least another year to promote and sell your record. In fact, once your record is completed and your promotional materials assembled, time counts for more than money. Making a coordinated sales, promotion, and performing plan and carrying it out thoroughly and relentlessly is what really matters. (See the promotion and sales plans on pages 17 and 36). The work is not difficult—just time consuming.

Time is your greatest ally. Most major labels schedule new record releases every month. If a record doesn't 'break' in that time, the majors simply go on to the newer ones. This formula works for them and makes them money, but often to the detriment of new artists who need more time spent than the month allotted. You can take that time. What will be difficult is believing that your plans will work, especially in the first four to six months when results are very slow. Just remember the time you put into learning your instrument and new songs. It's similar to the time it takes to succeed in selling records.

Time Plan. Here is a concise list detailing the two-year process as described above.

RESEARCH (TWO MONTHS)

► Conceive your record (songs, arrangements, personnel, recording method, recording location).

► Research your community (audience, retailers, distributors, media).

► Investigate services and rates (recording studios, graphic designers, printers, manufacturers, arrangers, producers, musicians, photographers, artists, lawyers, accountants).

► Obtain forms and information (copyright office, performance rights societies, business organizations).

FINANCING (TWO MONTHS)

► Prepare preliminary time plan and budget (Worksheets 1 through 11.)

► Contact investors.

► Set up legal and financial structures (corporation, partnership, proprietorship).

PREPARATION (TWO MONTHS)

► Establish your business (office, phone, stationery and supplies, accounting procedures, licenses, organizations).

► Make arrangements for recording (select songs, arrangements, personnel, recording method, recording location; plan sessions).

► Make arrangements for graphics (select graphic designer; determine cover concept; plan copy, photography, and artwork).

► Make arrangements for manufacturing and printing.

► Protect your songs (form publishing company; copyright your songs; join performance rights society).

Planning is really the hardest part of making records. Many of us have some sort of block about setting forth our grandest hopes and fears in broad daylight—let alone working out the future of our creative impulses in detail. Many of us also block out any rational thinking about selling our art. You've got to have a good plan (or a lot of luck) to have a ghost of a chance of getting back a fraction of the time, energy, and money that will go into making your record.

ED DENSON
Owner, Kicking Mule Records

Working through Cal State, Chico, had several advantages. There was, of course, the eventual degree. Of no small importance, the school helped me get the cash I needed to make my recordings. I have received money through scholarships and financial aid grants, through playing concerts for the school's performing arts program, and now through teaching. The school also provided a large number of talented musicians to interact with. I lifted most of my current band entirely from the school's jazz ensemble.

PETER BERKOW
Second Pressing Fund

► Obtain mechanical licenses (for other people's songs).

► Prepare preliminary sales and promotion plans.

RECORDING AND GRAPHICS (TWO MONTHS)

► Rehearse songs to be recorded.

► Record and mix songs according to session plan.

► Prepare graphic materials (copy, photography, artwork).

EDITING (TWO MONTHS)

► Sequence and prepare master tape.

► Prepare final graphic materials.

► Approve and proof camera-ready mechanicals.

► Ship master tape to disc-masterer.

► Ship camera-ready mechanicals to printer.

► Prepare promotional materials.

PRESALES (TWO MONTHS)

► Approve reference lacquers and test pressings.

► Approve bluelines and proofs.

► Prepare final promotional materials.

► Assemble final mailing lists.

► Book performances.

► Make final sales arrangements (salespeople, distributors, forms).

► Arrange for shipping and storage.

SALES AND PROMOTION (ONE YEAR)

► Copyright your record.

► Carry out coordinated sales, promotion, and performing plan.

MONEY

The foundation of any plan is a budget that sets out how much money your project will need and how much it can hope to return. It's important that you work out a preliminary budget of all your expected expenses and income before any money is borrowed or committed to designers, recording studios, printers, and manufacturers. Your budget will also help you to define your goals by indicating what you can reasonably hope to gain financially from your record project.

The pages that follow contain a series of worksheets which relate to each of the chapters in this book. Using the time and money sections at the end of each chapter and, more important, the information you have assembled in your research, estimate each of the expenses you will incur for each aspect of your project and enter them on the appropriate worksheets. Some of these figures will be based on rates for services which have been quoted you by designers, studios, and manufacturers. Others, such as the number of records you expect to give away, will be educated guesses on your part. Nevertheless, you will be better off to have at least put these estimates down in writing, even if you find later that you have to revise them. Just be sure that you base all your estimates on concrete thinking, so that if someone asks you how you arrived at a particular figure, you can tell them.

The final worksheet summarizes the figures from the individual sheets, and will give you your first overall picture of the profit (or loss) to be made from your project. This is the time to once again consider your reasons for making and selling your own record. Will the project make or lose money, and how much? Is this question the most important to you, or are there other gains to take into account? For example, are you willing to risk monetary loss to gain better bookings, reviews, possible access to major labels, or the chance to learn more about recording or business in general?

These questions are particularly important if you are borrowing money from others. Your family may be willing to lend you money that cannot be paid back from this project, but most investors will not. Even if it is your own money that will be lost, you should ask yourself whether you are willing to risk losing it.

In any case, you should try to revise your estimates so that they show your project breaking even or making a profit. Can you spend less on recording? Is there a way you can bolster sales? Can you save money by pressing fewer records initially and re-pressing later? Keep juggling your estimates on the individual sheets until the whole project falls into line. (Caution: resist strongly the temptation to save money by spending less on graphics or promotion.)

Eventually, you will come up with a budget you can justify to yourself and your investors. (It would be well for you to make copies of the blank worksheets, as you will be making revisions throughout your project.)

These worksheets will also be useful to keep track of expenses as your project unfolds, and to indicate whether your actual costs are exceeding your earlier estimates. Most important, preparing a budget will make you think through the entire project from beginning to end. If you can do that, your budget will be one of your strongest selling points in borrowing money, and a reliable guide as you carry out your project.

Two final tips: first, figure that your expenses will be a bit more than some of the definite bids you have. Costs have an uncanny way of creeping up as a project progresses. Also, figure your sales conservatively—don't plan on selling every last record, and don't be blinded by dollar signs in your eyes when you compute how much you'll make on re-pressings. Start with a realistic plan, and be pleasantly surprised when you meet with unexpected success.

Finally, don't begin spending any money until you have all the money your project needs in hand, or at least very firm commitments for getting your funds on specified dates. There's nothing worse than having to skimp on important tasks in the middle of a project because some 'promised' funds didn't come through.

The purpose of the following worksheets is to help you project income and expenses common to most recording projects. Because businesses vary greatly, you may find some items basic to your project missing from these worksheets. Be sure to add those items when projecting profit/loss probabilities.

This worksheet will help you to make some basic decisions regarding your promotional plans while estimating your costs for promoting your record. Estimating the number of names on your various mailing lists will help you gauge how many free records you are likely to be giving away. The number of names on your lists should also serve as a guide for the quantities of various promotional materials that you will be preparing.

The costs for these promotional materials should be for reproducing or printing. Any fees associated with designing the materials or having photos taken or artwork prepared should be included with your graphics expenses on Worksheet 3, Graphics. In many cases, you can save money by having these materials designed along with your album cover.

When figuring your continuing expenses, keep in mind that these will reflect somewhat the number of names on your lists and the quantities of materials you will be sending out.

If you plan on advertising or using independent promotional services, your figures for these items will show that these are by far the most expensive ways to promote your record.

1 Promotion

Mailing Lists

Priority media list

                                                NO. OF NAMES

Secondary media list   _____

Industry list   _____

Fan list   _____

                   TOTAL NUMBER OF NAMES   _____

Free Records Distributed

                                                _____
                                                NO. OF RECORDS

Promotional Materials (Reproduction)

The cost of preparing camera-ready artwork and shooting photographs should be included on the Graphics Worksheet.

	QUANTITY	COST
Photographs	_____	$ _____
Press releases	_____	$ _____
Press kit covers	_____	$ _____
Flyers/posters	_____	$ _____
Other _____	_____	$ _____
Purchase mailing lists	_____	$ _____
TOTAL PROMOTIONAL MATERIALS		$ _____

Continuing Expenses

	NO. OF MONTHS	PER MONTH	TOTAL COST
Phone	_____	$ _____	$ _____
Postage	_____	$ _____	$ _____
Photocopying	_____	$ _____	$ _____
Addressing/secretarial	_____	$ _____	$ _____
Transportation	_____	$ _____	$ _____
TOTAL CONTINUING EXPENSES			$ _____

Worksheet 1, Promotion

► CONTINUED ON NEXT PAGE

Worksheet 1, Promotion / continued

Advertising

The cost of preparing camera-ready artwork and shooting photographs should be included on the Graphics Worksheet.

	NO. OF MONTHS	PER MONTH	TOTAL COST
Display	______	$______	$______
Classified	______	$______	$______
Radio	______	$______	$______
		TOTAL ADVERTISING	$______

Promotional Services

	NO. OF MONTHS	PER MONTH	TOTAL COST
Airplay	______	$______	$______
Print	______	$______	$______
		TOTAL PROMOTIONAL SERVICES	$______

► ENTER ALL ITEMS MARKED WITH DOUBLE UNDERLINE ON WORKSHEET 11, PLANNING

On this worksheet, you will figure your sales income for your record project.

The first step is to determine what will be your prices and discounts in each of the sales categories. Then, after making sure that the number of records to be manufactured minus the number of free records to be distributed exceeds the total you plan on selling, make projections for your sales in each category and deduct your various selling expenses.

Your two major expenses will be the cost of servicing retail accounts you handle yourself and the cost of shipping and billing for records you sell through distributors. The total cost of your mail order package can vary greatly, depending on whether you plan on distributing the package personally at performances, mailing it to your fan list, or mailing it in greater quantities to lists of unknown groups or individuals.

As with all the worksheets in this book, you can use this form to make an estimate of your income and, later, to keep track of actual income. When making your initial projections, you will probably want to make several copies of the worksheet and experiment with various quantities of sales in each of the categories. Working out these numbers in advance will help you determine the most profitable and practical way to put together your sales plan.

2 Sales

Price/Discount Schedule

List price of record $ _____

Special performance price $ _____

Retailers' discount _____ $ _____
                      % OF LIST PRICE

Distributors' discount _____ $ _____
                        % OF LIST PRICE

Mail order price $ _____

Performance Sales Income

Number of records sold _____
                         NO. OF RECORDS

Gross (records sold x performance price) $ _____

Seller's commissions (subtract) _____   ($ _____)
                                  % OF GROSS

Sales tax (subtract) _____   ($ _____)
                      % OF GROSS

                              NET PERFORMANCE SALES $ _____

Retailers' Sales Income

Number of records sold _____
                         NO. OF RECORDS

Gross (records sold x retailers' price) $ _____

Seller's commissions (subtract) _____   ($ _____)
                                  % OF GROSS

Number of stores serviced _____
                           STORES

Number of months serviced _____
                           MONTHS

Cost of sales forms (subtract)   ($ _____)

Phone (subtract) _____ $ _____   ($ _____)
                  MONTHS   PER MONTH

Transportation (subtract) _____ $ _____   ($ _____)
                           MONTHS   PER MONTH

                              NET RETAILERS' SALES $ _____

▶ CONTINUED ON NEXT PAGE

Worksheet 2, Sales / continued

Distributors' Sales Income

Number of records sold	______ NO. OF RECORDS	
Gross (records sold x distributors' price)		$______
Shipping (subtract)		($______)
Billing, phone and postage (subtract)		($______)
NET DISTRIBUTORS' SALES		$______

Mail Order Package

The costs of preparing camera-ready artwork and shooting photographs should be included on the Graphics Worksheet.

Fan list	______ NO. OF NAMES	$______ COST
Mailing lists purchased	______	$______
Printing	______ QUANTITY	$______
Addressing	______	$______
Postage	______	$______
TOTAL COST OF MAIL ORDER PACKAGE		$______

Mail Order Sales Income

Number of records sold	______ NO. OF RECORDS		
Gross (records sold x mail order price)			$______
Sales tax		______ % OF GROSS	($______)
Record mailers (subtract)	______ QUANTITY		($______) COST
Postage for records (subtract)	______		($______)
Cost of mail order package, from above (subtract)			($______)
NET MAIL ORDER SALES			$______

► ENTER ALL ITEMS MARKED WITH DOUBLE UNDERLINE ON WORKSHEET 11, PLANNING

This printing worksheet separates the prepress costs, which you will incur only once, from the costs of presswork and fabricating. If you plan on printing extra cover slicks and holding them for fabrication later, list the excess cover materials you will have on hand when you go back for reruns.

If your printer quotes a package price, or if you are making use of a stock cover, be sure to note which of the various items are included.

3 Printing

Prepress

Halftones	$
Color separations	$
Negatives and stripping	$
Bluelines	$
Color keys	$
Press proofs	$
Plates	$
TOTAL PREPRESS	$

Presswork

	RECORDS MANUFACTURED	EXCESS QUANTITY	TOTAL QUANTITY	COST
Front cover slicks				$
Back cover slicks				$
Print on shorepack				$
Inserts				$
Labels				$
Stickers				$
TOTAL PRESSWORK				$

Fabrication

	QUANTITY	COST
Varnishing/lamination		$
Fabricate covers		$
Ship covers to pressing plant		$
TOTAL FABRICATION		$

▶ ENTER ALL ITEMS MARKED WITH DOUBLE UNDERLINE ON WORKSHEET 11, PLANNING

Worksheet 3, Printing

For the most part, your graphics expenses will be one-time costs for preparing the mechanicals for your cover, label, and promotional materials. It is not unusual, however, for professional photographers and illustrators to require additional fees for reuse of their artwork; it would be wise to clarify this before commissioning their services.

If you are going to be using stock or economy covers, be sure to inquire which of the items on this worksheet are included and which you must provide.

4 Graphics

Original Artwork

Art direction $ _____

Photography $ _____

Illustration $ _____

Logo design and production $ _____

Other _____ $ _____

                          TOTAL ORIGINAL ARTWORK $ _____

Cover

Design $ _____

Typesetting $ _____

Photostats/camerawork $ _____

Mechanicals $ _____

                                     TOTAL COVER $ _____

Label

Design $ _____

Typesetting $ _____

Photostats/camerawork $ _____

Mechanicals $ _____

                                     TOTAL LABEL $ _____

Inserts

Design $ _____

Typesetting $ _____

Photostats/camerawork $ _____

Mechanicals $ _____

                                   TOTAL INSERTS $ _____

Worksheet 4, Graphics

▶ CONTINUED ON NEXT PAGE

Worksheet 4, Graphics / continued

Press Kit Covers

Design $_____

Typesetting $_____

Photostats/camerawork $_____

Mechanicals $_____

                              TOTAL PRESS KIT COVERS $_____

Flyers/Posters

Design $_____

Typesetting $_____

Photostats/camerawork $_____

Mechanicals $_____

                              TOTAL FLYERS/POSTERS $_____

Mail Order Package

Design $_____

Typesetting $_____

Photostats/camerawork $_____

Mechanicals $_____

                              TOTAL MAIL ORDER PACKAGE $_____

Letterheads, Envelopes, Mailing Labels, Business Cards

Design $_____

Typesetting $_____

Photostats/camerawork $_____

Mechanicals $_____

                              TOTAL BUSINESS PAPER $_____

Summary

                              TOTAL GRAPHICS COSTS $_____

▶ ENTER ALL ITEMS MARKED WITH DOUBLE UNDERLINE ON WORKSHEET 11, PLANNING

Manufacturing costs are broken down into disc-mastering, plating, pressing, packaging, and shipping and storage expenses. If you re-press your record, you will not incur the disc-mastering and some of the plating costs again.

If your manufacturer quotes a package price, or if you are making use of a 'total package' that includes printing and manufacturing, you should determine which of the various items are included.

5 Manufacturing

Disc-mastering

Master lacquers (sides A and B)	$
Reference lacquers (sides A and B)	$
Shipping to plating facility	$
TOTAL DISC-MASTERING	$

Plating

Three-step process (master/mother/stamper)	$
Additional stampers	$
Shipping to pressing plant	$
TOTAL PLATING	$

Records to be manufactured

QUANTITY

Pressing

Test pressings		$
		COST
Pressing	QUANTITY	$
	TOTAL PRESSING	$

Packaging

	QUANTITY	COST
Collate records/covers		$
Inserts		$
Shrink-wrapping		$
	TOTAL PACKAGING	$

Shipping and Storage

	QUANTITY	COST
Ship to warehouse		$
Ship to distributors		$
Storage		$
	TOTAL SHIPPING AND STORAGE	$

▶ ENTER ALL ITEMS MARKED WITH DOUBLE UNDERLINE ON Worksheet 11, Planning

From *How to Make and Sell Your Own Record* by Diane Sward Rapaport. This form may be reproduced solely for private, noncommercial use. Copyright © 1979, 1984 by Diane Sward Rapaport and The Headlands Press, Inc. Copyright © 1988 by Diane Sward Rapaport. All rights reserved.

Worksheet 5, Manufacturing

Worksheet 5, Manufacturing / continued

Mastering

Cassette mastering $ _____

Compact disc pre-mastering $ _____

Compact disc mastering $ _____

                                        TOTAL MASTERING $ _____

Manufacturing

Cassettes $ _____
          QUANTITY _____

CDs $ _____
          QUANTITY _____

                                    TOTAL MANUFACTURING $ _____

Graphics

Cassettes $ _____

Cassette inserts $ _____

CD labels $ _____

CD booklets $ _____

CD inlay cards $ _____

                                        TOTAL GRAPHICS $ _____

Packaging

Collate CDs and graphics $ _____
          QUANTITY _____

Shrink wrapping $ _____
          QUANTITY _____

Other $ _____
          QUANTITY _____

                                       TOTAL PACKAGING $ _____

Shipping and Storage

Ship to warehouse $ _____
          QUANTITY _____

Ship to distributors $ _____
          QUANTITY _____

Storage $ _____
          QUANTITY _____

                                  TOTAL SHIPPING/STORAGE $ _____

▶ ENTER ALL ITEMS MARKED WITH DOUBLE UNDERLINE ON WORKSHEET 11, PLANNING

This worksheet is the first step in planning your recording sessions and beginning to estimate your recording costs. Make a copy of the form for each song you intend to record. List the artists for the song and the instrument (or vocal part) each will play or sing. Then, with the help of your arranger, producer, and/or engineer, assign each part a mike and track number. If you are recording by one of the less complex methods, these assignments may be fairly simple.

Once you have made a worksheet for each song, you can proceed to group the songs and parts into recording sessions on the following worksheet.

6 Recording: Songs

Title of Song _____ *Time of Song* _____ *Mixing Session No.* _____

ARTIST	INSTRUMENT/VOCAL	MIKE NO(S).	TRACK NO(S).	SESSION NO(S).

▶ MAKE A COPY OF THIS FORM FOR EACH SONG YOU PLAN TO RECORD.

Worksheet 6,
Recording: Songs

Make a copy of this form for each recording session. Using the song recording worksheets, indicate which songs and parts will be covered in each session, and what mikes and tracks will be involved. With this information completed, you should be able to estimate the number of hours needed for each session.

Make a separate form for each mixing session as well, and plan which songs you will mix in each one. This will help you estimate your mixing time.

As with all the worksheets, you can use these forms initially to plan your sessions and estimate costs and, later, to keep track of the actual recording and mixing sessions as they progress.

7 Recording: Sessions

Session No. _____ Hours _____   ☐ *Recording*   ☐ *Mixing*

SONG TITLE(S)	INSTRUMENT/VOCAL	MIKE NO(S).	TRACK NO(S).

► MAKE A COPY OF THIS FORM FOR EACH RECORDING AND MIXING SESSION.

Worksheet 7,
Recording: Sessions

This last recording worksheet is a breakdown of costs. Many of these will be determined by the number of sessions, the number of hours, or a combination. In addition to personnel and studio time, be sure to take into account any special equipment or instruments you will need, tape costs, and your personal expenses while you are recording.

8 Recording: Costs

Personnel

Producer(s)

NAME	NO. OF SESSIONS	NO. OF HOURS	$ COST
			$

Engineer(s)

NAME	NO. OF SESSIONS	NO. OF HOURS	$ COST
			$

Arranger(s)

NAME	NO. OF SESSIONS	NO. OF HOURS	$ COST
			$

Musicians

NAME	NO. OF SESSIONS	NO. OF HOURS	$ COST
			$
			$
			$
			$
			$
			$
			$
			$
			$
			$
			$
			$
			$
			$
			$
			$

TOTAL PERSONNEL $

Worksheet 8, Recording: Costs

▶ CONTINUED ON NEXT PAGE

Worksheet 8, Recording: Costs / continued

Studio Time

	NO. OF SESSIONS	NO. OF HOURS	COST
Recording			$
Mixing			$
Editing and tape copies			$
Location recording fees			$
Other studio costs _____			$
		TOTAL STUDIO TIME	$

Equipment and Instruments

	ITEMS	COST
Equipment rental		$
Equipment purchase		$
Instrument rental		$
Instrument purchase		$
	TOTAL EQUIPMENT AND INSTRUMENTS	$

Tape Costs

	TIME	FEET	COST
Multi-track			$
Half-track			$
Quarter-track			$
Cassettes			$
		TOTAL TAPE COSTS	$

Miscellaneous Expenses

		COST
Travel		$
Lodging		$
Food		$
Refreshments		$
Other _____		$
	TOTAL MISCELLANEOUS EXPENSES	$

► ENTER ALL ITEMS MARKED WITH DOUBLE UNDERLINE ON WORKSHEET 11, PLANNING

This worksheet is designed to keep track only of the costs involved in recording and publishing musical material. Any income you might receive from your songs being played on the air or recorded by other artists should be kept track of separately.

Be sure to note the mechanical license rates for each song you record which has been written by someone else. The total amount of these rates per record will have to be paid out of your income from your record project.

9 Song Rights

Mechanical License Fees

List each song recorded which is not assigned to your publishing company.

TITLE	PUBLISHER	LENGTH (TIME)	$ MECHANICAL LICENSE FEE PER RECORD

TOTAL MECHANICAL LICENSE FEES (PER RECORD) $ _____

Song Protection

	NO. OF SONGS	$ COST
Leadsheets		$
Photocopying		$
Cassette or tape		$
Song registration		$
Copyright registration (songs)		$
Copyright registration (record)		$

TOTAL SONG PROTECTION $ _____

Song Exploitation

ASCAP/BMI songwriter membership	$
ASCAP/BMI publisher membership	$
Legal fees	$

TOTAL SONG EXPLOITATION $ _____

▶ ENTER ALL ITEMS MARKED WITH DOUBLE UNDERLINE ON WORKSHEET 11, PLANNING

Worksheet 9, Song Rights

This worksheet covers the costs of setting up and running your office, professional services, and governmental fees and licenses, as well as various expenses associated with joining the record industry. Although some of these costs may seem vague or remote when you first start planning your project, be sure to budget some funds for them. Bear in mind that your legal fees can vary considerably, depending on the method you choose to finance your project (see Appendix).

10 Business

Office Expenses

The cost of preparing camera-ready artwork should be included on the Graphics Worksheet.

Letterheads, envelopes, mailing labels, business cards $ _____

Office equipment $ _____

Telephone installation $ _____

	MONTHS	$ PER MONTH	$ COST
Telephone	_____	_____	_____
Answering service	_____	_____	$ _____
Postage	_____	_____	$ _____
Supplies	_____	_____	$ _____
Rent	_____	_____	$ _____

TOTAL OFFICE EXPENSES $ _____

Professional Services

Legal $ _____

Accounting $ _____

	MONTHS	$ PER MONTH	$ COST
Bookkeeping	_____	_____	_____
Secretarial	_____	_____	$ _____

TOTAL PROFESSIONAL SERVICES $ _____

Fees and Licenses

Incorporation expenses $ _____

Fictitious name certificate $ _____

Seller's permit $ _____

Business license $ _____

Bulk mail permit $ _____

Trademark registration $ _____

TOTAL FEES AND LICENSES $ _____

▶ CONTINUED ON NEXT PAGE

Industry Expenses

PUBLICATIONS

Talent and Booking $ _____

Billboard $ _____

Other _____ $ _____

MEMBERSHIPS

NAIRD $ _____

NARM $ _____

NARAS $ _____

Other _____ $ _____

CONVENTION EXPENSES

Registration $ _____

Travel $ _____

Lodging $ _____

Food $ _____

OTHER INDUSTRY EXPENSES

_____ $ _____

_____ $ _____

                          TOTAL INDUSTRY EXPENSES   <u>$</u> _____

This final worksheet groups all the expenses and income from your recording project into sales income and initial costs, the cost of product, promotional and business expenses. Each of the entries on this worksheet should be taken from the appropriate totals on the preceding worksheets, which have been indicated by double underlines.

Looking at your project from this overall perspective will help you plan how much to spend on recording and graphics, how many records to press, and how many sales you will need to break even or show a profit. If the figures don't come out at first, go back to the individual worksheets if necessary and adjust your plans. Whatever you do, *don't* be tempted to make the figures show a profit by simply spending less on promotion.

This worksheet will also be helpful in figuring your profits should you sell out your first pressing and manufacture more records. You will not incur the initial costs again. Your promotional and business expenses will continue, though most likely on a different basis. By gearing the size of the repressing to your projected sales, you should be able to show a substantial profit.

11 Planning

Sales Income

	NO. SOLD		NET INCOME
Performances (from Worksheet 2)	_____		$ _____
Retailers (from Worksheet 2)	_____		$ _____
Distributors (from Worksheet 2)	_____		$ _____
Mail order (from Worksheet 2)	_____		$ _____

TOTAL NO. OF RECORDS SOLD ══════════

Mechanical license fees per record
(from Worksheet 9) $ _____

Number sold x fee per record (subtract)   ($ _____)

NET TOTAL SALES INCOME $ _____

Initial Costs

GRAPHICS

Total costs (from Worksheet 1) $ _____

PRINTING

Prepress (from Worksheet 3) $ _____

RECORDING

Personnel (from Worksheet 8) $ _____

Studio time (from Worksheet 8) $ _____

Equipment and instruments (from Worksheet 8) $ _____

Tape (from Worksheet 8) $ _____

Miscellaneous (from Worksheet 8) $ _____

MANUFACTURING

Mastering (from Worksheet 5) $ _____

SONG RIGHTS

Song protection (from Worksheet 9) $ _____

Song exploitation (from Worksheet 9) $ _____

TOTAL INITIAL COSTS $ _____

► CONTINUED ON NEXT PAGE

Worksheet 11, Planning

Cost of Product

PRINTING

Presswork (from Worksheet 3) $ _____

Fabrication (from Worksheet 3) $ _____

MANUFACTURING

Plating (from Worksheet 5) $ _____

Pressing (from Worksheet 5) $ _____

Packaging (from Worksheet 5) $ _____

Shipping and storage (from Worksheet 5) $ _____

Records to be manufactured (from Worksheet 5)   _____
QUANTITY

TOTAL COST OF PRODUCT $ _____

Promotional Expenses

Promotional materials (from Worksheet 1) $ _____

Continuing expenses (from Worksheet 1) $ _____

Advertising (from Worksheet 1) $ _____

Promotional services (from Worksheet 1) $ _____

Free records distributed (from Worksheet 1)   _____
NO. OF RECORDS

TOTAL PROMOTIONAL EXPENSES $ _____

Business Expenses

Offices expenses (from Worksheet 10) $ _____

Professional services (from Worksheet 10) $ _____

Fees and licenses (from Worksheet 10) $ _____

Industry expenses (from Worksheet 10) $ _____

TOTAL BUSINESS EXPENSES $ _____

Project Summary

Sales Income (from above) $ _____
                                                NO. RECORDS SOLD

Initial costs (from above)   ($ _____)

Cost of product (from above)   ($ _____)
                                                QUANTITY MANUFACTURED

Promotional expenses (from above)   ($ _____)
                                                NO. FREE RECORDS

Business expenses (from above)   ($ _____)

PROJECT PROFIT (OR LOSS) $ _____

In 1986 sales of cassettes totalled almost 2.5 billion dollars, ensuring that they will endure as a consumer format for many years. In almost all cases, the manufacture of cassettes is cheaper than records or compact discs. With cassettes, a record label isn't committed to producing a minimum run of 500 or 1000 copies as is common for the manufacture of records or CDs; quantities of 50 or 100 cassettes can be cost effective and profitable.

Once the music has been recorded, four major factors affect the sound quality of the cassette: the type of 'master' from which duplicates will be made; the type and quality of tape used; the cassette duplication method used; and the type of playback equipment the consumer will use to play the tape. A record company can control only the first three factors; it might deliver the highest quality cassette to consumers who will play it on inferior or even inappropriate, playback equipment.

MASTERING

Cassettes can be duplicated from a two-track tape, a ¼-track tape, or a cassette. You'll obtain the best results by using the master on which you recorded and edited your final mixes, in any of the above configurations. Bear in mind, however, that the wider the master tape used for recording (and the higher the recording speed), the better will be the quality of sound recorded, and the better the quality in reproduction. (See 'Tape Speed and Track Format' in Chapter 6, on recording procedures.) Each time information is transferred (tape to disc-mastering lacquer; 2″ tape to ¼″ tape, etc;) musical information is lost. The fewer transfers made between the recording and the cassette-duplication process, the better will be the sound quality.

TAPE FORMULATIONS

There are three basic kinds of cassette tape: ferric, chrome, and metal. Tape formations are also broken down into five 'types' assigned by the International Electrotechnical Commission (IEC): types 0 and 1 (commonly referred to as 'standard' or 'normal bias' tape) are ferric (or ferrichrome) tape; type 2 (commonly referred to as 'chrome' tape) has a chromium dioxide coating (or chrome coated with ferricobalt); type 3 (also chrome) is coated with dual-layered ferrichrome; and type 4 (metal tape) is a metal alloy tape.

Each basic kind of tape (ferric, chrome, or metal) has different abilities to receive and retain an audio signal, and each requires different magnetic strengths to record the signal properly. These characteristics in turn determine each tape's frequency response, dynamic range, signal-to-noise ratio (how much hiss will be present), and saturation levels (how much audio information the tape will hold before distortion or signal loss occurs).

On all types of audio tape, bias adjusts the magnetic field strength applied to the cassette tape during recording. Magnetic particles respond nonlinearly or disproportionately within any magnetic field. By adding the correct amount of an inaudible, very high frequency signal, the relative magnetization of the particles are charged to react proportionately. Without the proper amount of bias, the music being recorded will be distorted.

Another tape adjustment, equalization (EQ), corrects the fact that different tapes respond differently to different areas in the frequency range. Some tapes respond better to the bass frequencies than those in mid-range; other tapes have good mid-range response but poor low-end response.

Each type also displays general signal-to-noise characteristics. All blank cassette tape has a noticeable amount of noise, experienced by the listener as high-frequency hiss when no music is on the tape. The same hiss can still be heard when music is either recorded or played back at low volume or when quiet passages are recorded and played back.

The addition of noise-reduction capabilities to cassette recorders, most notably Dolby B and C, DBX, or HX Professional, helps quiet hiss. When noise reduction is used for cassette duplication, however, the critical requirement is constant attention to the alignment of the noise reduction to the tape recorder head. For this reason, some duplication facilities do not offer noise reduction, while some add the service for a slightly higher price. When noise reduction has been used during recording, tape playback will be at its optimum quality when noise reduction is also used during the playback of tapes.

Tape-player operating instructions tell consumers which kind of tape will give the best quality recording and playback for that particular machine. (Some cassette machines do not have recording capabilities and will only play back tapes.) Since not all duplicators or tape manufacturers use the same terminology, it helps to know the general characteristics of each tape.

Ferric tape (types 0 and 1) is far and away the most universal: it can be played back successfully on any type of cassette recorder, from the cheapest ghetto blaster or auto stereo to the most expensive professional machine. If no other designation appears in the manual, you can safely assume that ferric tape is recommended. For example, when sales literature refers to 'super' tape, and describes it as 'super standard bias tape for making serious records,' you will know they probably mean the highest grade of type 1 tape available.

Ferric tapes require a 120-microsecond EQ and the normal 100% bias current. Their general characteristics are that the frequency response can be expected to fall within ranges of 10,000 to 15,000 cycles (depending on the method of duplication and the type of playback equipment used). There are varying grades of

ferric tape, classified according to their frequency response and their signal-to-noise ratio.

Type 0 tapes, for instance, have limited high-end response and noticeably more hiss than type 1 tapes. They are most commonly used for spoken-word recordings.

Premium type 1 tapes display excellent response to bass frequencies, good response to mid-range frequencies, and deliver a higher output level.

Types 2, 3, and 4 tapes are commonly referred to as 'high bias' tapes. They require bias currents starting at 150% and a 70-microsecond EQ, and display a number of improvements over normal bias tapes: better tape saturation, lower hiss, greater ability to reproduce high-frequency sound, and greater ability to reproduce music of wide dynamic range. In general, the higher the bias required by these tapes, the better are the above characteristics.

Metal tape, for example, is successfully used for live recording, because it can deliver a high-end overload capability comparable to open-reel tape formulations.

There are, however, some drawbacks to chrome and metal tapes. One is that they cost more than ferric tape. Another is that chrome and metal backings are highly abrasive and tend to wear the heads faster on the recording equipment. The last but perhaps most important drawback is that these types can only be successfully played back on cassette machines that offer that capability. Manual settings, usually located on the front panels of cassette players and labeled 'standard,' 'chrome,' or 'metal' (0, bias/EQ), change the internal calibration so that the player will respond optimally to each kind of tape (during both recording and playback). Although a chrome or metal tape can deliver higher quality reproduction, using it will limit sales to those people who own proper playback equipment.

Not surprisingly, therefore, most chrome and metal tape is used for home recording situations in which the recording and playback are done on the same machine and where the consumer has the proper equipment to take advantage of the overall excellent performance of these tapes. The consumer needs not only a cassette recorder that can be calibrated to meet the bias and EQ requirements of chrome or metal tape, but also the audio components (speakers and amplifiers) that can deliver the dynamic range and frequency response of which the tapes are capable.

The notable exception is this: chrome tape can be recorded in such a way that it can be played back on the normal or ferric setting, thus giving it the same universal applicability as ferric tape. In this instance, the duplicator will re-calibrate the cassette recorders to record at the 120-microsecond EQ needed for ferric tape. The bias requirement will not be changed. If you wish to take advantage of this service, you should expect to pay a higher price both for the tape and the duplication service itself, and you may need to shop around for the service, since not all duplication firms offer it. If you use chrome tape recorded in this way, you must also make that fact clear on your packaging so that the consumer understands that the tape can be played on all cassette players, and that when the cassette player gives the choice between ferric and chrome playback, the ferric setting should be used. The chrome tape recorded at the 120-microsecond EQ will sound strange when played on the chrome setting on your cassette recorder.

TAPE DUPLICATION METHODS

The quality of sound is also affected by the method of cassette duplication and, to some extent, attention to tape recorder calibration and maintenance. At this time, two different methods are used: real-time and high-speed duplication.

Real time. In this method, the master tape is not only duplicated to play at the speed at which it was recorded, (7½, 15 or 30 ips) but it is played at the same running time. If it takes 42 minutes to play the music, it takes 42 minutes to duplicate the music.

In real-time reproduction, the frequency response and dynamic range of the master tape are transferred almost exactly, depending on the quality of the master tape, the speed at which the master was recorded, and the type and quality of the tape used. The method reproduces the highest quality audio fidelity possible in cassette recording.

High-speed Tape Duplication. In this method, both the master tape and the cassette are run at higher speeds, the common ratios normally being 8, 16, 32, or 64 times the playing speed. In general, the greater the speed, the greater the loss in high-frequency information and the greater the hiss. For this reason, most cassette duplicators reproducing music of wide dynamic range or much high-frequency information will seldom duplicate at speeds higher than a ratio of 32:1. Duplicators operating at ratios of 8 or 10 to 1 claim that the audible differences in quality are minimal compared to those in real-time duplication, and that these audible differences can only be perceived on excellent audio components by those with educated and/or 'caring' ears. Between a chrome tape duplicated at a low ratio of 8 to 10 on excellent and well-maintained equipment, and a chrome tape duplicated in real time and well-maintained equipment, the audible differences are minor. The average consumer, the claim goes, won't hear it.

In-cassette Duplication or Bin-loop? Cassette duplicators are currently using two systems for transferring the music from the master tape.

In-cassette duplication means that the tapes are already in their cassette housings. The method is most commonly used for real-time duplication. At high-speed duplication, mechanical problems interfere with the electronics, the most common problem being a variation in tape speed, which can lead to drop outs, loss in level, etc. When high-speed duplicators use an in-cassette system, they mediate against the problems by using oversized pressure pads and a tape known for its above average lubrication to keep it gliding smoothly in its plastic housing.

The bin-loop system is used by most high-speed duplicators. In this system, material is recorded several times in sequence on large pancakes of cassette tape and loaded afterwards into individual cassette shells. A master tape is made whose head and tail ends are spliced together to form a long loop. The loop is played over and over, while the cassette recorders duplicate them on the pancakes in reel-to-reel fashion. Each time the head of the material on the master tape is recorded, a 6 Hz tone signals the beginning of the tape. As the loading machines read the tones between each tape, the machine automatically cuts the tape and loads it into shells.

Price. Prices for tape duplication have become extremely competitive. In 1982, real-time duplication was, without exception, double or triple the price of high-speed duplication; the higher the speed ratio, the lower the price. And premium ferric tape was significantly cheaper than chrome.

In mid-1984, however, at least two duplication facilities offered lower prices for real-time than high-speed duplication. Prices for all ratios of high-speed duplication varied widely, and in a few cases, notably large centers of recording activity, salespeople in duplication facilities were unwilling to send out price lists and preferred that you tell them what you wanted so that they could make a bid, much as construction firms do. In quantity, premium ferric tape and chrome tape were only cents apart in price.

When researching prices, a good method is to call the duplicator and ask for the sales representative. First describe the type of music you are reproducing in terms of its dynamic range and frequency range. You don't have to be technical: you can simply say, for example, that the music contains a lot of bass information or lots of cymbals and bells. Tell the person what type of master you are delivering (½ track; cassette, etc.), what the total running time is, and how many copies you want. Then ask the following questions:

▶ What kind of machines do you use for duplication?

▶ Do you use the in-cassette or bin-loop system?

▶ What type of tape would you normally use for my kind of music?

▶ At what speed are you duplicating (if not in real time)?

▶ At this speed, what are the tape's frequency response and dynamic range likely to be for my type of master?

▶ What type of noise reduction do you use?

▶ What is the price and what will it include?

If the sales rep can't answer these questions, ask to speak to a technical person or an engineer.

When you have narrowed your choices to three possibilities, ask each if they would be willing to make a copy of your tape using their method of duplication and the type of tape recommended. Be sure you indicate a willingness to pay for that demo, though in some cases, firms will do it for free as an incentive. If they agree, send the best *copy* of your master tape that you can afford to make—be it ½", ¼", or cassette. At the same time, ask for references you can use to check their reputation: the names of other bands who have used the duplicator's services. If you are satisfied with the results of the demo, make sure your final contract specifies that the cassettes will sound at least as good as the demo made from the tape copy you sent.

Here is a range of prices encountered in mid-1984 for 1000 C-60 cassettes duplicated from a two-track master tape.

Real Time	*High speed 8:1*	*High speed 32:1 or 64:1*
$1.35–$3.50	$1.30–$1.75	$.90–$1.50

To add to the confusion, some prices include labels and boxes; some offer the added attraction of four-color two-panel inserts including color separations, and so on. Where a bin-loop system is used, most manufacturers will charge you a one-time fee for copying the material onto the bin-loop master. Forty dollars is an average price.

GRAPHICS AND PACKAGING

Cassette Graphics. As with album covers, an attractively designed cassette package draws attention to itself and encourages sales. Poorly designed graphics lead to suspicions that the music may also be inferior.

The most common cassette package is a shrink-wrapped box containing a labeled cassette and a four-panel insert. The insert's front and back panels, visible through the box, contain the necessary information, while the reverse sides are commonly printed with supplementary information. More elaborate cassette packages contain six- or eight-panel inserts.

Another kind of cassette package is now finding its way into the market. The boxed cassette (with insert) is being repackaged in a transparent plastic bag, approximately 4″ by 12″, which can be hung from a pegboard. The larger size enables the record company to include more materials, such as a flyer, business card, postcard order form, and so on.

Just because a cassette insert is smaller than an album cover doesn't mean it will cost less to design. Creating effective graphics on a small scale makes challenging demands on a designer's skill: he or she has much less space in which to deliver a potent message. As a result, you can expect to pay the equivalent of album cover design prices to achieve good results. (See Chapter 4, on graphics.)

You can help your graphic designer greatly by providing at the very beginning all the words to be included in your package. The graphic designer will have to design, size, and integrate the words aesthetically to make the information easy to find and read.

You can also help your graphic designer by asking the firm that will be printing the inserts to provide him or her with the layout specifications. This will ensure that the artwork is properly sized for printing.

The following checklists of information are labeled 'mandatory' for information that must be included on your cassette package, and 'optional' for supplementary information that can be included when and if you feel you have the extra room. (For information organizing the words efficiently for your de-

signer, read 'Preparing Copy for Typesetting' in Chapter 4.)

CASSETTE LABEL: MANDATORY

► Cassette title

► Your name (or your group's) if different from the title

► Record company name

► Record company logo

► The letters 'A' and 'B' or the words 'Side One' and 'Side Two'

► Tape playback information: type of tape; EQ setting required if different from that normally associated with the type of tape used; type of noise reduction used, if any; stereo or mono indication. Example: 'High Bias Chrome, 120 EQ, Dolby, Stereo.'

► Copyright notice for the songs†

► Copyright notice for the cassette†

► ASCAP or BMI affiliation†

CASSETTE LABEL: OPTIONAL

► Song titles in sequence

► Lengths of songs

► Total length of playing side

In 1979 I started researching statistics and found that one cassette was sold for every six records. I also found that cassette decks were selling quicker than turntables. Today the statistics for cassette sales are much higher.

NEIL COOPER
Reachout International Records

► Address of record company

► Name(s) of song publisher(s)

CASSETTE INSERT: MANDATORY

► Front cover:
Cassette title
Your name (or your group's) if different from title

► Spine:
Cassette title
Your name (or your group's) if different from title
Name or logo of record company
Cassette catalog number*

► Back cover (and/or reverse of panels):
Song titles
Sequence of songs
Name(s) of composers
Name(s) of publisher(s)
Names of primary musicians and instruments played
Copyright notices for the songs†
Copyright notice for the cassette†
Copyright notice for the cover design†
ASCAP or BMI affiliation†
Tape playback information: (1) type of tape; (2) EQ setting required if different from the one normally associated with that type of tape; (3) type of noise reduction used, if any; (4) stereo or mono indication

CASSETTE INSERT: OPTIONAL

► Name and mailing address of your label (although this is not mandatory, it is extremely important if you are an independent)

► Mail order price

► Credits for other musicians, vocalists, producer, engineer, arranger, graphic designer, photographer, illustrator, recording studio, manufacturer, printer

► Biographical material or information about the music, lyrics, and musicians

---

*The cassette catalog number is an arbitrary number you select for quick reference to each cassette title you issue under your label. Number future cassette releases sequentially. Don't get tricky; #101 or #1001 are good starts. Numbers like 1405 or THS 627 are illogical and hard for dealers and distributors to work with.

†Publishing and copyright are discussed in Chapter 9, "Song Rights."

► Lyric sheets

► Other records or books you might have for sale

► Mail order form

► Cassette dedication or special thanks

Printing Prices. Fortunately, in contrast to design prices, the cassette's smaller format does mean lower printing costs for cassette labels and inserts compared with album covers. Generally speaking, the majority of cassette-duplication firms almost always quote duplication prices that include label printing

Reachout International Records (ROIR) is the first cassette-only label specializing in rock recordings. For this insert for One Way System, *Kishi Yamamato, an artist living in England, conceived of one overall graphic to work with four folds, a unique concept and effective design solution.*

(one color only) and the box (but not shrinkwrapping). Some firms also include the printing for a two-panel insert with color on the front and black and white on the back. Here are some average prices when printing prices are quoted separately.

► Cassette labels (one color): 10¢ label/side

► Shrinkwrap: 7¢/box

► Inserts (black and white): $90 to $125/1000

► Inserts (full color front, black and white back, includes color separation): $300 to $350/1000

Assembling inserts and cassettes into boxes is usually included in the price for printing and/or duplication.

Because pricing and services are highly competitive, be sure you are clear about what you will be paying for. A good method for asking for printing price quotations is first to describe the desired quantity, color, and size of insert, and then to ask the following questions:

BLACK AND WHITE (OR ONE-, TWO-, OR THREE-COLOR PRINTING)

► Price per thousand?

► Charge for half-tones (black-and-white photographs that need to be converted for printing)?

► Charge for additional ink colors?

► Charge for set-up, if any?

FULL COLOR

► Price per thousand?

► Price for color separations and/or stripping?

► Additional charges?

As with the duplication of the tape, request samples of printing, particularly if you are printing in full color.

SALES AND PROMOTION

Most of the information you will need to sell and promote your cassette effectively is included in Chapters 1 and 2, 'Sales' and 'Promotion.' Not included there is the pricing of your cassette for sale.

Most independent cassettes are priced according to the length of the music, the amount of money spent for both recording and duplication, the type of tape, and the target market. At the time of this writing, most major record labels are asking that 45-minute cassettes retail for $8.98. This is the standard against which you will be competing. Remember: you, not the retail store, decide on the retail price.

As an incentive for both the store and the consumer to buy, some independents sell cassettes to stores at slightly below the price commonly asked by distributors. They also use the lower prices to bargain for key display space or in-store play of the music.

Once you have set your retail price, the next step is to decide what your store wholesale price will be when you sell to record stores directly, and at what price you will sell to distributors. At this time, most distributors sell to stores at approximately 55 to 65% of the retail list price (or between $4.75 and $6.00). Distribuors buy from record companies at approximately 25 to 40% of the retail list price (or between $2.30 and $3.50).

Appendix II

Manufacturing Compact Discs

SINCE THEIR INTRODUCTION IN THE FALL OF 1982, digital audio compact discs (CDs) have made a dramatic impact. In 1986, statistics from The Recording Institute of America (RIAA) showed CD sales totalling more than $930.1 million dollars, close to the same dollar volume as sales for LPs/EPs during the same year. The Consumer Electronics Association's Annual Review showed factory sales of compact disc players totalling $630 million dollars. Industry predictions are that sales of both CDs and CD players will continue to skyrocket.

A CD is a polycarbonate disc, coated with a reflective metal and sealed with plastic, that digitally stores music (or other audio information) in micrometer size pits arranged on a continuous spiral track on one side of the disc. The information is read optically by the laser beam in the compact disc player while the disc rotates. The digital signal is processed and amplified through the audio playback system.

The sound you hear is crisp and clear, without distortion, hiss, wow, flutter, modulation noise, frequency or mistrack distortion, provided of course that your master tape is free of these as well. Background noises common to cassettes or records are nonexistent, unless they were digitized from an analog tape that already contained these noises. CDs have a wide dynamic range (over 190 decibals) and an essentially flat frequency response from 5 Hz to 20,000 Hz.

Compact discs come in two sizes. The 4¾" long playing CD holds a maximum of 74 minutes of music. The new 3" CD single, introduced by Sony Corporation in the summer of 1987, holds up to 22 minutes of music. Sony Corporation introduced a patented plastic adapter that surrounds the CD single so that it can be played on any compact disc player.

PREMASTERING

CD mastering is begun by converting your music to the universal standard used by CD manufacturers: a ¾" U-Matic video tape, prepared in Sony PCM 1610 or 1630 format with a sampling frequency of 44.1 KHz.

Some CD manufacturers will accept tapes prepared on JVC ½" VHS video tape or JVC ¾" U-Matic video tape with a sampling frequency of 44.1 KHz. They will, however, convert the data to the universal standard by making a tape transfer or using a format converter that changes the data directly.

For the best conversion to digital audio video tape use the same master from which you recorded and edited your final mixes, not a second or third generation copy. Producers preparing master tapes for cassettes or records may prefer to remix the master tape for CD conversion because of the greater dynamic range available in CD format.

Music recorded with a different sampling rate than 44.1 KHz, must be converted to that standard. The preferred method for converting differing sampling rates is to use a transcoder (such as a Studer SFC-16), a signal processor that translates from one sampling rate to another, while the signal is in the digital domain. Degradation generating methods that first convert the music back to an analog master before making another conversion to video tape should be avoided.

As some manufacturers experience difficulty in accommodating playing times that approach the maximum limits stated previously, check with them about time tolerance limits before premastering begins.

Once the conversion has been made to digital audio video tape, a recording engineer will fill out a SMPTE Time Code Log to specifications set by each CD manufacturer. The log tells precisely where each track of music starts and stops in terms of video frames (absolute time).

Your engineer will indicate whether a high frequency boost or emphasis was used in recording any track by writing 'on' or 'off' for each track of music; will indicate whether any cross fades were used; and will note exact locations of any disturbing effects or noises. An accurately filled out SMPTE log is extremely important because a CD manufacturer uses it to insert the PQ subcode on the compact disc. This conveys information to your compact disc player about the total number of selections on the disc, start time, total start and stop times of tracks, index points, preemphasis on/off and other information. If your SMPTE log is inaccurate, compact disc players may not properly reproduce the music on your disc.

Before sending the tape for manufacturing, you and the engineer should listen to it very carefully. What you hear is what you'll get on your CDs. The manufacturer will duplicate what you send. Unlike disc mastering, where some enhancement can be added or deleted, there is no such thing as 'fixing it during

Senior Audio Engineer Ed Thompson premasters for compact disc manufacturing at the studios of Discovery Systems, Dublin, Ohio, a compact disc manufacturer. Equipment pictured: DMR 4000 (2); Audio Editor DAE 1100; Cue Editor DAQ 1000; Sony 1630.

disc mastering' once the digital master tape has been prepared. If there is an error on your tape, there will be an error on your disc. Your engineer should also make sure the tape is free of hold errors and mutes, and that the tracks and track times noted on the tape are consistent with what is noted on the SMPTE Time Code Log. Many premastering companies will analyze your tape with a digital tape analyzer, such as the Sony DTA-2000.

The conversion of your master tape to required industry standards and an accurately filled out SMPTE Time Code Log are best done by a facility specializing in CD premastering.

Charges for premastering (including analog to digital conversion) range from $100–$150 an hour. When the transfer is being made from an analog tape without additional remixes or enhancements, the transfer and preparation of the SMPTE log will take approximately 1½ to 2 times the length of the recorded music. If additional editing or enhancement is required prior to conversion, get a time and money estimate first.

MASTERING

The mastering and manufacturing of CDs requires a combination of lasers and robotics as well as very high standards of quality control and cleanliness. Numerous steps in the manufacturing process occur in cleanrooms, since even the smallest particles of dust will affect the final product. Employees working in these cleanrooms wear special clothing, face protectors and gloves. Each step of the process is carefully checked for flaws.

Once the CD manufacturer receives your video tape, an engineer will listen to verify that any discrepancies, noises or errors are logged on your SMPTE Time Code Log and verify that it is accurately filled out.

Next, he or she will insert the PQ subcode, the time, display and control data needed for the compact disc.

Two different processes are used to convert the digital information on video tape to a master disc and then to stampers for mass production.

The most common is glass mastering. The digital information on your master video tape is used to control a laser beam. Its light exposes a layer of photo sensitive material that has been applied to a carefully ground and polished glass master disc. When photographically developed, the exposed areas become microscopic pits (the information bearing formations on the disc). There are close to 3 billion of these pits on a long playing CD; viewed through a microscope, they look much like Morse code dots and dashes.

The glass master is then coated with a thin layer of metal in order to render the pit surface electroconductive and played on a master player to check for defects, track numbering, phase depth, tracking and RF signal.

Negative metal masters ('fathers') and positive metal masters ('mothers') are generated to make the metal stampers used for CD production by a process known as electroforming. These techniques are similar to those used in making stampers for records except that they occur in cleanroom conditions.

Because these processes differ from manufacturer to manufacturer, glass masters or stampers generated at one manufacturer cannot be used to make CDs at a different manufacturer.

Direct Metal Mastering was developed by Teldec Schallplatten GmbH, the same manufacturers who developed Direct Metal Mastering for LPs. This technology is still under development.

In this process, a thin copper layer is 'sputtered' over a glass substrate and pits are 'embossed' on the metal layer with the digital information from your video tape. A 'galvanic' process is used to prepare stampers for CD production. A good technical description of this process may be found in Ken Pohlmann's excellent article "DMM for CD" in the February 1987 issue of Mix Magazine.

Advantages of the DMM process for a CD manufacturer are that the mastering equipment costs less than glass mastering equipment and the process does not have to occur in cleanroom conditions. Those advantages may get passed on to you as decreased mastering costs when DMM for CD is commercialized.

Mastering Costs. Costs for glass mastering vary from approximately $900–$1500; and for CD singles from $350–$500. The price includes making stampers. Some manufacturers charge extra for PQ encoding; some include it in the mastering price.

Some will make a reference CD that is analogous to the glass master. It can be played many times, just like a manufactured CD, but no copies can be made from it. The price per reference disc will be approximately the same as for the glass master. Like reference lacquers for records, the reference CD verifies the accuracy of the transfer from the master tape.

MANUFACTURING

Once stampers have been made, injection molding techniques are used to manufacture final discs. Optical grade polycarbonate is used and processes occur in cleanroom conditions.

Then each disc is coated with a thin layer of metal, usually silver or aluminum, to create a reflective surface. In cases where optimum quality and price are demanded, gold may be used. The surface on the pit information side of the disc is hermetically sealed with an ultraviolet cured plastic coating to protect it from scratches and oxidation. The CD label is printed on the protective coating using silk screen techniques and ultraviolet cured ink.

Most manufacturing facilities do a final quality control check by 'reading' selected discs for any defects and either playing them on high speed test equipment or listening in real time.

Once the discs are approved, they are ready to be packaged and shipped to the record company.

Manufacturing Costs. Manufacturing costs for discs range from $1.50–$3.50 each. Although prices have yet to be set for CD singles, executives from Sony Corporation expressed the hope that they

Compact discs receive their reflective metal coating in a cleanroom, 1000 times cleaner than a hospital operating room, at LaserVideo, Inc., Anaheim, California.

would be "under a $1.00". A few manufacturers are happy to run small quantities (40–500). Most prices include the silk screening of single color labels if you use the standard colors offered by the manufacturer.

The average delivery time for CD manufacturing is 3–6 weeks.

Good places to research CD facilities are Mix Magazine or the Billboard International Buyers Guide.

GRAPHICS

CD Graphics. The graphics commonly packaged with discs are booklets and inlay cards (sometimes called tray cards) seen through the back of a 'jewel' box. The main part of the inlay card is the approximate size of the booklet but has two perforated edges that can hold some printing.

The common CD packages are:

► The transparent plastic jewel box, just large enough to hold the CD and graphics. When packaged for sale, the jewel box will be polywrapped, like a record or cassette.

► The windowless 6"X12" long box (or spaghetti box) that contains a jewel box and its graphics. The long box is generally printed on the outside with similar cover graphics used on booklets or inlay cards.

► The generic box is a long box that has a die cut

window through which the jewel box is displayed.

► The blister pack is a clear plastic version of the long box. The booklet is placed in the top portion of the pack and the jewel boxed CD in the bottom.

Before mastering begins, all graphics and packaging materials must be in the hands of the manufacturer. These include positive film for the compact disc label, booklets, inlay cards, any printed materials for alternative packaging and preprinted packaging materials such as the generic box or long box. CD manufacturers supply the jewel boxes and blister packs.

Common errors that hold up manufacturing are graphics that are incorrectly submitted or sized. Your CD manufacturer will provide you with exact graphic requirements, including size specifications and color selection for labels. They will also provide specs to help meet the following copy requirements: (1) the universal CD logo; (2) origin of manufacture, particularly if your CDs are manufactured outside of the USA for sale in the USA. To avoid problems clearing customs, CD labels must be printed with words showing the manufacturing origin such as "manufactured in Japan". If CDs manufactured in the USA are to be shipped to other countries, use the words "Manufactured in the USA".

A word of caution: some record companies that manufacture records, cassettes and compact discs add a few extra cuts of music to the compact discs and forget to include the information on their graphic materials. This mistake usually occurs when the graphic designer simply shrinks the record album graphics down to the size necessary for compact discs without adding the additional information.

The following checklists are labeled 'mandatory' for information that must be included on your compact disc label and other packaging materials; and 'optional' for information that can be included when and if you have the room.

Universal CD logo.

COMPACT DISC LABEL: MANDATORY

► Compact disc title

► Compact disc catalog number

► Universal compact disc logo

► Record company name and logo

► Copyright notice for the songs†

► Copyright notice for the CD†

► ASCAP or BMI affiliation†

COMPACT DISC LABEL: OPTIONAL

► Song titles in sequence

► Lengths of songs

► Name(s) of song publisher(s)

► Total length of playing side

► Origin of manufacture

CD BOOKLETS AND INLAY CARDS: MANDATORY

► Compact disc title

► Compact disc catalog number

► Universal compact disc logo

► Record company name and logo

► Copyright notice for the songs†

► Copyright notice for the CD†

► Copyright notice for the graphic designer†

► ASCAP or BMI affiliation†

► Song titles in sequence

► Lengths of songs

► Name(s) of song composer(s)

► Name(s) of song publisher(s)

► Names of primary musicians and instruments played

► Name(s) of producer(s)

► Total length of playing time

CD BOOKLETS AND INLAY CARDS: OPTIONAL

► Origin of manufacture

► Universal Price Code (UPC Code)

► Name and mailing address of your record label

► Mail order price, ordering information, mail order form (with information about other records, compact discs, cassettes or other materials your company sells).

► Credits for other people or firms involved in your project

▶ Biographical material or information about the music, lyrics, and musicians

▶ Lyric sheets

▶ Any special dedications or thanks

CD INLAY CARD SPINE: MANDATORY

▶ Compact disc title

▶ Compact disc catalog number

CD INLAY CARD SPINE: OPTIONAL

▶ Record company name and logo

▶ Universal Price Code (UPC Code)

Printing and Packaging Prices. Prices are average and are not quoted for all color or booklet page variables.

▶ Average prices for 1000 inlay or tray cards printed in 1 color on book stock are $165; for 5000, $270; and for 25,000, $725. Prices include scoring for folding.

▶ Average prices for a 4-page CD booklet with 4 color covers and 1 color (black) insides printed on book stock: 1000, $575; 5000, $750; 25,000, $1875. Prices include inlay cards, folding, stitching and scoring.

▶ Average prices for printed long or spaghetti boxes in four colors on board: 2000, $480; 5000, $1025; 25,000, $5605.

▶ Jewel box with graphics booklets: $.25 each.

▶ Polywrapped jewel box and graphics: $.35 each.

▶ Long Box: includes jewel box, disc and graphics: $.50 each.

▶ Blister pack: includes jewel box, disc and graphics: $.60 each.

▶ Estimates for additional services such as promotional stickers or other inserts will be quoted separately.

▶ Shipping prices are FOB. Ask for an estimate.

*The CD catalog number is an arbitrary number you select for quick reference to each CD title you issue under your label. Number future CD releases sequentially. Don't get tricky; –101 or #1001 are good starts. Numbers like 1405 or THS 627 are illogical and hard for dealers and distributors to work with.

†Publishing and copyright are discussed in Chapter 9, "Song Rights".

SALES, PROMOTION AND PRICING

Most of the information you need to sell and promote your CDs effectively is included in Chapters 1 and 2, 'Promotion' and 'Sales.'

The undiscounted retail list price of most long playing CDs is $16.99. $10.99 and $12.99 are the most common discounted prices. At the time that Sony Corporation announced manufacturing capabilities for its CD single, industry guesses were that the retail price would be 'under $5.00'.

Although you set the price, the above prices are industry standards against which you will be competing. Once you have set the retail price, the same industry standards apply for wholesale discounts to distributors and stores set forth in the sales chapter.

The common sales packages seen in record stores are the long box or the blister pack; a polywrapped jewel box is most often used when filling mail orders.

Many radio stations prefer to play CDs because they deliver a crisper sound over the airwaves. Stations also prefer their compactness and durability. When querying radio stations during your preliminary market research, ask about preferred airplay formats.

Grateful Dead Merchandising has rereleased Bob Weir's "Ace" on compact disc and has made it available to fans only through mail order.

Appendix III
New Technologies

by Craig Anderton

Craig Anderton is the author of Home Recording for Musicians, The Digital Delay Handbook, MIDI for Musicians, Guitar Gadgets, Electronic Projects for Musicians *and* The Electronic Musician's Dictionary. *He is also the editor of* Electronic Musician Magazine. *He does production and technical consultation for Narada Records and several individual artists, with most preproduction occurring in his MIDI-based home studio.*

Sony Digital Audio Tape Recorder.

THE ART OF RECORDING IS CONSTANTLY CHANGING and new technologies and techniques make life more exciting and confusing. Important advances in recent years are digital audio, low-cost cassette-based multi-track machines and the 'tapeless studio'.

DIGITAL RECORDING

For years, signals were recorded on tape via analog techniques; in other words, the taped signal was similar to the original sound source. Digital techniques, however, operate in a different manner and what is recorded on tape bears no sonic resemblance to the original sound source.

Digital recording requires an *analog-to-digital converter* between the sound source and the recorder. The device takes a series of 'snapshots' of the audio signal—typically 44,100 snapshots per second—and determines the voltage level of the signal at the time of each snapshot. This voltage level is translated into a numeric code; it is this code that gets recorded on tape.

Then a *digital-to-analog* converter is needed at the output of the recorder to convert the coded digital signal into analog.

Why take this roundabout route? A number recorded on tape is not subject to the same degradation as an analog signal recorded onto tape. When an analog signal picks up noise, you hear noise mixed in with the signal. If a digital signal picks up noise, the digital-to-analog converter recognizes only the numbers and not the noise (or hum, or myriad other problems). Thus, the decoded output signal is virtually identical to the encoded input signal.

Many people feel that digital recording and signal storage are the wave of the future and that before too long all recording will be done digitally. Others feel that while digital recording holds great promise, there are some problems with it in its present form. The problems most often identified are harshness in the treble regions and unnatural distortion characteristics (soft passages are more distorted than loud passages). Some listeners go so far as to say that listening to digitally recorded music is more fatiguing to the ear.

Nonetheless, for a technology that is in its infancy, digital recording yields impressive results. In fact, only high quality analog equipment can equal the sound quality of even low end digital recording equipment.

While hourly rates for digital multi-track recording are well beyond the recording budgets of most independent labels, a cost effective alternative for digital live recording is available. Several manufacturers offer equipment that converts analog signals into digital audio signals suitable for recording on videocassette machines (VHS or Beta) using consumer grade videotape. The specs are impressive: dynamic ranger greater than 86 dB, THD less than 0.01%, and virtually flat frequency response. The most common digital audio adapter is the Sony PCM-F1; many compact disc manufacturers are set up to accept PCM-F1 masters. Although the tape cannot be edited easily, it is possible to use two VCRs and one PCM-F1 to create extremely high fidelity sound-on-sound recordings.

Even more promising is the Digital Audio Tape recorder (DAT). Using technology that borrows from, but miniaturizes, the digital audio devices mentioned above, DAT recorders meet or exceed the fidelity of the compact disc and offer two hours of music on a tape cartridge smaller than a standard audio cassette. DATs have had a controversial birthing; their introduction in this country has been delayed because some record companies want Congress to require the installation of circuitry that would make it impossible to copy CDs, thus discouraging home taping of copyrighted material. When DATs become available, they will offer tremendous audio capabilities to small studios for about $1,000 and it will be economical to buy two DATs to do album assembly and editing.

LOW-COST CASSETTE-BASED MULTI-TRACK MACHINES

Several companies (including TEAC, Fostex and Yamaha) manufacture four-track recorders that use standard cassette tapes rather than reel-to-reel tapes. This reduces the size of the transport (thus cutting manufacturing costs) and reduces the cost of operation (cassettes are inexpensive compared with open-reel tape). Virtually all cassette multi-tracks include noise reduction and some run the tape at twice normal speed. When you use high-quality tape, these features help achieve surprisingly good results. Some cassette-based multi-tracks are stand-alone units, but others are packaged with an integral mixer and sometimes other controls or patch points as well.

THE "TAPELESS" STUDIO

There are two ways to implement a tapeless studio. One is to digitize the audio signal and store it in a computer storage system, typically a computer's hard disk. Once stored, the signal can be manipulated and edited with great precision—far more so than with razor blades and splicing tape. This approach is very expensive at present, even for limited recording time, but we can expect hard disk-based tapeless studios to cost under $15,000 before too long.

A less costly method involves synchronizing a MIDI sequencer to tape. MIDI (Musical Instrument Digital Interface) is a way to communicate musical data between elements of an electronic music system (synthesizers, samplers, drum machines, even MIDI-controlled signal processors). Playing a MIDI keyboard sends out data that describes your performance in terms of notes, dynamics, amount of pitch bending, tempo, and so on. If you record this data in computer memory (and you don't need much memory since you're recording a computer 'shorthand', not digitized audio for their performance), then you can play it back and recreate the performance. This is analogous to the way a player piano works, except that you're storing notes in memory instead of on paper rolls—and editing is easy. A MIDI sequencer can hold dozens of tracks of data, each of which can drive an individual MIDI instrument.

Synchronizing a sequencer to tape lets you record acoustic tracks on tape and electronic tracks on the sequencer. During mixdown, the multi-track and se-

Composer and Producer David Litwin's San Francisco recording studio. Pictured here, left to right and top to bottom are: Apple Macintosh Plus with Performer sequencing software and Sound Designer sound modeling software; Customized sequential Six-Trak analog synthesizer; Sequential Drumtracks digital drum computer; Sequential Prophet-5 analog synthesizer; Sequential Polysequencer; Yamaha DX-7 digital synthesizer; TEAC Model 2 mixer (for drums); Otari remote control for Otari Mk III 8 eight-track recorder; ARP 2600 analog synthesizer; Sequential Prophet-2002 digital sampler; Otari 5050-B 2-track tape recorder; UREI 964 digital metronome; Yamaha FB-01 FM Sound Generator; Oberheim synthesizer expander module; Technics SL-B200 turntable w/Grado M+ stylus; Tapco 2200 graphic equalizer; Yamaha RV-7 digital reverb; Barcus-Berry 402 sonic maximizer; Sansui SC 3110 cassette deck; Fostex 3180 reverb; DeltaLabs Effectron 2; Furman Parametric EQ; Sansui amplification; Otari Mk III-8 eight track recorder; Symetrix 528 voice processor; TEAC 3300 2-track recorder; RAMSA WR-8210A console; dbx 4-channel noise reduction; dbx 2-channel noise reduction; dbx 161 compressor/limiter; Auratone speakers; JBL 4311 speakers; Network Sound Effects library (89 albums). Numerous equipment is not pictured including other tape recorders, amplifiers, sound generators, equalizers and so forth.

quencer are synched together. This plays taped acoustic tracks and 'live' electronic tracks into your master simultaneously. Thanks to MIDI, automated mixing, automated signal processing changes and audio/video synchronization are now within financial reach of small studios. Time spent learning about MIDI will be well worth your while.

Recording has progressed significantly since its inception and continues to grow. It is easier than ever to ensure that what you record on tape is the most accurate representation of your sound.

Appendix IV
Financing Recordings

*by Edward R. Hearn
and J. Gunnar Erickson*

This article has been prepared by Edward R. Hearn, an attorney with offices in Palo Alto and San Jose, who specializes in entertainment and computer matters, and by J. Gunnar Erickson, a partner with the law firm of Armstrong, Hendler & Barnet in Los Angeles. The firm specializes in entertainment law. Mr. Hearn is a Director of California Lawyers for the Arts (CALA), a bar association, based in San Francisco that focuses on the legal needs of artists and art groups. Messrs. Erickson and Hearn are co-authors, with Mark Halloran, of Musician's Guide to Copyright, *published by CALA.*

THERE ARE MANY APPROACHES TO CONSIDER WHEN planning the financing of your recording project. An initial decision to make is whether to handle all phases of the project (including financing) yourself or to approach an existing record company.

FINANCING AN INDEPENDENT RECORDING

Independent recordings are financed in one of three methods: self-financing, borrowing or profit sharing. This section will discuss these methods and the advantages and drawbacks inherent in each.

Self-financing. Self-financing can be the most desirable way of funding an independent record venture. It is the only technique that allows you to be free of financial obligations to lenders and gives you maximum artistic and financial control. Although it means that you must bear all the risk of the project, it also means that you will enjoy the benefits.

Frequently, financial control results in artistic control of the recording. Tension can develop between financial backers, who want things done in a certain way to insure the project makes a profit, and the artist, who feels pressured to compromise the music.

Self-financing also minimizes the paperwork, record keeping, and other business complications involved in producing a record.

One technique of self-financing, in addition to the obvious one of drawing on savings, is to presell the record to friends. This technique should be used with extreme caution and only when you are very close to production and are absolutely certain that the record will be issued. Limit these types of sales to sympathetic friends. Failure to deliver can constitute fraud and invite hassles in the form of lawsuits or proceedings by governmental consumer fraud units. It can also destroy your credibility with your most loyal friends.

Borrowing. Borrowing is the second basic technique for raising funds. By 'borrowing' we mean accepting a loan for a fixed sum of money and agreeing to repay that sum plus a specified percentage of interest by a certain time. Arrangements where the return to the lender depends on the success of the record will be discussed under the section on profit sharing.

There are two possible sources of loans. The first is commercial sources. They include banks, finance companies, savings and loan associations, pawn shops, and credit cards with cash advance provisions.

Interest on commercial loans secured by such collateral as a home, an auto or even a co-signature of a person in whom the bank has confidence will usually be lower than interest on unsecured loans. The reason is obvious: the risk is lower. No commercial lender will take unproven records or songs as collateral. Loans backed up with collateral or the co-signature of a credit worthy individual are also easier to secure.

In addition to a written business plan, commercial lenders may ask for personal financial statements and income tax returns if the loan is to be made to an individual. They will certainly check your credit history. The reasons are obvious: they need to know you have a sound financial plan and that you are financially responsible.

If the loan is being made to your business, commercial lenders will want to see the profit and loss statements of your business for the past two to three years.

Since commercial lenders make money lending money, you should shop for the best deal.

A second source for loans is family and friends. Usually they will lend money at a rate lower than that of a commercial lender. The important thing to consider when borrowing from friends is, because of the close relationship and the potential for straining it, strong pressures for timely repayment may result which would be greater than the legal obligation to repay.

When you borrow from friends, the usury laws of most states come into play. These statutes limit the amount of interest which a private lender can charge a borrower. Banks and other commercial lenders are generally exempt from the usury limits and can charge higher rates.

Whether you borrow from friends or from commercial lenders, you will want to structure a written repayment plan that states the amount loaned, the rate of interest, and the method of repayment.

This can be a simple written promissory note: "On or before June 15, 1989, John Debtor promises to pay Sally Lender the sum of $2,500 plus 9% interest from January 1, 1988, (signed) John Debtor."

The note from a commercial lender is more complex, but it will contain the same elements. Sometimes commercial loans are structured so that you pay a smaller monthly amount the first two years and a larger one the next two to three years. Once again, shop for the most favorable terms, interest and monthly payback amounts.

Profit Sharing. The third technique for raising funds is profit sharing arrangements where an investor puts funds (or time) into a project and gets a return based on the success of the recording.

The arrangement can take several forms, depending on whether the investor is 'active' or 'passive'.

Active Investors. Active investors are individuals who put up money to finance a project for another person and become involved in the project (or fail to take adequate action to insulate themselves from responsibility). They assume all of the risks of the business, including financial liability for all losses, even if the losses go beyond the amount invested.

The forms of business in which the participants have this financial exposure could be a general partnership, a joint venture or a corporation and the profits or losses of such businesses are shared among the participants according to the nature of their agreement.

A general partnership is co-ownership of an ongoing enterprise in which the partners share both control and profits. A joint venture is a general partnership which either has a very short term or a limited purpose. The production of a single record could be termed a joint venture.

The general partners and the joint venturers are each personally liable for all the debts of the enterprise. The liability is not limited to the amount that they invested nor to the debts which were incurred with their approval. All of the personal assets of each of the general partners or joint venturers are liable for repayment of the debts incurred by the enterprise.

Generally, such persons are responsible for the obligations of the business even if they have not given their approval or have not been involved in incurring business debts.

If a corporation is formed, then even if the project is a total failure, only the assets of the corporation are vulnerable to the business creditors. A corporation is a separate entity formed under state laws. Its ownership is divided among its shareholders.

A corporate structure provides limited liability to the shareholders. If you are thinking about setting up a corporation, you'll need some sound legal advice.

If you are interested in learning more about the structuring of partnerships or corporations, your local library should have some good books on setting up a small business that will provide the information you need.

Passive Investors. A more complex category of investments is that in which backers provide money for the project but take no role in the management and affairs. Such backers are passive investors who are hoping for a return on their money based on the success of the project.

The primary advantage of profit sharing arrangements from the point of view of the independent is that the downside risks are shared. If a recording fails to sell, the borrower is not obligated to repay the investors. Offsetting this advantage are several problems that make profit sharing the most complicated form of financing an independent recording.

The foremost of the problems are the security law requirements. Any time one enters into an agreement in which someone gives money for a project with the understanding that part of the profits are to be shared with them and the investors do not actively participate in the management of the funds or the operation of the business, a 'security' has been sold. A security can be a promissory note, stock, points or any other form of participation in a profit sharing arrangement, whether written or oral, where the investor's role in the business is passive. Because general partners and joint venturers are actively involved in the business, their participation is generally not considered a security.

Limited partnerships, promissory notes structured with profit sharing, corporate stock and contracts providing for points participation are clearly securities, and the securities laws of state and federal statutes must be satisfied when these types of funding are used. Failure to comply can have serious civil and criminal consequences.

What does this legal talk mean to you? Why should you have to worry about it if all you want to do is raise some money to record some music? The securities laws were enacted to protect investors from being harmed by the fraud of others, by their lack of sophistication or even their inability to afford to lose the money they invest in the project. The legal burden falls on the one seeking to raise the money to make certain the investor is getting a fair deal and fully understands the risks involved. "Let the seller beware" is the rule that operates.

If you want someone else to invest money in your project without allowing them a hand in controlling the project, then you should be willing to accept some responsibility to them. Willing or not, state and federal statutes place responsibility on you.

Repayment of Loans Conditional on the Success of the Venture. In these types of loans, the debt is evidenced by a promissory note and repayment is conditional on the success of the funded project. Because such a loan is a security, the note should set out the terms of repayment, including interest rates and payment schedules.

A common form of this kind of loan is a 'point' arrangement in which a percentage (called 'points') of the sales of the record are shared with a producer who only puts in time; or some other investor who only puts in money. This arrangement could be provided for in a written contract rather than in the form of a conditional promissory note.

Limited Partnerships. Like a general partnership, a limited partnership also has co-ownership and shared profits, but only some of the participants are entitled to control or manage the enterprise. These are termed the general partners. The other investors are called limited partners and their only involvement is the passive one of putting funds into the project.

A partner receives that percentage of the business profits or losses set out in the agreement between the partners; for example, 10% of the net profits up to $10,000 and 5% of the net profits after the first $10,000. The term of the partnership is often limited to a specified period; for example, three to five years. If the project has not earned the hoped for return to the investor by the end of the term, the investor has to absorb the loss.

There are also rules in the federal law and in several states that apply to limited partnerships and other security investments, if the investments are structured as a private offering, which are easier to qualify under the law than are public offerings. For example, in California, the investments may not be taken from more than 35 persons; there can be no advertising of the investment offering; the investors must represent that they are making the investment for their own keeping with no intent of transferring it to others and, either the person investing the money must have a preexisting business or personal relationship with you, or they or their professional financial advisors, because of their business experience, can reasonably be presumed to have the ability to protect their own interests.

Corporate Shares. A third way to raise investment capital is through the sale of shares in a corporation. Corporate shares are securities and are usually sold for a stated number of dollars per share. That money is then used to operate the business or pay for a specific project. A shareholder owns whatever percentage of the corporation his or her shares represent of the total number of shares sold.

Shareholders participate in the profits of the corporation when they are distributed as dividends and vote on shareholder issues according to their percentage of ownership.

Whatever method of financing you choose, it is wise to check with your lawyer and to set up a good financial record keeping system with your bookkeeper.

Appendix V
Negotiating Record Contracts

*by Edward R. Hearn
and J. Gunnar Erickson*

*This article has been prepared by
Edward R. Hearn, an attorney with
offices in Palo Alto and San Jose, who
specializes in entertainment and com-
puter matters, and by J. Gunnar
Erickson, a partner with the law firm of
Armstrong, Hendler & Barnet in Los
Angeles. The firm specializes in enter-
tainment law. Mr. Hearn is a Director
of California Lawyers for the Arts
(CALA), a bar association, based in
San Francisco that focuses on the legal
needs of artists and art groups. Messrs.
Erickson and Hearn are co-authors, with
Mark Halloran, of* Musician's Guide to
Copyright, *published by CALA.*

AN ALTERNATIVE TO RAISING FUNDS TO PRODUCE your recording is to approach independent record companies. Within the last decade, independent record labels specializing in particular styles of music have become very successful in reaching and developing niche markets. By researching these labels, you might find one that successfully markets music that fits your style and might be interested in producing, manufacturing and/or distributing your record.

If you succeed, you will have to negotiate and sign a contract. Careful consideration must be given to the terms of the contract, since it will be the road map by which the rights and responsibilities between the label and you will be determined.

Before examining the major issues involved in negotiating with a record company, it would be useful to summarize the major advantages and disadvantages between producing, manufacturing and distributing your album through your own effort, as compared to turning some or all of that responsibility over to a record label.

Pros and Cons of Being Your Own Record Company. Retaining full control over production, manufacturing and distribution, enables you to determine and identify the marketing style and image you wish to project. You retain quality and aesthetic control over all the elements involved and realize a larger amount of the income that results from the sale of your albums, thus providing a quicker return on your investment.

The disadvantages of retaining your own distribution include: limitations of the geographical scope of distribution you can handle; the difficulty of collecting money on sales from record stores or intermediate distributors; financing the costs of production, manufacturing and inventory as well as marketing, promotion and distribution. These activities take substantial amounts of time and money and must be weighed against using that time and money to further develop your talents.

Pros and Cons of Making Arrangements with a Record Company. The chief advantage of releasing your album with an independent record label is it generally has the distribution mechanism in place. It is organized to handle the time and costs of financing and administering the production, manufacture, marketing and distribution of records. It can absorb the financial risk, including the risk of collecting money from the buyers of records. In addition, the company may have developed a reputation in the music community for a certain style of music and can move a greater volume of records in a wider geographical territory.

The negative aspects of distributing through a record company include: seeing less income per unit sold, as well as a longer period of time to receive that income; giving up control over elements of your career or music and making a long term commitment for future recordings as a partial exchange for the company assuming the financing, production, manufacture, marketing and distribution of your records.

One of the realities of the music business is that the distribution artery is the most congested when it comes to the flow of money to the seller of the albums. Both major and independent record labels have experienced difficulty collecting from distributors and record stores—particularly when record chains and distribution companies suddenly go out of business, declare bankruptcy, or sell their businesses. Frequently, there is a substantial delay between placing the albums in the market and the return of income to the artist. Consequently, any distributor or record label selected should be carefully investigated to determine its success level and reputation for honesty and financial responsibility.

RECORDING DEALS

The amount of money that you will realize from signing with a record company depends on the type of recording deal that you make. The following section outlines various options and some of the industry standards regarding possible financial returns.

Straight Distribution Deals. In this type of deal, you deliver fully manufactured and packaged records, cassettes or compact discs to a record company. Some labels may only distribute records, while you do the marketing and promotion, others may do everything. In Canada, many small labels have made deals with major record companies for distribution only, a practice that may eventually make its way to the United States as independent distribution networks continue to erode.

In a distribution only deal, the record label will either contract directly with stores or deal with networks of independent distributors or both, selling to them at wholesale prices in the ranges mentioned elsewhere in this book. They may also sell you your records at a wholesale distributor price or less so that you can sell them at performances or to your fan mailing list.

In a distribution plus promotion arrangement, the label distributes your record and promotes it.

In either case, you will receive money only on records actually sold and paid for. The amount paid on a straight distribution deal typically ranges between 20–30% of the wholesale selling price. If the company also picks up promotion and marketing costs, then it will charge that cost against the money owed to you, or structure the deal to pay a royalty to you that will leave the company with a sufficient margin to cover all of its costs and a reasonable profit. When negotiating this type of deal, ask that any percentages be specified as a net cent per unit.

Production and Distribution Deals (P & D Deals). In this type of deal, you deliver a fully mixed recording master and artwork to the record label, which then assumes the responsibility of manufacturing, marketing and distributing your records, cassettes or compact discs.

If the company only distributes your record, you will receive a sum equivalent to the wholesale price, minus a fee of 20–30% and other direct expenses that you authorized the company to pay. If marketing and promotional duties are involved, then these expenses could be deducted as direct costs, or the deal could be structured on a royalty basis, with a royalty of anywhere from 10% of retail to 16–18% of retail.

You will receive money only for records actually sold and paid for.

Production Deals. In this type of deal, you sign as an artist with a production company. The company is responsible for recording your music and for obtaining distribution through independent distributors or a record company. In many cases, contracts for these deals are structured similarly to record contracts because the production company will most typically make a P & D deal with a record label and then contract with you for a percentage of the royalty paid to it by the record company.

For example, a production company may have a P & D deal with a record company that pays 18% of the retail selling price on records sold. It might then contract with the artist to pay a royalty from between 6% and 10% of the retail selling price.

RECORDING CONTRACTS

The following outlines the major negotiating areas included in almost all record contracts, as well as industry standards. Major and independent labels tend to have obtusely written contracts which have been developed over a long period of time they are reluctant to change.

However, smaller independent companies sometimes work out arrangements that do not mirror these standards. These companies may be willing to step away from obtuse and confusing language to create a contract in plain English that is balanced between the interests of the record company and those of the artist; namely, to more equitably share the economic benefits realized from the skills and talents of the artist and the business expertise and mechanisms of the recording company. For example, some small labels encourage the artist to buy records from them at a substantial discount so that the artist can sell direct through mailing lists or at performances—a practice actively discouraged by most major recording labels.

Duration of the Contract. Recording contracts often obligate the artist to a 1 or 2 year period for the initial term and subsequent option periods of approximately 1 year each. The record company usually retains the authority to decide whether to exercise any options. The actual duration of the recording agreement can be anywhere between 5 to 7 years and sometimes longer, with the artist being obligated to produce anywhere from 5 to 10 albums.

The advantage of long duration contracts for a record company is it increases the chances to profit from the time and money spent developing your career and a market for your records. Contrary to media hype, fame and fortune are seldom achieved 'overnight'. In fact, a small label may insist on a long term commitment since its investment in you will have a greater financial impact than a major label's investment.

From the artist's perspective, the best approach would be to limit the term of the agreement to a 1 to 3 year period, with 1 album to be produced during each year of the contract. Limiting the term of the contract provides the opportunity to negotiate a more substantial agreement with the company or going with another label if that seemed to be the best course to follow in advancing your career.

If a major label deal is your goal, a limited duration contract would increase your opportunity to sign with one without it having to buy out the small label's agreement with you.

Bear in mind, though, if a small lable invests time and money in your career and is successful in generating a reasonable level of income for you in the process, you should carefully weigh the benefits of signing with a major label (where you probably will be one of many) against staying with the smaller one (where you may be the star!). Far too often, these benefits are discovered only after an unhappy relationship with a major recording label occurs.

Royalties. Different record companies use different formulas to identify the royalty percentage paid to an artist. The percentage can be based on the retail selling price for albums sold and paid for or on the wholesale cost to distributors or record stores.

Industry standards for first albums vary, but an artist royalty range, not including fees or percentages paid to a producer, typically varies from 6% of retail to 10%. The wholesale standard varies from 12% to 20%. Some companies base that royalty on 100% of sales, while others base it on 90% of sales.

Some companies agree to increase royalty percentages based on success. For example, an artist might earn a royalty of 6% up to the sale of 100,000 records; 8% on the sale of up to 250,000 records; and 10% when sales reach 500,000 records.

Some record companies deduct a sum for packaging, which ranges anywhere from 10% to 20% of the retail or wholesale royalty.

The most important thing you or your lawyer can do when negotiating royalties is to ask for a "net cents per unit". Being told that you will get a certain percentage per record without determining how it translates into actual "net cents per unit" will not provide you with the information you need.

For example, one label may offer you 10% of an $8.98 retail price, with a 15% packaging deduction, based on 100% of sales. The net cents per unit would be $.763.

Another label may offer the same 10% on an $8.98 retail price, with a 20% packaging deduction, based on 90% of sales. In this case, the net cents per unit would be $.646.

Record labels often provide a certain number of "free goods" to retailers and wholesalers for every identified number of units purchased. Generally, no royalties are paid on free goods.

For example, on the purchase of 100 units perhaps 15% are free and 85% are billed. In the examples given above, your net cents per unit would be further discounted by another 15% when measured against the actual number of units shipped.

By the same token, the free goods amount to a per unit discount on every 100 units shipped, resulting in less money per unit received by the record company.

The bottom line is to determine exactly the net cents per unit you will receive as a royalty. Since that royalty is paid only after bonus advances, production, and recording costs are recouped (sums that can be specified in your contract), you should figure out how many records the company will have to sell to recover those costs and you see your first dime.

Foreign Sales. Most contracts address the distribution of albums in foreign countries. For such sales, the amount of royalty paid to the artist is 50% to 75% of the domestic royalty. The rationale for this deduction is the record label is licensing an independent company in another territory to manufacture and distribute the albums in that territory. If the arrangement for foreign distribution is made with a company that has no relationship with the record company itself, then there is justification for the reduction in royalty. If, however, the foreign company and the record company are related, the justification is weakened, although not completely eliminated, since the foreign affiliate has its costs of doing business and generally must prove itself as a free standing profit center. The arrangement with the record company should provide for an alternate scale of foreign royalties depending on the relationship, if any, the record company has with a foreign distributor and what the distributor is paying the record company. (Read also "Selling Your Record in Foreign Markets" on page 176.)

Recoupment of Expenses and Advances.
Typically, a record company advances the costs of producing, manufacturing, promoting and distributing

the record and charges the production and recording costs against the artist's future royalties. For this reason, it is extremely important to nail down a ceiling cost for these expenses in your contract.

Sometimes companies advance a bonus sum for signing to the artist as well as costs for touring and videos. These are charged against the artist's future royalties.

Financial Statements. Your contract should specify the receipt of financial statements from the record company on a quarterly or semi-annual basis. Your first statement should itemize the amount spent on album production that will be recouped from royalties. In addition, the first and all subsequent statements should show the amount of records that have been distributed and whether those records were given away as promotional copies or actually sold. The total amount of money earned will either show as a debit or credit.

Authority to Use Your Name. The record company will want the authority to use your name, likeness and biographical material in its promotional activity for the album. You will have to give the record company the authority to do that. You should strive to have the record company grant you the right to have a say in how it will be promoting you, so that you will feel comfortable with the image to be projected.

Merchandising. Some record companies will try to acquire ownership rights for merchandising. These include the right to use your name or image or the artwork on your album for T-shirts, posters, concert booklets, etc. Since this activity can mean additional income for you, particularly when touring, you should strive to retain these rights.

Promotion. Critical in any arrangement with a record company is the promotional commitment that the record company is willing to make. It will do little good to have a record contract and an inventory of records with no commitment from the company to actively promote the album. While it may seem strange that a record company would spend money to produce and manufacture records and not promote them, such events do occur.

You should try and get the record company to commit to a minimum promotional level and perhaps work out a promotional plan of attack with them. This may include the record company advancing costs for touring. Most record companies, however, resist making contractual commitments, arguing that they want to wait until after the music is recorded. In this situation, your ability to retain good communication with key people in the record company may provide your best guarantee that your record will be actively promoted.

Publishing. Many record labels, both small and large, ask that publishing rights be assigned to them. You should remember that publishing in the music business often involves large sums and that whoever owns the publishing rights winds up with most of those dollars.

In the last decade, artists (and their lawyers) have been successful in not assigning publishing rights to record labels, arguing that a record label's primary job is to sell records. A publisher's job, they argue, is to sell songs, and since most record companies do not actively provide that service, the artist should be free to assign that right to a publishing company of his or her choice.

On the other hand, record companies will argue that participation in publishing income helps offset their investment risk in producing and marketing the record.

The purpose of this article has been to make you aware of options, suggest ways of investigating those options and help you understand the primary considerations involved in reviewing any contract proposed by a record or production company. It is always advisable, when faced with a financial or contractual situation, to solicit the advice of an attorney or accountant who is familiar with the music business and the way recording and publishing contracts are structured.

Appendix VI

Selling Your Record in Foreign Markets

by Holger Peterson

Holger Petersen is the Managing Director of Stony Plain Records, a Canadian independent label that releases about 15 albums per year and specializes in licensing deals. Stony Plain's catalog includes Ricky Skaggs, Amos Garrett, Maria Muldaur, King Biscuit Boy, Chris Hillman, David Grisman, The Whites, Bim, and Diamond Joe White. Mr. Peterson is also on the Board of Directors for the Canadian Independent Record Production Association and Alberta Recording Independent Association.

SALES OF RECORDS IN FOREIGN MARKETS HAVE BECOME a lucrative source of income for many independent record companies. An added advantage, of course, is that sales often lead to airplay and concert tours, thus stimulating additional income and the opportunity for foreign travel for their artists.

You can reach foreign markets in any of three ways: by finding a distributor who regularly exports to foreign markets, by licensing your master tape to a foreign record label, or by contracting with a foreign subpublisher. You must balance the desire to investigate or use these resources, however, with a realistic appraisal of *how* sales will be stimulated. Having a record in the bins of a record store in Australia or Japan does not guarantee it will sell.

The major reasons export distributors, foreign record labels, or publishers might be interested in doing business with you are these:

▶ An already perceived market exists and has been developed for the type of music you are recording. For independents, this often means non-mainstream recordings such as jazz, folk music, bluegrass, computer music, and so on.

▶ Your music has received airplay in your own country and/or enjoys a substantial reputation that can be exploited as promotional sales leverage in a foreign market.

▶ You will be touring in that country. As always, performances stimulate sales and provide a 'hook' or platform on which a promotional campaign can be mounted.

Export Deals. The simplest way to sell records in a foreign country is to find a distributor who regularly exports to foreign markets. The foreign distributor operates in the same way as a domestic one: the distributor buys your records at a discounted distributor's price and sells them at a wholesale price to record stores.

Ideally, you will find a distributor who can simultaneously distribute your record domestically. Then you can ship a minimum quantity (such as a box of records) to test the market potential at little risk to you or to the distributor.

Abroad, your record will retail for a price 30 to 100% higher than the domestic retail, depending on the price paid by the store to the distributor, the strength of the foreign currency, shipping costs, import duty, and local taxes.

As in most distribution deals, you will be paid on the basis of records actually sold. The monies are usually paid to your distributor within 30–90 days after the records are received by the record stores. (Remember, it sometimes takes weeks for shipments of records to arrive and clear customs in foreign countries.) Your distributor will then pay you within 30–90 days of receiving these monies. Thus, it may take as long as 6–9 months before you actually receive any monies due you.

Although most distributors have an established range of prices they like to pay for records for foreign export, the price is negotiable. There are several questions you ought to ask before a final price is agreed on. What volume of sales might you expect in a year? What is the retail price of the record likely to be and how will the price compare with those of the competition? Who pays shipping, taxes, and duty (you or the distributor)? How often will you receive an accounting?

Import distributors generally deal with a relatively small and specialized market compared with the major labels and their distributors. They seldom allocate promotional budgets for any one title because they don't do enough volume to justify them. For this reason, expect little or no promotion in the foreign market with an export deal.

LICENSING FINISHED MASTERS (LEASE DEALS)

When you make lease deals, you provide a master tape and art mechanicals to a foreign record company who will manufacture, market, promote, and distribute your record. The foreign record company covers the costs for all this, and you are paid a percentage of each sale. Lease deals have several advantages over other export arrangements:

▶ The record will have the backing of a label that may be nationally distributed by a major record label or by an already established network of independent labels. In Canada, for example, many established independents are themselves distributed by major record labels, even though they are producing non-mainstream records. The label might also have an existing catalog of and reputation for a particular genre of music it has helped establish.

► Compared to stores dealing with imports, retail stores dealing with established domestic record labels or distributors generally have better and more convenient return privileges and deal in more volume.

► Your record will be sold at a more competitive price and generally have wider distribution and some promotion.

► The potential for touring is enhanced. The label itself may help in connecting you with the right agent and will sometimes help negotiate tour support. The support can come in various forms, ranging from advertising your concert dates to picking up a portion of travel costs.

Licensing Contracts. All the general advice about terms in the appendix "Raising Money and Negotiating Record Contracts" by attorney Edward Hearn applies to foreign licensing. Remember: you should always consult an attorney who specializes in entertainment law when negotiating or finalizing any deal.

The percentage paid by the record company in a typical licensing contract is between 10 and 15% of the base price on 100% of records sold. The base price is the agreed-on retail list price less taxes, duties, and packaging. A fair packaging allowance might be 10% for an album jacket, 12% for cassettes, and 15% for foldout jackets or special packaging (including 12″ EPs).

Sometimes you can negotiate escalating percentages for increased sales. For example, you might receive 12% on 10,000 records sold and 13% on all subsequent records sold.

Advances against royalties are negotiable and depend on your stature as an artist, the sales potential you and the record company perceive, and your (or your attorney's) negotiating savvy.

The term of the agreement can vary, but three to five years is an average length. In many cases, the label will also want the incentive of an option for one or more future recordings.

All licensing contracts should contain an accounting-frequency clause. Contracts typically agree to issue financial statements and payments 30 to 60 days after each quarter or semi-annual time period. In most cases, you can only assume that the financial accounting is accurate, but, since licensing deals are conducted on the basis of mutual trust, most record companies work hard to maintain a reputation of honesty. (Certain avenues for checking that reputation are suggested later in this appendix.)

However, you will find it wise to include an audit clause in your contract in case a dispute over your financial statement should arise. The audit clause guarantees your right to dispute a financial statement through the request of a formal audit. The clause will outline auditing practices and will also stipulate the circumstances under which the record company might become responsible for audit costs. A typical clause might read, "In the event that an audit discloses a discrepancy equivalent to or greater than 10% of the money dispersed, the difference, interest, and cost of the audit is paid by the company."

FOREIGN SUBPUBLISHING

A foreign publisher, sometimes referred to as a "subpublisher" to distinguish it from your principal (domestic) publisher, has two main duties to perform on behalf of your publishing company: to administer the collection and payment of mechanical and performance royalties and to exploit (promote) songs, either by stimulating airplay or by getting other performers to record 'covers.'

The system works like this: most countries have a society that collects mechanical royalties from the record companies and performance royalties from radio stations and television stations. The society that collects mechanicals then pays the local publishers the amounts owing and the publisher in turn pays your publishing company. Thus, in order to collect foreign mechanical royalties, your publishing company must be represented in that territory by a local publisher. If you have no representation, the monies collected by each society are paid into an escrow fund, known as the "Black Box" fund. If no local publisher steps forth within seven years to claim the monies on behalf of a foreign record company, the fund is divvied up among local publishers. The amount each local publisher receives is determined by the publisher's annual gross income and years in business! What is really astonishing is that the amount paid into the fund per year is a whopping $20–22 million. The result is that foreign publishers have an income source that North American publishers don't have.

Foreign publishers also make more money from a successful record than their North American counterparts, since they receive a higher mechanical rate per record sold (in most European countries, for example, the rate is 8% of the retail price) and performance royalties are higher. For this reason, foreign publishers have a great incentive to exploit songs and diligently collect royalties. In fact, in some instances the foreign publisher, not the record company, plays the primary role in securing airplay for records. As a result, some artists find that it increases their leverage in getting a foreign licensing record deal if they make a publishing deal first. And in some cases, the foreign publisher actually helps secure a licensing or export deal. Artists who already have export deals may find it beneficial to make a subpublishing deal as well.

SUBPUBLISHING AGREEMENTS

A standard subpublishing agreement might be that 25% of all publishing income goes to the foreign publisher, with an increase to 50% for local covers on a specific composition. This gives the foreign publisher an incentive to persuade an artist in the assigned territory to record your composition.

How Do I Find the Right Company? As in any other business, your success in the music industry depends on establishing and maintaining contacts. If you don't have the contacts, you need to find someone who does, such as an entertainment lawyer, an artist's manager, or the owner or distributor of a record company doing business in foreign countries.

As you meet people in the industry, and before you enter into any agreement, keep these questions in mind:

► What is the history of the company? What is its reputation?

► What distribution systems does it have? How many stores does it do business with?

► What kind of catalog does the firm have—for example, what kind of music does it specialize in, if any?

► What kind of promotion does it normally give its records?

► Is the company financially solvent? Does it pay its bills on time?

You can ask all these questions—including that about solvency—directly to the company you are seeking to do business with. You should also ask them of companies who have done or are currently doing business with that firm.

For export deals, the logical place to look for contacts is through the distributor with whom you already do business who exports to foreign territories. If you want to establish contacts with a new distributor, investigate the export catalog, which you can request in writing. Then, to check the firm's reputation, contact the record companies it does business with.

For licensing and foreign publishing deals, a good place to start is with an entertainment lawyer who deals with foreign contracts.

When starting out, new label owners and distributors (and lawyers!) have found it helpful to attend trade conventions where information is shared and traded. One organization that holds such events, the National Association of Independent Record Distributors (NAIRD), is discussed in Chapter 10 under the heading 'Joining the Industry.'

Two other trade shows specialize in international deals: MIDEM and MUSEXPO. MIDEM (International Record and Music Publishing Market) was established in 1966. Every year at MIDEM's trade convention in Cannes, France, more than 7000 music-industry 'wheeler-dealers' from more than 55 countries gather for five days of nonstop activity. Most established record companies and publishers attend MIDEM to negotiate licensing and publishing deals or to maintain already existing deals.

MUSEXPO, established in 1974, holds its annual international record- and music-industry trade show in Acapulco, Mexico, and draws about 2500 participants.

Going to these major trade conventions, however, is by no means the only way to learn about the business. In the last ten years, seminars and all-day workshops conducted by key industry people have made information about all aspects of the music business available to newcomers. Many independents have made their first contacts at these seminars. Learn to take advantage of these programs; they are advertised in music stores and local and alternative music magazines, as well as regional and national magazines. And when you attend, ask lots of questions. You will find that most people are willing to help.

Directory and Bibliography

ORGANIZATIONS

American Federation of Musicians
(AF of M)
1500 Broadway
New York, NY 10036

American Federation of Television and
Recording Artists (AFTRA)
1350 Avenue of the Americas
New York, NY 10019

American Guild of Authors and
Composers (AGAC)
40 W. 57th St.
New York, NY 10019

American Society of Composers, Authors
and Publishers (ASCAP)
1 Lincoln Plaza
Broadway at 64th St.
New York, NY 10023

Audio Engineering Society
60 E. 42nd St.
New York, NY 10017

Broadcast Music Inc. (BMI)
40 W. 57th St.
New York, NY 10019

Electronic Industries Association
2001 Eye Street NW
Washington, D.C. 20006

Harry Fox Agency
110 E. 59th St.
New York, NY 10022

MIDEM
Perard Associates Inc.
100 Lafayette Dr.
Syosset, NY 11791

Music and Entertainment Industry
Educators Association (MEIEA)
c/o Richard Broderick
School of Music
New York University
239 Green Street, Suite 300
New York, NY 10003

MUSEXPO
International Music Industries, Ltd.
1414 Avenue of the Americas
New York, NY 10019

The National Association of Independent
Musicians and Educators
(NAIME)
3713 Kimble Road
Baltimore, MD 21218

National Academy of Recording Arts and
Sciences (NARAS)
303 North Glen Oaks
Burbank, CA 91502

National Academy of Songwriters
(formerly Songwriters Resources and
Services)
6381 Hollywood Boulevard
Los Angeles, CA 90028

National Association of Independent
Record Distributors (NAIRD)
c/o Richman Brothers
6935 Airport Hwy. Lane
Pennsauken, NJ 18109

National Association of Recording
Merchandisers, Inc. (NARM)
1060 Kings Highway North, Suite 200
Cherry Hill, NJ 08034

Recording Industry Association of
America (RIAA)
1020 19th Street, N.W., Suite 200
Washington, D.C. 20036

Register of Copyright
Library of Congress
Washington, DC 20559

Songwriters Resources and Services
(*see* National Academy of Songwriters)

Songwriters Showcase
PO Box 93759
Hollywood, CA 90093

INDUSTRY DIRECTORIES

The number of record companies in
America has outgrown the capacity of
this book. Lists of the independents can
be found in *The Billboard International
Buyers Guide, The International Discography
of the New Wave, Music Industry Resources,
Phonolog* and the *Schwann Record and Tape
Guide.* Up-to-date lists of U.S. trade
magazines, record labels, music, radio
and print media are databased and updated
regularly in *Music Industry Resources;* for
Canada look to *Music Directory Canada.*

The Billboard International Buyers Guide
1515 Broadway
New York, NY 10036

International Discography of the New Wave
B. George and Martha DeFoe
Omnibus Press/One Ten Records
110 Chamber Street
New York, NY 10007

Music Directory Canada
832 Mt. Pleasant Road
Toronto, Ontario, Canada M4P 2L3

Music Industry Resources
The 1987/88 Music Business Directory
The 1987/88 Music Radio Directory
The 1987/88 California Music Directory
PO Box 190
San Anselmo, CA 94960

New Music Distribution Service
500 Broadway
New York, NY 10012

The Pan Network
PO Box 162
Skippak, PA 19474

Phonolog
Music Department
10996 Torreyana Road
San Diego, CA 92121

Schwann Record and Tape Guide
535 Boylston
Boston, MA 02116

BOOKS

This is the author's selected list of books
on particular aspects of recording and
business. For a more complete bibliography, write to the Mix Bookshelf,
2608 Ninth Street, Berkeley, CA 94710.

The Craft and Business of Songwriting
John Braheny
Writer's Digest Books
Cincinnati, Ohio, 1987
A practical guide for songwriters

Home Recording for Musicians
Craig Anderton
Music Sales Corporation, New York,
New York, 1978
Comprehensive guide to recording at
home. Now being updated

Just for the Record
Shad O'Shea
PO Box 11333
Cincinnati, Ohio 45211
How the entertainment industry really
works

Making Money Making Music
James W. Dearing
Writer's Digest Books
Cincinnati, 1982
A practical guide to earning money

*Making Music: The Guide to Writing,
Performing and Recording*
Editor: George Martin
William Morrow & Company
New York, New York, 1983
Good insights into the work habits of
famous musicians

MIDI for Musicians
Craig Anderton
Music Sales Corporation
New York, New York, 1987

Mix Annual Directory
c/o Bookshelf Dept.
2608 Ninth Street
Berkeley, CA 94710
U.S. and Canada reference guide to recording studios; studio designers and
equipment suppliers; mastering, pressing
and duplication facilities; audio, video
and music manufacturers; video production and post-production facilities

Modern Recording Techniques
Robert E. Runstein and
David Miles Huber
Howard W. Sams & Co.
Indianapolis, Indiana
Third Printing 1987
Reference text

Principles of Digital Audio
Ken Pohlmann
Howard W. Sams & Company
Indianapolis, Indiana, 1987

Music Business Handbook and Career Guide
David Baskerville
The Sherwood Company
Denver, 1982

Musician's Guide to Copyright
Edward R. Hearn, J. Gunnar Erickson,
and Mark Halloran
Bay Area Lawyers for the Arts,
San Francisco, 1979
Song publishing and copyright

The Musician's Manual
Mark E. Halloran and the Beverly Hills
Bar Association
Hawthorn/Dutton, New York, 1979
Business practices and sample contracts

The Platinum Rainbow
Bob Monaco and James Riordan
Swordsman Press
Sherman Oaks, Calif., 1980
Practical advice on the music business
from two insiders

*This Business of Music
More About This Business of Music*
Sidney Shemel and William Krasilovsky
Billboard Publications, New York, 1977
Guides to the music business

Index

Accountants, 121
Accounts, service of, 24, 25, 27
Acetates, 59, 60
Acoustics of concert hall, 96
Advertising, 16, 17
mail order sales, 35
AF of M, 106, 126, 179
AFTRA, 106, 126, 179
AGAC, 179
Airplay, 3, 5, 15, 16, 166
royalties for, 115
Alignment
heads, 73
tape, 73
tones, 59
American Federation of Musicians.
See AF of M
American Federation of Television and
Radio Artists. See AFTRA
American Guild of Authors and
Composers. See AGAC
Analog, 167
time processor, 71
Analog-to-digital converter, 162, 167
Arrangements, 87, 88
Arrangers, 99
payment of, 106
ASCAP, 52, 111, 115, 179
Attenuation, 76
Attorneys, 121, 175, 177, 178
Audience
and cover design, 48
identification of, 5, 6
for mail order sales, 34
Audits, 175
Authorship of songs

Baffles, 81
Band members, payment of, 107
Bank accounts, 121
Bias control of tape recorder, 73, 79, 156
Bids from printers, 43
Billboard, 6, 179

Billboard International Buyer's Guide, The,
29, 30, 124, 125, 164, 179
for manufacturers, 64
for printers, 41
Billing distributors, 31
Bin cards, 27
Bin-loop cassette duplication, 157–158
Black Box fund, 166
Block recording rates, 104
Blueline proofs, 40, 44
BMI, 52, 111, 115, 179
Booking agents, 12
Bookkeepers, 121, 171
Borrowing money, 169–170
Brownline proofs, 40
Budget covers, 55, 56
Bulk mail permits, 18, 37, 122
Burwen noise reduction system, 76
Business, 121–127
worksheet, 153
Business cards, 122, 123

Calibration, 73
Calligraphy, 57
Camera-ready mechanicals, 54
Cardioid microphones, 71
Cashbox, 6, 178
Cassette-only releases, 21, 155–161
Cassette tapes
chrome, 155, 156, 157
duplication of, 157–158
ferric, 155, 156, 157
graphics for, 158–160
labels for, 157–160
mastering, 155
masters, 156, 158
metal, 155–157
prices of, 158
printing, 161–162
printing prices, 160–161
sales of, 2, 3, 21–22, 155, 161
sound quality, 155, 156
tape duplication, 157–158
Catalogs, 32–34
Click tracks, 91
Club owners, 12
Club performances, sales at, 22, 23
C.O.D., discounts for, 30
Collating records, 66
Collection from distributors, 30–32
College courses, 108
College radio stations, 7, 15
Color keys, 40
Color, in printing, 39, 44, 45
Color separations, 39, 44
Common law copyright, 112
Compact disc
airplay, 2, 3, 166
graphics, 164–166
manufacturing, 162–166

mastering, 163–164
mastering costs, 164
packaging, 164–165
premastering, 162–163
printing prices, 166
sales, 2–3, 21–22, 162, 166
SMPTE, 162, 163
Compression method, 61
Compressors, 78
Concept of cover, 48, 49
Concert promoters, 12
Concerts
recording at, 96, 97
sales at, 23, 36, 37
Condenser microphones, 70
Consignments, 25, 27
sample form, 26
Contracts
with band members, 107
with independent labels, 172–177
Conventions
NAIRD, 29, 30, 125, 126, 178
NARM, 126
MIDEM, 178
MUSEXPO, 178
Converted masters, 61
Converted stampers, 61
Cooling records, 61
Copy for cover, 49, 51, 52
Copying tapes, 85
Copyrighting records, 113
Copyrighting songs, 111–114
Corporations, 171
Cover of album, 9
budget covers, 55, 56
concept of, 48, 49
copy for, 49, 51, 52
economy covers, 55, 56
graphics, 47–57
information included on, 52
package manufacturing deal, 66, 67
paper for, 40
as press kit cover, 12
printing of, 39–45
production of, 49–54
stock covers, 55, 56
Critics, 6
on mailing list, 8
researching of, 7
Cross talk, 74
Crystal microphones, 70
Cue sends, 76
Cue system, 96
Curing records, 61

Damaged records, 37
DAT, 75, 167–168
DBX, 59, 75, 76, 155
Decibels, 70

Decoding, 75
Demos, 108
Designers, 47–49
choosing of, 54, 55
fees, 57
for stationery, 122
Digital delay, 71, 78
Digital recorders, 75, 167–168
live recording, 75, 167
Digital-to-analog converter, 167
Direct boxes, 72
Direct metal mastering, 163, 164
Direct-to-disc recording, 93, 94
sales of, 25
Direct to two-track, 88, 89, 167, 168
time for, 103
Directional microphones, 70, 71
Disc jockeys. See DJs
Disc-mastering, 59
hourly rates for, 65
mono mixes made in, 84
preparation for, 84, 85
Discount prices, 21
Discounts, 21, 25
and distributors, 30
Distortion, 70, 73
testing for, 82
Distribution by record companies, 173
Distributors, 2, 3, 27–32
and performance sales, 23
for foreign markets, 176–178
DJs
late night, 7
at performances, 14
records to, 15
researching of, 7
Dolby noise reduction systems, 59, 75, 76,
155
Duplication, cassette, 158–159
Dynamic microphones, 70

Echo, 78
Economy covers, 55, 56
Encoding, 75
Engineers, 98, 99
hiring of, 106
Ensemble multi-track recording, 90
Environments for recording, 94–97
EPs, 21
EQ. See Equalization
Equalization, 73, 76, 79, 156
Equalizers, 71, 78
Equipment for recording, 69–79
checking of, 80, 81
Expanders, 78
Exploitation of songs, 114–119, 175
Export deals, 174, 176–178

Fabrication, 41, 45
Faders, 76

Fans
  list of, 9
  mail order sales, 34
  performances, 22
Feature stories, 14, 15
Federal ID number, 124
Federal regulations on mail orders, 35
Federal Trade Commission, on mail
  orders, 35
Ferric cassette tape, 155–157
Fictitious name certificates, 114, 123
File cards for mailing list, 8
Filters, 78
Financing, 169–171
Flash, 61
Flutter, 73
Flyers, 11
Foreign markets
  distributors, 176–178
  export deals, 174
  sales in, 157, 176–178
  subpublishing, 177, 178
  trade conventions, 178
Format of records, 2, 3, 21, 22
Four-color printing, 39
Free records, 9, 10, 12, 14–16, 32, 174
Frequency response, 70
Friends
  and financing, 169
  and promotion, 5, 6
  and store sales, 27
Fringing, 74
Full color printing, 39
Full protection matrixing, 61, 65
Full-track mono, 73, 74

Galleys, 53, 54
Gang runs, 40
General partnerships, 170
Ghost, 81
Giveaways, 9, 10
Government regulations, 123, 124, 171
Grammy Awards, 126
  for album covers, 47
Graphic equalizers, 71, 78
Graphics, 47–57, 158–160, 164–166
  and designers, see Designers
  on mail order package, 34
  and promotional materials, 11, 12
  worksheet, 139

Halftones, 39, 44
Half-track stereo, 74
Harmonic distortion, 70
Harry Fox Agency, 117, 179
Head alignment, 73
Headphones, 79, 82
  preparation of, 80
  in studios, 96

High bias tapes, 157
High speed duplication, 158
Home studios, 97
  costs of, 105, 106
  semi-professional equipment, 79

ID number, federal, 124
Illustrators, 49, 57
Image and cover design, 48
Impedance, 71, 72
Industry list, 8, 9
Injection method, 61, 62, 164
Inserts, 41, 66
In-cassette duplication, 157–158
In-store play, 27
Insurance of shipments, 63
Intermodulation distortion, 70
International conventions.
  See Conventions
International Record and Music
  Publishing Market. See MIDEM
Interviewing audiences, 6
Inventory control form, 28
Investors, 170–171
Invitations to performances, 12
Invoicing distributors, 31

Joint ventures, 170

Labels, 41, 45
Labor Unions, 126
Lacquers, 59, 60, 65
Lamination of cover, 41
Lawyers. See Attorneys
Leadsheets for copyrighting, 112
Lease deals, 172–173, 176–177
Ledgers, 121, 122
LEDs, 76
Library of Congress, 33, 34, 179
Licensing contracts, 172, 177
Limited partnerships, 171
Limiters, 71, 78
Line art, 39
Lists, mailing, 7–9
Local business license, 124
Location recording, 96, 97
  rates for, 104, 105
Logo, 48, 49
LPs, 21
Lyric sheets, 51

Magazines, 6, 7
Magnetic tape recorders, 72, 73
Mail order package, 34, 35
Mail order sales, 34, 35
Mailers, 66
Mailing costs, 37, 122
Mailing lists, 7–9
  for mail order sales, 34

Mailing services, 122
Making a master, 61, 163
Making a mother, 61, 163
Making ready, 40
Manufacturing, 59–67, 157–158, 164, 165
  worksheet, 141
Master lacquers, 60, 65
Masters, 61, 155 163–164
Materials for promotion, 9–12
Matrix number, 54, 85
Matrixing, 60, 61, 65, 85
Mechanical licenses, 117, 119
Mechanical royalties, 114
Mechanicals, 39, 158, 160, 164–165
  for labels, 42, 159–160, 164–166
Media
  mailing list for, 8
  releases to, 10, 11
  researching of, 6, 7
Metal cassette tape, 156, 157, 158
Metal parts, 60
Methods of recording, 88–94
Mic/line switch, 76
Microphones, 70–72
MIDEM, 178, 179
MIDI, 168
Mixing, 82–84
Mixing console, 71, 76–78
  in semi-professional equipment, 79
  two track recording with, 89, 90, 168
Molds, 60, 164
Monitor speakers, 78, 79
Mother, making a, 61, 163
MTV, 7
Multi-track, 74, 75
  cassette-based, 79, 168
  ensemble recording, 90
  mixing for, 83
  overdubbing recording, 90–93
  premixes, 93
  tape prices, 105
  time for recording, 103
MUSEXPO, 178, 179

Name
  authority to use, 175
  on cover, 48
NAIRD, 2, 29, 30, 125, 126, 178, 179
NARAS, 126, 127, 179
NARM, 29, 30, 126, 179
National Academy of Recording Arts and
  Sciences. See NARAS
National Association of Independent
  Record Distributors. See NAIRD
National Association of Recording
  Merchandisers. See NARM
Negative masters, 61
Negatives, 39, 40

New Music Distribution Service.
  See NMDS
Newspapers, 6, 7
NMDS, 29
Noise reduction systems, 59, 71, 75, 76, 155

Offset printing, 39
Ohms, 72
One-color printing, 39
One-for-ten policy, 30
Options in recording, 87–101, 167–168
Other peoples' songs, use of, 119
Outdoor concerts, sales at, 23
Output impedance, 71, 72
Overdubbing, 74, 164
  and arrangements, 87
  on multi-track recording, 90–93
  time for, 103

Packaging manufacturing deal, 66, 67
Package printing prices, 42
Packaging, 62, 63, 158–160, 164–165
Pan pots, 76
Paper for covers, 40
Parametric equalizers, 71, 78
Partnerships, 170
PCM, 75, 167–168
Performances, 12, 14
  arrangements from, 87
  and distributors, 32
  plan for promotion, 17
  rights to, 114, 115
  selling at, 22–24
Personnel
  hiring of, 106, 107
  for recording, 97–101
Phase shifters, 78
Phonograph Record Labor Agreement,
  127
Phonolog Reporter, 32, 33, 179
Photo stories, 15
Photographs, 11
  for album cover, 49
  fees for professional photographer, 18,
  57
  reproduction costs, 18
Pick-ups, 72
Ping-ponging, 93
  time for, 103
Plan for promotion, 17
Plan for sales, 36
Plan for time, 130
Planning worksheet, 153
Plastic leader, 84
Plating, 60, 61, 65
Playback, record and, 82
  cassette, 155, 158
Point arrangements, 171
Postal services, 122

Postcards, 11
Posters in stores, 27
PR firms. *See* Public relations firms
Preliminary design of cover, 49
Premixes, 93
  time for, 103
Preparation of equipment, 80, 81
Press kits, 11, 12
Press lists, 18
Press releases, 10, 11
  duplication costs, 18
  remailing of, 14
  to stores, 25
Pressing records, 61, 62
  charges for, 66
Pricing, 21, 22, 30, 161, 166
  of cassettes, 21, 22, 161
  of compact discs, 21, 22, 166
  of records, 21, 22, 30
  for distributors, 21, 22, 30
  special prices, 22
Printing, 39–45
  worksheet, 137
Procedures for recording, 69–85
Process of recording, 79–85
Producers, 99–101, 107
  fees of, 107
Production of cover, 49–54, 57
  for cassettes, 161–162
  for compact discs, 164–166
Profit sharing, 170
Promissory note, 169–170
Promotion, 2–3, 5–19
  and album cover, 49
  and distributors, 32
  and sales at concerts, 23
  sample promotional plan, 17
  video programming, 7
  worksheet, 133
Proofs, 39, 40, 44, 52, 53
  checking of, 40
  of cover copy, 52, 53
Public relations firms
  fees of, 19
  independent, 16
Publishing, 114–119, 175
  forming your own company, 114
  rights, 175
Pulse Code Modulator.
    See PCM

Quarter-track stereo, 74
Questionnaire for audience, 6

Radio stations, 2–3, 7, 15, 16, 83, 166
Real time, 158
Record mailers, 37

Record and playback, 82
Recording contracts, 172–175, 176–178
Recording
  cassette, 168
  costs, 103–107
  options, 87–101, 167–168
  procedures, 69–85
  session tips, 107–109
  sync track, 167, 168
  time, 103
  worksheets, 143–147
Reference lacquers, 59, 60, 65, 164
Register of Copyrights, 111, 113, 177
Regrind, 61
Regulations by government, 123, 124, 171
Rehearsal of songs, 108
Repro copy, 54
Resale license, 123, 124
Researching the media, 6, 7
Retail list price, 21
Reverb, 78
Reversed areas on cover, 40
Reviewers. *See* Critics
Reviews, 14
Rhythm tracks, 91
Ribbon microphones, 70
Rolodex cards for mailing list, 8
Royalties
  for airplay, 115
  album sales, 117, 174
  for songwriters, 115, 117

Safety masters, 85
Sales, 21–37
  and airplay, 15
  sample sales plan, 36
  of songs, 117, 118
  worksheet, 135
Sales tax, 124
Sliders, 76
Schlesinger, Alfred W., 112, 113
Schwann Record and Tape Guide, The, 32,
    33, 179
Scores for copyrighting, 112
Second pressings, 63
Securities, 171
Self-financing, 169, 170
Seller's permit, 123, 124
Semi-professional recording equipment, 79
Sequence of songs, 84
Service of accounts, 24, 25, 27
Session tips, 107–109
Set-up
  for concert recording, 96
  of equipment, 81
Shipping, 63
Shore-pak covers, 40, 45
Shrink wrapping, 62, 161, 164, 166
Signal processing equipment, 77, 78

Signal-to-noise ratio, 70
Slicks, 40, 44
  printing of, 67
Sliding scale discount, 30
SMPTE, 163–164
Solo switch, 76
Song Registration Service, 112, 179
Song rights, 111–119
  other people's songs, use of, 118
  worksheet, 149
Songsharks, 118, 119
Songwriter/Publisher Agreements, 118
Sound reinforcement companies, 104
Speakers, 78, 79
Specialty journals, 6
Specifications, 70
Speed of tape, 73, 74
Stampers, 60
Statements by record companies, 175
Stationery, 122, 123
Stock covers, 55, 56
Stores, selling in, 24–27
Storing records, 63
Stripping, 39, 40, 44
Studio musicians, 99
  costs of, 106, 107
Studios, 95, 96
  prior visits to, 107, 108
  rates for, 103, 104
  size of, 94
Submixes, 93
Subpublishing, 166–168, 177
Switches on mixing board, 76
Sync track recording, 168
Synthesizers, 168

Talkback switches, 76
Tape, 72–75
  alignment, 73
  costs of, 105
  speed of, 73, 74
Tape heads
  alignment, 73
  cleaning, 80
Tapeless studio, 168
Tape recorders, 72–75, 79, 167–168
  semi-professional, 79
Tax returns, state and federal, 124
Technology, new, 167–168
Telephone bills, 18, 36
Telephone for business, 122
Television, 7
Test pressings, 62, 66
Testing, 81, 82
  for concert recording, 96
Time, 129–131
  code, 164
  graphics, 56, 57

manufacturing, 65, 66
printing, 42–45
promotion, 17–19
recording, 103
sales, 36, 37
time plan, 130, 131
Track format, 73, 74
  semi-professional equipment, 79
Trucks, shipping by, 63
Two-track
  digital, 75, 167–168
  direct to, 88, 89
  with mixer, 89, 90
  time for recording, 103
Typesetting cover copy, 52, 53
Typing press release, 11

U-Matic video tape, 162
Unions, 127

VHS tape, 162
Video programming, 3, 7
Vinyl, 61
VU meters, 76

Warped records, 37
Wholesale prices, 21
Window displays, 27
Worksheets, 133–154
Writers. *See* Critics
Wow, 73

We would like to correspond with more independent record companies and hear your music. We hope to be able to update our directory of independent labels and help foster a network of people making and selling their own records. Please fill out this form, answering whatever questions you wish. If possible, include a copy of your record and promotional materials. When completed, mail to:

How to Make and Sell Your Own Record
Post Office Box N
Jerome, Arizona 86331

If this book is not available in your local book, record or music store, you can order additional copies by sending $14.95 plus $2.05 postage and handling (total $17.00) to: Jerome Headlands Press, Post Office Box N, Jerome, Arizona 86331. Please allow four to six weeks for delivery.

Feedback

NAME OF LABEL/RECORD COMPANY

NAME OF OWNER/OPERATOR   TITLE

ADDRESS

CITY   STATE   ZIP

TITLE OF RECORD

ARTIST/GROUP

NUMBER DESIGNATION   DATE ISSUED   45 ☐   EP ☐   LP ☐

NO. OF RECORDS FIRST PRESSING   ADDITIONAL PRESSINGS

METHOD OF RECORDING

LOCATION OF RECORDING

RECORDING BUDGET   GRAPHICS BUDGET   PROMOTIONAL BUDGET

INDEPENDENT DISTRIBUTORS USED

PERFORMANCE SALES   RETAILERS' SALES   DISTRIBUTORS' SALES   MAIL ORDER SALES

PUBLICATIONS WHICH HAVE REVIEWED THE RECORD

RADIO STATIONS WHICH HAVE GIVEN IT AIRPLAY

Do you have any comments, information, or suggestions for revisions which might be included in future editions of this book?

Enclosed: ☐ copy of record   ☐ promotional materials

Mail to *How to Make and Sell Your Own Record,* Post Office Box N, Jerome, Arizona 86331